JUMPING OUT
OF THE
MAINSTREAM

An American family's year in China

Savor the adventure!

BY
CAROLINE DEPALATIS

Published by CreateSpace, North Charleston, South Carolina, USA
Printed in the United States of America
First edition, 2017

First edition publication through CreateSpace
ISBN-13: 978-1975959081
ISBN-10: 1975959086

Layout: C. DePalatis
Cover Design: C. DePalatis, Luke DePalatis

For inquiries about this book, please contact us at:

www.cultureweave.com/jumping-out-book
Email: caroline@cultureweave.com
Facebook.com/cultureweave
Instagram: @cultureweave
Twitter: • @cultureweave

Author's note: Most names throughtout this book, other than the author's and those of her immediate family members, have been changed to maintain privacy & security.

Disclaimer: To the best of our knowledge, the information contained herein, both narrative stories and information/data, is accurate and reliable as of the date of publication; however, we do not assume any liability whatsoever for the accuracy and completeness of the included information.

TO DALE,
my companion, delight, lover & best friend.
Your patience is as deep as an ocean,
your character as steady as a rock,
and your love for God & people
as high as the rugged mountains
of your native Alaska.

Thanks for cheering me on at every turn.
Here's to the adventure ahead!

*"There is no greater agony
than bearing an untold story inside you."*

– Maya Angelou, Author

Contents

Challenges & Celebrations

Interlude

Springing Forward

Traversing the Middle Kingdom

Home Stretch

Goodies at the End

~~~~~~~~~~

This book is actually a collaborative effort of our family, to some extent. You will hear the voices of each family member via occasional blog posts highlighted and inserted throughout this manuscript. Many were written during our year in China, but some came to life years later, as reflections. We've included them to give you a fuller picture. And for fun!

INTRO | Make the dream your reality

"In the end, we only regret the chances we didn't take."
– Lewis Carroll, Author

As you open these pages, you are embarking with our family of five on a journey across an ocean, cultures, languages and perspectives. Our year abroad changed each of us in meaningful, but different, ways. This book chronicles how.

We'd like to invite you to leap into the story with us, as we jump out of the mainstream of American life, explore and discover an ancient land and its newer elements, and most of all, its people.

But, who are you? And why would you be interested in this story?

You may be someone who is intrigued by the idea of doing something different, of stretching beyond your comfort zone, of jumping out of your own mainstream, routine life to experience another culture and another part of the world. Maybe you've even done it already. Or maybe not.

My hope is our story will inspire you to do so soon.

If you're single or a newly married couple, you can enjoy and benefit from our story. It may help you to envision your future.

The same applies for you who are in the season of babies, toddlers and preschoolers.

Why? Because even in the midst of the daily demands of getting food on the table, paying bills, changing diapers, and general survival, we want to help you raise your eyes from the mundane to consider a future of living abroad – at least for a season – with your family.

Parents of children in the 5–15 year-old age range will benefit the most from this book. These are the "memory-making years" for children, the season of childhood from which both identity and defining childhood memories arise. This period is most crucial to the healthy development of parent–adult child relationships too.

I believe one goal 21st century parents should have is to expand the hearts and minds of their children, transcending the slew of media messages hurled their way. No question – if you are raising kids now, they *will* learn about a larger world out there. But you, as a parent, play the greatest role in *what* and *how* they learn, and what messages stick. And your impact can be the greatest in the 5–12 year-old age range.

You might be tempted to think this book is only relevant for Americans since it is written by an American and is about an American family's experience in China (and a few other places). But I believe our story can find a broader audience because living abroad and getting into another culture impacts and changes those who do it. The essential ingredients are a curious mind, an open heart, receptivity to diverse ways of living, and a desire to stretch beyond your comfort zone. You can do this whether you are living as an Australian family in Peru, a Pakistani family in Canada, or a French family in Japan.

Jumping Out of the Mainstream focuses mostly upon the narrative account of our year living abroad as a family. Most of all, it is story. I hope you'll leap right in!

For those who want the nuts and bolts of *how* to get your own family abroad, whether for a year, more, or less, consider our online course, *YourFamilyAbroad,* available through the Courses section of our website, **CultureWeave.com**. On our Blog and in our Resources section you will find a number of reflections and insights, along with how-to's and other handy material, for you to successfully make that jump with your family!

1 | Shanghai teahouse moment

Tea is the elixir of life.
– Lao Tzu, Chinese Philosopher

A sense of pure contentment passed over us as we sat together, as a family, soaking up the ambiance of the Shanghai teahouse. The hot, heavy August air didn't seem to matter. The sense we had now "arrived" prevailed. It was a moment of finality, recognition the transition had been made, and we were now, officially, here.

We were no longer back home, stuck in endless to-do lists and piles of stuff. There was no more packing, no more anticipating. We had made it! And we were even beginning to overcome jet lag as well.

As the delicate, traditionally clad woman began to prepare our tea, I made a mental snapshot of her – and this moment – in my mind. I didn't want to lose it, ever.

Our Chinese language was limited to a few greetings and niceties. And pointing. Using these "tools," each of us was able to make our choice of tea. Then we watched our hostess do her work.

Strange – it was messy and humid outside, but inside this little air-conditioned oasis we managed to forget all about that. Oddly, hot tea on a muggy August day in Shanghai seemed a good thing. Even our eight-year-old was swept up by the experience. All of us settled into the moment.

I chose rose tea. The aroma transported me to another place entirely. As I closed my eyes and let the puffs of fragrant steam fill my nostrils, I envisioned the rose garden of my sweet older friend and mentor, Sue – now on the other side of the planet.

I looked around at my family. My husband, Dale, appeared as content in the moment as I was. With 23 years of marriage under our belts, it only seemed to be getting better with the years. Not easier, just better. And now we were on this new adventure.

Next to me sat Justin, our 14 year old. His mahogany locks framed his emerging adult visage. "Where did that chin stubble come from?" I wondered. He had just finished a banner 8th-grade year, riding the wave of friendships and the newness of social media, a middle school graduation privilege. But at this point, he was eager for the adventure as well. He, too, soaked in the moment, forgetting the oppressive heat outside.

Then there was our 12-year-old daughter, Erika. She had pulled her long chocolate-colored locks back into a singular braid. Our most independent child, she had learned to take care of such things at an early age. She, too, seemed to revel in the moment.

Last came Luke, our eight-year-old, squeezed between Dale and me. This impish little guy, with protruding adult front teeth and scraggly hair, mimicked his brother at every turn. Born with a distinctive shock of blond right across the front of his otherwise dusty brown hair ("the place where God kissed you," I would say), Luke had been the most consistently happy one in the bunch.

That moment in this Shanghai teahouse in the architecturally traditional – and also touristy – shopping area of *Yùyuán* (豫园) seemed to affirm our journey. We *could* do this, as a family! Until now, resistance had been formidable. But now, as we melted into the moment, our efforts gained a new sense of clarity and purpose.

You know those moments when everything within you feels all is right in this world (even when it's not)? Well, that Shanghai teahouse moment was one of them for us. Much lay ahead, true. But so much had been accomplished just getting here. Our family – imperfect, discombobulated fish out of water – had arrived.

And we lifted our tea cups to the occasion!

Decision & Preparation

2 | Opening the atlas, opening the mind

"The day we stop exploring is the day we commit ourselves to live in a stagnant world, devoid of curiosity, empty of dreams."
– Neil DeGrasse Tyson, Astrophysicist

I remember the atlas. For me as a young child, it literally held the world. Oh, how I loved that atlas, with its weighty and elegant ivory cover embossed with the golden letters "Rand McNally."

I was the one in my family who kept the dust off the atlas. Its maps, especially the one of our solar system, never failed to capture my attention. "Maybe she'll be an astronaut someday?" my parents pondered.

But space, itself, wasn't what drew me. Rather, it was the adventure and the unknown lands beyond my rather ordinary, suburban American upbringing. Like Carl and Ellie in the Pixar hit *UP*, I somehow came to believe at a young age that "adventure is out there!" And I was determined to find it.

In those early years, I also found that adventure in the pages of *National Geographic* magazines. Those yellow-rimmed tomes opened up worlds of wonder to me. I longed to know more with every article I read and every picture I admired.

When I was 14, my dad scored a big business deal and decided to take our family on a cruise in the Caribbean to celebrate. Of course, I didn't drag my feet. I had never strayed outside the U.S. before, other than stepping over the border into Tijuana and Enseñada, Mexico, and passing through Vancouver, British Columbia. I was ready!

And I was a teenager. With hormones. My parents knew it and, from their perspective, the real memory they hold about the time was how their 14-year-old, limit-pushing teenager had a romantic dalliance with another passenger about her age. It was passing – I assure you – and wasn't really much. But my parents found it quite amusing and have teased me about it over the years.

I won't deny it; that's probably what characterized the time for me – on the surface. But something else happened deep down when we pulled into Port-au-Prince, Haiti.

While I had encountered the homeless on U.S. streets and Baja California before, this visit to Haiti opened my eyes to the brokenness and disparity of our world in a new way.

Our family had just walked off a white, gleaming cruise ship docked in the Port-au-Prince harbor. Here we were, among the elite, living like kings and queens on that ship, eating almost around the clock, enjoying every amenity imaginable on that mammoth vessel.

And then we stepped off.

Hawkers swirled around us, trying to sell us all sorts of items. But I managed to pull out of that mess. What caught my eyes was a girl about my age. Her clothes tattered, she begged on the street, not as a hawker but as one in true need. Our eyes locked. I gave her the few dollars I had on me, but I was confused about what I really should do.

I thought about that girl for a long time. Our lives and resources were so different, but probably many of our hopes and dreams were the same. I can still see her eyes today. That experience both haunted and changed me, much more than the surface "cruise ship romance" ever would.

While I remained reflective about the Port-au-Prince moment, the self-absorption of adolescence began to push out that introspection over time. I wish I could tell you otherwise, but I'd be lying.

Then, after seeing a random flyer I brought home from school one day, I apparently convinced my parents to start to rent out their extra room for short-term English-language-learning students. At first, since Japan's economy was on the rise, most of these students came from Japan to attend a local ESL (English as a Second Language) program.

I had never thought much about Asia. But, as I got to know a few of them, I started to think about their part of the world. *What was it*

5

like? Why did they want to (need to?) learn English? How was their culture different from mine?

These exchange students were all older than I. As I learned more about where they came from and why they tried so hard, I came to really take an interest in their journeys. And in Asia.

Those early experiences with the short-term Japanese exchange students left an indelible mark upon me. They opened up to me a world so very different from my own. They whet my appetite for new foods and for language learning.

These encounters also made me realize how ease of travel and communications were forcing people from diverse cultures to interact with one another. But to do so, I reasoned, we have to grow in our understanding. I longed for that myself. I recognized this greater understanding would become a key to my own personal and professional success in this increasingly interconnected, multicultural world.

3 | Our home: A mini-UN

"Having a soft heart in a cruel world is courage, not weakness."
– Hans Hubermann, character in *The Book Thief*

Before my husband and I exclaimed "I do," we had determined a few non-negotiables for our upcoming life together. First, we were clear the foundation for our marriage would be rock-solid faith in Jesus. We had both been through our spiritual searches before meeting each other. Although I was a much younger Christ-follower – and had gotten sidetracked several times along the way – we were both committed to following this path by the time we married.

Another non-negotiable was our desire to raise a family. If natural childbirth wasn't possible, we were open for adoption, and were especially intrigued by the prospect of international adoption.

But we weren't in a rush to start a family. Indeed, my husband always told me he wanted me to take the lead when it came to timing. He knew pregnancy and childrearing, if it were to happen, would likely impact my life choices the most. As would adoption. So he never pressured me on this matter and was very patient.

That meant almost 10 years of marriage before Baby #1, our son Justin, arrived on the scene. Then our daughter Erika leapt into our lives less than two years later. And finally, after a miscarriage, came Luke about three-and-a-half years after that.

A final non-negotiable in raising our children was to nurture in them a mindset of compassion and love for our world and its peoples. We wanted to help our children see the people of the world as God sees them – without prejudice or discrimination, as individual human beings of dignity, and as unique, creative expressions of His love. We also wanted to inspire our children to see themselves as ambassadors of God's gracious love and peace.

During those childbearing years, especially after I miscarried, we explored the possibility of adopting internationally. We thought it might be a way to both bring international flavor to our family and love an orphan (or two) as our own. But, eventually, we realized this was not the path designed for us.

Dale and I had often discussed the idea of raising our children overseas well before our kids emerged on the scene. But a few years before Justin's arrival, a door opened that changed all that. We became involved in an outreach to international college and university students in our city.

The international students loved our little kids, no question! All of our children – to varying degrees – were "pass-around babies," held by international friends from countries all over the world. As they grew older, the international students played with them and babysat them. I'll never forget one time, when our Lithuanian friend Regina (who now has three boys of her own) babysat Justin, Erika and Luke. We came home to find out they (playfully) had been holding her prisoner in a chair, tying her up with rope! (We put an end to *that* behavior!)

We'd take the international students on hikes with our family as well. One time we went on a day-long hike at a national park a couple hours away. That day, a colorful and playful young man from Kazakhstan, Aibek, took particular interest in our two boys and challenged them as we climbed. He was a really fit guy, running circles around the rest of the group (up and back while we were still on our first leg up). But the boys loved him, creating a special bond.

There were trips to Yosemite and to the mountains for skiing and snow play. Rich, intensive times of relating with numerous international friends, while in the car, on the slope and on the trail. We tried to make sure, always, the kids knew they came first. After all, *they* were the ones on whom we wanted to have the most lasting impact.

Still, multitudes of other international students became part of our daily lives. Hamza and Alayna and their two daughters worked their way into our hearts. Erika played multiple times with the two little girls, and they looked up to her as a big sister. Anya from Korea developed an instant bond with our children, especially Erika. Now Anya has four children of her own; she got some good training hanging out and playing with our three many times.

Another was Nassra from Oman, a sweet friend who frequented the gatherings at our home and stayed with us several times. She grew close to all three of our children. I remember well the time Nassra invited me and Erika over to her place and revealed to us her long flowing hair! Seeing her without *hijab* (head covering) for the first time was both a shock and delight!

Our friend, Mabior, hailing from the nation now known as South Sudan, left a lasting impression on our children. Mabior was a "lost boy" who had made his way to the U.S. under toilsome circumstances. He and fellow classmate, Geoffroy, from the Congo, occupied our makeshift garage guest room for a few weeks before they settled into places of their own. During that time, our family grew close to these young men from faraway parts of the world.

Although our children really didn't seem to notice the differences in skin color, pitch-black Mabior with his shining white eyes and teeth proved an exception. One day 10-year-old Justin, unfiltered, exclaimed out loud, "Wow, Mabior is the blackest person I've ever seen!" We all, Mabior included, got a good laugh out of that one.

We remain in contact with these friends – and so many more – to this day. It was, we imagine, quite a blur for our kids, with new people coming in and out of our house all the time. As they got older, we didn't force the relationships but gave them space to choose to engage or not. But we did make it a priority to help our kids understand where these new friends came from and to learn from them. I believe it enriched their lives in deep and lasting ways.

We found other avenues to cultivate this in our children as well. We started filling shoeboxes for children in tough parts of the world through Operation Christmas Child when it first started up. We did this with the international students and our kids together, year after year. Our kids loved going out and selecting items for "their" shoebox. So did the small groups of international students. Together, we'd have a packing party in our living room. It was a small but impactful way we could remind them of the world beyond their borders.

We also participated in a child sponsorship program through

Partners International. Each of our children developed a pen pal relationship with a child in the Philippines. Over the years, these relationships blossomed, and we got to meet all three of the children years later. We've remained close to one of the families and, thanks to email and social media, continue in our relationship with them to this day.

An excellent opportunity arose to visit the Philippines when Justin was 11 years old. Our then-pastor and his wife had been missionaries to the Philippines for 13 years prior. They had tons of connections and planned to take a select group from our church there for a 10-day short-term missions experience. Hearing about this one Sunday, my heart leapt. I sensed this would be an excellent opportunity for Justin to develop a real connection with his sponsored child. And I was right!

A similar opportunity emerged a couple of years later. This time, it was destination Thailand for Erika, then 11, and me. While a different trip entirely, it again was an eye-opening, mindshifting experience for both of us.

4 | The dream no longer deferred

*"One thing I've found... the road rarely rises up to meet you
until you've begun walking."*
– Michelle Jennae, Author & Creativity Coach

If rolling back time were possible, there is little I would change about how our family life unfolded. The exception, however, is I wish we had explored the possibilities of heading overseas much earlier in our childrearing years.

I'm sure most parents would agree: Once you embark on the adventure of raising children, life becomes so very *daily*. This is a term a mentor of mine coined for me. It proved so apt. Just making it through the day sometimes took Herculean effort!

Although I tried hard to live in the moment while my kids were young, sometimes I longed for that day when I could take a shower without interruption … or have an adult conversation without interruption … or, most importantly, get a night of sleep without interruption.

Even with the challenges, however, I did love those years. Chaotic, messy, blissful, sing-song craziness. In the midst of going through them, though, it sometimes seemed as if we could barely come up for air, much less "strategize" our lives.

Then, as Justin entered 8th grade, reality struck. "Are we *ever* going to do what we had envisioned? Namely, give our children an experience so different from that of most American children, as well as from that of our own, stateside upbringings?" And, with Justin's entrance into 8th grade, we began to see how he was differentiating from us. Indeed, it wouldn't be too long before he could simply say "No! I don't want to go." At that point we'd have little recourse but to give in.

Please be clear: all our kids were on board with the idea of going overseas. But each one, at various times, had their moments – or stretches – of resistance. It wasn't always smooth sailing. Years later, however, each of them has separately assured us they were glad we went, and that doing it made their lives richer overall.

Not only was Justin on the edge of independence (at least in his mind!), but we also recognized the problem of him missing a crucial year of high school in the U.S. In particular, we were concerned how that would affect his preparations for and applications to college. So, in many ways, we felt as if the window for a year abroad was starting to close. Rapidly.

I blame our procrastination to take those first steps on the daily demands of life. But, as I reflect, I realize it was so much more. A powerful force can arise when you begin to "plant" yourself in a community, developing roots. You shoot those roots downwards and spread them out. You become a part of the community. And, most significantly, you become comfortable.

Something in me from an early age balked at that ubiquitous American quest for comfort. While I wanted stability in my life – such as knowing where I'd sleep on any given night – I didn't want comfort for comfort's sake. I wanted to live a life markedly distinct from what I perceived as the typical American suburban lifestyle.

This time imperative really put the fire under us to make some choices. Were we going to take the steps necessary to move ourselves abroad, or not? It was time to act. So Dale took the first step, and both applied and received permission for a yearlong sabbatical from his teaching job.

Now the question was where? And what? By this time, we had friends scattered all over the world. Perhaps we could find something through them, we wondered.

One of the early opportunities we discovered was the Fulbright Teacher's Exchange program. Dale decided to apply. We had a few different location options but in the end we threw in our hats for Turkey. While we were waiting on Fulbright, we thought it best to explore other avenues. We began to email friends living in other countries. Our criteria? We wanted the location to be moderately to highly challenging for our family. Not Switzerland (although, we admit, it's a pretty gorgeous place!).

Why did the level of challenge for our family matter to us? I know for some, simply getting overseas to a different culture is enough. And I get that. But for us, we were looking for something to jolt our system and push us all out of our comfort zone. Because we had raised our children in a relatively affluent area of the U.S., we wanted them to experience, at least for a year, how the majority world lives. For us, we believed this meant living in a developing country. Or, at least, in an emerging one.

So during this time of waiting on Fulbright, we explored possibilities in Kazakhstan, China, Indonesia, India, Nepal, Ethiopia, South Africa, Oman, Costa Rica and Albania. Many of our friends wrote us back with enthusiasm. But another criteria were jobs to cover our living costs, and that proved more difficult. A few of our friends had something in mind. In particular, a friend in Ethiopia, who ran a school, thought we might be able to teach there.

But around that time an older friend of ours pulled us aside to persuade us *not* to go to Ethiopia. He and his wife had been missionaries in Ethiopia for 16 years, giving birth to two of their three children while there.

"Don't take your family there," he warned. "It'll just be too much. Conditions there still aren't stable and can change at any time. It would be too hard on your kids."

When we heard those words, I'll be honest, we wanted to prove him wrong. "Of course, we all can handle it!" Dale and I secretly thought. But in the end, I believe he was right.

We remained hopeful with the Fulbright Exchange. Dale learned of his acceptance into the program as we turned into the new year. We began to bring our kids more into the picture, letting them know Dad was taking a sabbatical and we were exploring possibilities overseas. This was about eight months before we would leave. We wanted to make sure they had time to process the change.

Then in March of 2009, we heard back from Fulbright. They had been unable to find a Turkish teacher to exchange with my husband. I'll admit – we were crestfallen for at least a few days. Because Dale had made it to the next round of evaluation, we had already been talking about Turkey, just the two of us, as if it were a reality. We had begun reading articles on Turkey and developing a mindset in that direction. And then the news.

So we scrambled. One American friend who had spent a good deal of time in China was living in our area during this time. Jon told us of several contacts with whom he could share our résumés. "Go right ahead," we told him. "We are open."

That move led to three new opportunities at universities in China. Once the doors had opened, the Foreign Affairs Officers at each of these schools began recruiting us through email.

At the same time, some college friends who had lived in Costa Rica for several years got in touch about an opportunity there as well. They had found a school where Dale could teach, and it looked quite promising.

China seemed like a good option because over the years of working with international students many Chinese had crossed our paths, especially in more recent years. This was quite different when it came to students from Latin America, where we only had a few friends. Still, the Costa Rica opportunity intrigued us. Living in Central America, we could learn Spanish and that might give us an "in" to Latino culture in California. We were struggling with the decision.

At that point our friend Phil came to mind. "He's in the field of Decision Analysis," I thought. "It sure seems like he might be able to help us – even if it's just through a simple phone call."

So we rang him up. And sure enough – he was more than willing to help us out.

"Let me suggest this," he offered. "Why don't you let me email you a few documents? The two of you can work through them together, get them back to me, and then we'll arrange a time to talk more."

As we worked through those documents – evaluating our needs, wishes, hopes and expectations – the answer began to emerge. It got sharper and sharper until we could no longer deny it: China.

When we got back with Phil for a second session, our conclusion became clear to him as well. His tools worked! Among the three China options, again, one stood out more than the other two. It was at Ningbo University (宁波大学 – *Níngbō Dàxué*), in a city of about 7.6 million (greater area, 2010 census), approximately two hours south of Shanghai. This opportunity appeared the best fit for us largely because of the hard-working efforts of the Foreign Affairs Officer. She went by the English name "Ellen" and seemed ambitious and accessible. This was not the case for one of the other two.

So we began the journey to Ningbo, working with Ellen through all the paperwork and details. She stayed on top of the communication, responding promptly to our questions, even when the details weren't immediately clear. We learned much later that unclear details were part of the experience, and we'd need to learn to adjust.

5 | The path & the resistance

To fly we have to have resistance.
– Maya Lin, Designer & Artist

As we began to get clearer on the Ningbo choice, we started to sharpen our direction on the home front. Dale finished up the paperwork with his district to finalize the sabbatical year.

We also began talking with my employer, a non-profit called International Students, Inc., about the steps I needed to take. Because of the international focus of my work, a reassignment of location and focus was all that would be required. But this also necessitated a fair amount of paperwork, explaining what we were doing and, more importantly, why. We also needed to show how a year in China would benefit my employer and other interested parties.

We encountered resistance at many levels. Sometimes it was within ourselves; it is a lot of work to go against the status quo. Doubts and questions arose, especially when the action would involve our kid's lives. We faced challenges in the logistics of making the move; at times we'd find ourselves drowning in details.

And we ran into attitudes of family, friends and even mere acquaintances who were either befuddled by our decision or completely against it. Questions would arise: "Why would you *ever* do this? Why would you take your children out of school, mess up their lives?" "Why go through all the hassle to make this happen? Can't you just be satisfied staying here?"

One acquaintance of mine who owned a local coffee shop at the time questioned, "China? Why China? Why not somewhere beautiful and relaxing, like the Greek Isles?" (Note: This was *before* the migrant & refugee crisis.)

My father pulled Dale and me each aside on separate occasions. "Why do you have to do this with them [his grandchildren]? How do you know *they* want to go? Can't you just let them make their own decision when they grow up?"

A lot of people simply didn't understand what we were trying to do. Indeed, why *would* you mess up your simple, predictable lives?

But for Dale and me, it made complete sense. We were looking for the shake up, something not easy but a memorable challenge to experience as a family. We wanted to expose our kids to ways of life very different from that in our tiny corner of the world, not just through the lense of a tourist, but through the actual experience of living there day-to-day.

Many of the logistical elements of this move fell into place. But one major challenge for us on the home front was just that: the home. We live in a rather unaffordable part of the U.S. But over ten years earlier, we received an unexpected blessing – the opportunity to purchase a home for half the market value.

Without question, this was a miracle for us, arriving at just the right time. We had a two-and-a-half year-old, and an eight-month-old baby. We had been looking for places for a few years. With our modest salaries, we were priced way out of the market.

But a miracle came our way through inclusionary housing – a federal program administered at the local level for low-to-moderate-income, first-time homeowners. We were able to purchase our three-bedroom, two-and-a-half bathroom home for a price we could afford.

Part of the terms included a statement requiring us to be the primary residents of the property. The contract did say we could live away from the property for up to 15 months. If, however, we wanted someone else to live in our home while we were gone, they, too, would have to go through the rigorous income-screening process.

And this is where things got sticky.

One day a friend at our church checked in with us about our house and what we were planning to do with it while gone. She had some military friends expecting to move into the area. It turned out later, however, her friends Mark and Emily needed a larger house for their four kids.

But what happened next was the weird part. Or the miracle, depending upon how you choose to see it. Mark, Emily and their family were within a few weeks of returning to the U.S. from Japan. While driving on base there, they had a flat tire and were on the side of the road. Mark was attempting to fix it when another car came alongside. "Hey, you guys okay? Anything we can do to help?" came the friendly voice out of the passenger side.

The other American military couple, Nancy and Steve, popped out of their van to lend a hand. The four of them struck up a conversation as Mike and Steve focused on getting the flat off and the new tire on.

In the stream of information shared during those few minutes, Nancy learned Emily and Mark were headed to our city next. She got a gleam in her eyes. "You're not gonna believe this," she announced.

"What?" shot back Emily.

Nancy gestured to her cousin, Kelly, and her husband, Matt, tucked away in the van, introducing them as she did.

"Kelly and Matt, or *Liú Mínghuá*, are headed to the same city where you're going. They've just spent a couple years living in China. Matt will begin a job soon at the DLI [Defense Language Institute] teaching Chinese."

"No kidding!" Emily exclaimed.

"No kidding," responded Kelly. "Yes, we're trying to figure it all out now. But we have no idea where we'll live, or just about anything else."

Emily's mind got spinning. "I know of a couple who are taking their family to China for a year and are looking for someone to rent their house while they're gone."

The rest is history. But the process wasn't a slam-dunk. Working with our county housing authority took a lot of patience on both ends. Suffice to say, in the end, Matt and Kelly ended up living in our house along with an international student friend for the year we were gone. It was a great blessing to know that our home would be in good hands while we were out of the country.

6 | Preparing heart & mind

"Destiny waits in the hands of God, shaping the still unshapen..."
– T.S. Elliot, Author

I wish I could write something blithely romantic such as, "Our family always had a heart for China, and we prepared for years before we left, so we would be culturally and linguistically competent for the journey." Or, "In the footsteps of Eric Liddell, the Olympic runner made famous through the movie *Chariots of Fire*, "We followed the missionary call on our lives to China."

But that is not the truth.

China seemed to make sense for us from a number of different perspectives. It seemed appropriately challenging for our family, but not over-the-top. We knew we couldn't blend in easily, so we'd be dealing with that. And the door opened wide for us.

But that was after most other doors closed. And, in the end, it was a rush to get everything in line so we could make it to our posts at Ningbo University on time.

How were our children dealing with the impending changes? We found each handled what lay ahead differently.

Our almost 14 year old, Justin, was in a happy place of his life, after meeting much success in his final year at middle school. He seemed genuinely enthusiastic about doing something different and heading to China for a year. Most likely, it's because he didn't really know what to expect, so the curiosity seemed to propel his eagerness.

Erika, our 12 year old, was a different story altogether. I'm pretty sure China would've never been on her radar. For her, I imagine, it was just too…different. Also, as a lover of fiction and romantic stories involving princesses (which seemed to take place mostly in Europe), going to Asia probably wasn't her first choice.

Being someone who often thinks and plans ahead, Erika began to deal with some rising anxiety. She wasn't a continuous bundle of nerves; rather, it came out in spurts. She didn't want to miss the friendships and events of her seventh-grade year. Especially the Yosemite trip Justin had raved about and the Renaissance Faire hosted by the seventh graders every year.

That sense of missing out proved a recurring cry for her. But it only rose up in the dark hours as we'd put her down for bed. Worries. Concerns. She just didn't want to leave that which she knew. We would assure her, "It'll be all right." But she didn't always buy that. We would pray with and for her to get comfortable with the idea. It took time.

But then something happened. As summer progressed and the boxes started to pile up in our garage – and especially as she put the contents of her known life to this point into boxes herself – Erika seemed to realize this was going to happen, whether she wanted it to or not. She consciously made a mindset shift. In her words later she told us, "I realized it was out of my control. So I made a decision then and there, I'm going to make it the best I can. Make it great, even. Get the most out of the year I could."

To me even now, that's a remarkable step for a 12 year old. But that's exactly what she did.

Finally, our youngest, Luke. He was an eight-year-old bundle of energy and enthusiasm at the time. Raw, funny and charismatic. And very much the copycat of his older brother. Whatever Justin did, Luke wanted to follow. It would drive Justin crazy, but we assured him this, too, would pass. So, like Justin, Luke was just full of bubbly enthusiasm towards the vague "concept" of going to China. He didn't realize at the time how much it would rock his world.

That summer Dale commented to me, "We're going to need to keep an extra eye on those two boys," he suggested. "They seem all right now, but I suspect they'll face struggles after we get to China."

I never could have imagined just how prophetic those words would be.

We also had the job of putting together an educational plan for each child so they wouldn't miss a year of school in the U.S. Because my husband is an educator, this fell mostly in his territory. Luke would do 4th grade in China. The curriculum for him was flexible relative to the older two. Dale spoke with one of the potential 4th grade teachers and got some outlines for grade-level requirements. We spoke with some friends who were homeschooling parents about curriculum options for this age. In the end, we chose a curriculum from a well-respected company called Calvert Education. Part of this program required age-level reading books which we could load onto one of two Kindles. Those two very basic Kindles opened up worlds to all of us – especially Luke and Erika. It proved quite easy to line up Luke's curriculum.

For Erika's 7th grade year, Dale connected with each of the teachers she would have had if we had remained stateside. Since Justin had been through 7th grade only two years earlier, the material was fresher in our minds. The teachers were helpful in passing along syllabi, booklists, and anything we needed. The school also allowed us to borrow a few needed textbooks for the year. Along with the Kindle books plus some paperback biographies, Erika was set!

Justin, entering his freshman year, was the most complicated one on the education front. We wanted to make sure his first year of high school living abroad would meet the graduation requirements back home. In the end, the only state-approved curriculum for independent study abroad at the time came out of Brigham Young University, or BYU, so we used their online courses for most of the required study. We also got a handful of materials from the high school, including all the books for the Honors English I Curriculum which Dale had helped design, along with a supplemental textbook for Algebra II.

This was 2009-10. Internet study offerings and homeschool curriculums were much more limited at that time. Now, with more selection, parents can tailor their choice to meet their needs and the child's learning style.

Still, all this required adjustments, both for us and for our children. Although we had always woven teaching and learning opportunities into their upbringing, we had never done any formal homeschooling. So our learning curve proved steep as well.

7 | The six-and-a-half-foot angel

*"Each friend represents a world in us, a world possibly not born
until they arrive, and it is only by this meeting
that a new world is born."*
— Anaïs Nin, Essayist and Memoirist

From the moment we met Yongzheng Li (李勇正 – *Li Yǒng Zhèng*), or YZ (as we came to know him), our trajectory towards China not only became more certain, but also more possible. If there were a guardian angel presiding over our year in China, this was the guy.

Almost every year in June Dale and I attend a conference for International Students, Inc., and this year was no different. Even though we'd be leaving for China in just a couple months, we didn't go to the conference with any specific agenda. But we are certain meeting YZ was a divine connection. In fact, that relationship has been an ever deepening and enduring one.

When we met him, YZ was an international student in Southern California, and two of my coworkers there had invited him to attend as a guest. He came to the conference to share his testimony about how he had come to faith in Jesus Christ.

YZ's story had the entire audience on the edge of their seats, captivated for the 10 minutes he was given.

Tapped to be on the Chinese National Volleyball team at the ripe age of 16, the Chinese government was grooming YZ to compete internationally, including at the Olympics. All seemed to be going well; he was a rising star. And then, one day at 20 years-old, YZ experienced a sudden and severe pain in his head while at practice. The coaches rushed him off the court and to the hospital.

He had a brain aneurysm.

Coming out of critical care, YZ had lost all functioning on the left side of his body. He also had lost some of his memory but miraculously was still able to speak. Still, he had to learn many basic functions all over again.

He shared with the audience about that time. At first, it was very dark. But some people came into his life to encourage him. Teammates visited him. His coaches spoke words of hope into his life. He began, slowly, to view the only path forward as one of complete recovery.

He told us, "One reason why I could recover relatively quickly with my body was because I was an athlete. I understood the basic functioning of the human body. I knew I needed to work with a physical therapist – and there were relatively few at that time in China – in order to regain motion on my left side. So I set my mind to do it. I didn't want to remain helpless the rest of my life."

As he recovered from surgery via physical therapy, he enrolled at Fudan University (复旦大学 – *Fùdàn Dàxué*) in Shanghai. During this time, YZ learned through a friend about a scholarship program for athletes – specifically volleyball players – at a university far away, in Southern California. YZ decided to apply in the off chance he might get accepted. He knew he could no longer play for the Chinese national team.

A few months later, he was on an airplane, set to begin a new life in California.

Landing at Los Angeles International Airport, YZ sensed a different mood from his native China. While he had been to Hong Kong, Australia, and a few European countries previously with the Chinese National Team, as he landed in the U.S. he sensed a freedom he couldn't really put his finger on. *Something* was different, new, clear. He told himself right then he would make this experience count. He realized he had been given a second chance.

YZ makes friends easily. He is upbeat, jovial and inviting. This bode well for him in the new environment. He slipped into school and onto the volleyball team in a seamless way. Most people would not be able to tell his body had been through the trauma it had. As an international student, he wasn't expected to have perfect English. He could function in this new environment!

And he wasn't the only recruit from abroad. His team boasted a Ghanaian and a German player as well. He felt as if he had been brought into an international brotherhood of sorts, one that he never could have imagined even a year earlier.

But more was to come. You see, it was California Baptist University, or Cal Baptist / CBU that had recruited him. YZ, an atheist from China, was now surrounded by a bunch of Christian professors, classmates and teammates.

Most significantly, however, all international students at CBU got matched with host families. These were not living arrangements; YZ lived with other students in the dormitories. Rather, these were families – in YZ's case, a mature couple – who made time to spend with their CBU international student on a regular basis.

Bob and Betty shared their love with YZ from the get go. And they lived out and spoke about their faith as if it were second nature. They were seasoned volunteers and lovers of all things international. And now they brought YZ into their lives.

In time, YZ began to see the reasoning behind putting his faith in Jesus. But he still had some sticking points. He wondered if this would only apply for him in the States. How would it work back in China? And what about all those who didn't get to hear about Jesus? Like his parents, grandparents and friends back home? Did that mean they wouldn't go to heaven? And did he really believe these "foolish stories," as he had been raised to believe? Were they really true?

These questions – and more – kept YZ in spiritual limbo for some time. He enjoyed his Christian host family and the other Christians he met through CBU, but he wasn't sure he was destined, long term, to be one of them. So he kept them – and Jesus – a polite arm's distance away.

Then one weekend everything changed. He was on road trip with some teammates to an early Saturday morning practice and then game in San Diego. The accident happened at almost 70 miles per hour on Highway 101. YZ was in the back seat, passenger side. Not long afterwards, he was in the emergency room.

As he lay on the bed, bruised on the forehead, scraped all over, with some broken ribs and what seemed to be a dislocated collar bone, IV dripping and hospital staff buzzing around, the shock sensation spread like a warm liquid throughout his body, engulfing him. This was not where he expected to be.

"What about his friends?" he immediately thought. One, his Ghanaian friend in the passenger seat, was in intensive care. He had suffered the most. He was in a traumatic coma. But the doctors felt he was going to make it.

At that moment, YZ called out to God. "If you are there, God, save my friend. And help me get out of here healed and healthy. I want to believe in Jesus. But I'm asking you for these things first."

Bob and Betty visited YZ and his friends as they recovered. YZ shared his prayer with them. Bob looked at him with gentle eyes and asked, "Are *you* ready now to put your trust in Jesus? Even if you don't get the exact results of your prayers?"

YZ admitted he was ready, so Bob led him in a quiet prayer to invite Jesus into his life.

Everyone recovered, although the CBU team that year suffered in its run for the state championship. But they captured it the next year, with recovered athletes and a renewed commitment to play hard.

From that time until the moment he stood on stage before us at the conference, YZ continued to grow stronger in his newfound faith.

When our coworkers introduced us to YZ later, we saw his eyes light up as he heard about our family's plans. It was an immediate connection.

YZ immediately invited us to stay in his apartment in Shanghai upon our arrival. He suggested we rest there while recovering from jet lag. YZ owned the apartment with his parents; he had been able to contribute to its purchase with some of the money he had earned as a national athlete. His parents, however, would not be in town at that time, and neither would he, so the apartment would be ours to use.

We were amazed at the prospect of having a place to stay for free in the expensive city of Shanghai as we recovered and acclimated to our new time zone and surroundings. What a gift!

YZ told us how he had recently graduated from CBU and was waiting on his OPT, or optional practical training visa, in order to remain in the U.S. for at least another year. He expected to hear in the early fall at latest. So he would not be in China when we arrived.

He did offer, however, to set us up with one of his good Fudan University friends, Andy. Once Andy finished his exams, YZ told us, he would be available to help us figure things out. We would not know how much all this would mean until we were on the ground in Shanghai.

Indeed, the emergence of our angel – all six-and-a-half feet of him – appeared to us a remarkable sign we were headed in the right direction.

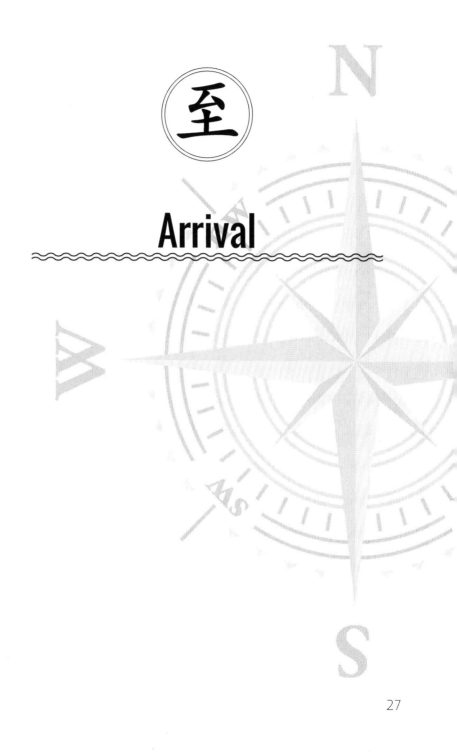

Arrival

8 | Taking off, touching down

"Nothing ever becomes real 'til it is experienced."
– John Keats, English Romantic Poet

The day had arrived. With sleep still in our eyes, but with energy and anticipation in our hearts, we jumped out of my parents' two cars curbside. They had offered to walk us in, but that seemed as if it would be too much for them, especially since they could only go with us up to Security.

I could see the mix of hopefulness and reluctance in my father's eyes. So, as we stood on the curbside hugging goodbye, I whispered in his ear, "Don't worry, Dad. It'll be all right. We will see you in a year. And we'll let you know we arrive there safely."

He is the more emotional of the two. My Mom is the more pragmatic one. She was excited for us, it seemed. I glanced towards my Dad and could see the slight wetness in his eyes.

I, too, felt a bit choked up, even though I was eager to go. Mostly because of my parents. Both in their seventies, they seemed on the borderline of old. But both remained remarkably sharp. At 71, Mom was physically fit, still walking most mornings.

At the back of my mind was this question, "Would they be here in a year?" When we moved to Japan early in our marriage, Dale and I had arrived at our new home in Hokkaido greeted by some shocking news. Dale's dad had just undergone emergency triple bypass surgery! Although his dad made it through the surgery fine, it had been difficult to be far away during that time. I know we *all* need to be prepared for the eventuality of death, but as people age the possibility grows. Now poised in their early-to-mid seventies, I thought about my parents in those terms a little more. I held each one of them in a longer-than-usual embrace.

Our family had 10 bags total, a large check-in and a carry-on, plus purse or backpack. While it looked like a lot of stuff, for a family of five heading abroad for a year, it was a reasonable amount. And everyone could take care of their own stuff. Even Luke, our now eight-year-old, could pull his smaller bag on his own. Justin, at 14, took turns with Dale managing Luke's large bag. Somehow it felt so freeing to be able to get around that airport with capable kids carrying (mostly) their own weight. I realized had we done this just a few years earlier, such would not have been the case.

As our plane approached Shanghai's Pudong International Airport, our sleepy eyes opened wide to take in the rows upon rows of high-rise apartments, the sprawl of the city, and the grey-yellowness of the air. It was mid-morning the next day. We still had a full day to live through before we were technically "allowed" to sleep. But the excitement of exiting the capsule that had contained us for 15 hours proved palpable.

We didn't have anyone meeting us that early August morning, so we had to figure out things ourselves. YZ had given us some instructions and we were following them. After passing through Customs, our first task was to find the train taking us into Shanghai's main station.

I recalled the first and last time Dale and I had arrived in China, in 1988. What a different world in 2009! Any Chinese would tell you that. I had even had some young people tell me, "They are not even the same countries." But immediately, at the modern, shiny Pudong Airport, I could tell the difference.

For one, we were not an oddity. It truly was an *international* airport among the best. Although predominantly Chinese, people from all ethnic backgrounds and races milled through the gleaming atriums, up and down slick escalators, pushing polished silver carts. The service workers seemed welcoming and hospitable.

My first impressions of *this* China were of a land of prosperity, of advancement. I secretly wondered, "Would this even be *nicer* than back home? And, if so, would we accomplish our goal of challenge?"

But it didn't take long to realize there would be plenty of hurdles ahead. One step out of the airport train, onto the gritty streets of Shanghai, where we hailed two taxis, made it clear: this was not like home. We were foreigners in a foreign land.

The August heat, thick and heavy, assaulted us. At that moment, the contrast between this present reality and the easy climate and clean air back home struck me. Although all of us had encountered humidity before, this time its effect assailed our tired minds and bodies. I had to pinch myself to start thinking clearly. "After all," I thought to myself, "These kids are depending on you!"

Thanks to YZ, we were able to pass a couple of notes with scribbled addresses on to the two taxi drivers. Both nodded their understanding. They didn't speak much to us. And what we heard coming from their mouths didn't sound *anything* like the Rosetta Stone Mandarin several of us had begun studying.

Arriving at YZ's place, up the narrow stairs with our bags, through the mottled heat, we heaved a collective sigh. It felt like bedtime, of course. But it was midday. Dale and I resolved we wouldn't give in to the jet lag.

Opening the door using the key YZ had arranged to be under the mat, we looked in. The apartment's simple, nondescript decor didn't get in the way of our feelings; right now, this place felt like heaven. *Pure heaven.*

As we entered, though, I felt everything in me cave. The sense of exhaustion and overwhelm engulfed all of us. None of us had slept much on the flight. The prospect of going through another full day without any sleep seemed impossible. So we decided to give ourselves a few hours. And we told the kids why we were doing it this way. While they seemed to understand, even more, they just were craving sleep.

We fell onto the beds and discovered a startling truth: These mattresses were hard, almost as if sleeping on the floor! We hadn't been prepared for that. But propping ourselves in various ways with blankets and pillows, we made due. We all fell into a deep slumber within minutes.

Dale's alarm rang three hours later, waking us with a start. Disorientation. It took a few minutes to gain composure and to reckon with reality. We had to get up.

As I sat up, I realized hunger was setting in. Combined with the travel and heat, the weakness felt almost crippling. And it became clear the others were feeling similarly.

What to do? Where to go? A sense of dread cascaded through me. There wasn't much in the apartment, just some dry goods, and it wasn't clear whether or not we could use them anyway.

Suddenly I realized how ill-equipped we were for this moment when our kids would need food, and we had no idea how to get it. This moment when the reality hit: We are in China, as a family, and we have no idea what we're doing. We can barely say anything. We don't know the system well enough to get around. We have, at the very moment, no one to actually help us. In an instant, panic overwhelmed me.

9 | Navigating new territory

"It's never overreacting to ask for what you want and need."
– Amy Poehler, American Actress & Comedian

Shaking off the disorientation, fatigue and panic, Dale stepped up and offered to go try to find some food we could cook in the apartment. The rest of us remained groggy and listless. So my hunter-gatherer husband set out on his quest with some of the money we had exchanged at the airport.

After what seemed like hours later (though probably only 20–30 minutes), he returned with five packages of instant ramen. "Well, I thought we could figure this out, and it would at least get us going," he explained. We found two pots, filled them with water, and figured out the gas stove. Within minutes, we had ramen for all five of us in a variety of bowls.

That meal tasted so good! Just hot noodles and a few freeze-dried vegetables. But we were so hungry we all gulped it down, wishing we had more. Now we needed to get ourselves up and out to explore the area around us.

The boys were lagging. They just wanted to stay put. This time, we chose not to fight that battle. Justin was old enough to remain with his little brother in an unfamiliar apartment in a city we did not know, thousands of miles away from home, right? Well, so we reasoned. We'd be gone for just a bit.

But when Dale, Erika and I hit the outside, we realized we had no orientation, no sense of where we were and...no smart phone! In fact, we had no phones. Not so startling of course, since Dale and I had only the most basic of cell phones back home. It was 2009. Most people didn't rely upon them in the crazy, obsessive way we do today. Still, our own lack of preparation for this moment struck us yet again.

At almost three in the afternoon, the humidity seemed turned up to its highest level. I was mopping my face every few minutes with a pack of tissues I had managed to swipe from the apartment. "*This* will take some getting used to," I thought. But I had been in heat like this before, many times. *I could do this!*

We wandered along streets with colorful food vendors selling grilled octopus on sticks, dumplings (饺子 – *jiǎozi*) and steamed stuffed buns (包子 – *bāozi*), calling out to us and motioning us with their hands to come try their fare. We offered them half smiles but declined. We just weren't sure we – nor our stomachs – were ready for that!

We stumbled upon a market where we could use our limited Chinese – *really limited Chinese, at the moment* – combined with the universal pointing finger, to purchase a handful of items all could eat back at the apartment. We were looking for items we could identify. While Dale and I are rather experimental with our food choices usually, this time we knew it best to err on the conservative side. There would be time. So we looked for what we knew and could make with little worry. And it boiled down to (literally and mostly) instant ramen, fruit and a few green veggies. We would wash all those well. I just couldn't trust the meat – not yet, anyway!

For the first few days, in the haze of jet lag and humidity, meals and moods were haphazard. Thankfully, even Luke, our youngest, seemed to realize things would get better. We spent an inordinate amount of time in YZ's apartment, grateful for the rattley air conditioner which made it all bearable. We found ways to prop ourselves up on pillows at night to adjust to the hard beds. The kids did better with it than we did. I realized, having given birth three times, some body parts had shifted….

We found ways to keep amused with only laptops and some limited (but often unstable) internet access. We kept in touch with family and friends back home to assure them, yes – we had arrived and were adjusting, albeit gradually.

But most "earth-shaking" for us – and especially for Justin – is what happened in China almost 2500 miles (3900 km) away, in

Ürümqi, the capital of Xinjiang Province, only a month earlier. Riots against the Chinese government in this predominantly Muslim area triggered Beijing to cut off access to Facebook and Google nationwide. The government claimed the protesters used both platforms for their communications.

Suddenly, we felt cut off. But the one who struggled most with it at first was Justin. With his recent 8th grade graduation, we now allowed him his first social media account. He was having a good time using it to connect with friends over the summer before we left.

The Chinese government's move affected us on a very practical level. Being Gmail users and earlier Facebook adopters, we struggled, at first, wondering how we'd communicate with the world outside China. Fortunately, my husband did have access to his teacher's email back home, run on a different server. That is how we got our first messages out, beyond China's "Great Firewall."

In truth, China doesn't feel like a police state all that much. At first. But if you keep your eyes open, if you try to press into the boundaries, and if you somehow transgress the accepted, you will feel it. Our first encounter came in the deep disappointment of our 14 year-old son.

In time, we found ways over and around the wall using a VPN (Virtual Private Network), and that served us beautifully for the year. And while we really didn't have anything to hide, as foreigners proffering resumés / curriculum vitaes splashed with references to our Christian faith, we wondered if this might be – or eventually become – an issue.

Then a surprise came to us about three days in. The water suddenly went off in the entire building! We were trying to get some cooking done at the time. I turned the tap and...nothing! At first I wondered if it was limited to our apartment, but then I went across the hall to knock on the neighbor's door and check with them, a bit anxious about this first linguistic challenge.

The woman who opened the door, probably in her early thirties, smiled demurely at me. She had a baby in her arms.

I took a breath, then in my rehearsed Mandarin began.

"Wǒ bù zhīdào zhōngwén. Nǐ zhīdào yīngwén ma?" (我不知道中文。你知道英文吗? – "I don't know Chinese. Do you know English?") Even with all the practice, I'm sure I still got the tones terribly off.

"Yes, a little," she responded shyly.

"We are friends of Li Yǒngzhèng. We are staying in his apartment for a short time."

"Ah, yes, Li Yǒngzhèng. He is in the U.S. now?"

"Yes. Do you know why the water is off?"

She didn't. And she didn't have water, either. But she told me her husband would try to find out and help us as well.

It took one-and-a-half days. Suddenly, we were out exploring Shanghai more than we might have planned. With purchased bottles of water, mind you. That's something we could find and recognize!

10 | Shanghai subway surprise

"All things are ready, if our mind be so."
– William Shakespeare, Henry V

I'm glad we had snatched that bundle of tourist material written in Chinese and English as we left the airport. At the time, I wondered if the fliers would simply find their way into the trash. But now, these brochures were helping us figure out Shanghai's subway system.

Subways! They are a favorite of mine in Asia (and in European cities, too). Years earlier, while doing a summer internship for Fuji Xerox in Tokyo, I felt such a sense of accomplishment when I felt I had "mastered" the Tokyo subways. It was one of those personal heroic moments where no one applauds but you realize you've conquered a behemoth.

Now, Dale and I were ready to take on this new challenge in Shanghai. I liked the system's circular structure – very much like Tokyo's. I can't lie; something comes alive in me when I get into airports, train and subway stations. I love the movement, the energy, the drama happening all around me in those places.

We found ourselves located on Line 8, the dark blue line. Our exit, Huangxing Park (黄兴公园 – *Huáng Xìng Gōngyuán*) sported a nice, clean station. We purchased our tickets to the center of the city, People's Square (人民广场 – *Rénmín Guǎngchǎng*) and got ready to explore. Finally we were venturing out.

Among the throng of people, including many foreigners, we managed to blend right in. Well, kind of. We were eager to find the restaurants YZ had told us about since by now our stomachs were grumbling again. The ramen for breakfast, lunch and dinner only went so far! This time, Dale and I resolved we'd get our family some real food in a restaurant.

Around us stood Shanghai old and new. Parts of the square memorialize China's Communist heroes. But we found more of an emphasis on the new. Cranes swaggered against the sky alongside modern highrises all around. We headed towards one of them, a seven-story shopping mall on the southeast corner of the bustling square.

YZ had told us to look for something there called *Lillian Dàntà* (蛋挞). It's a shop that makes these Portuguese custard tarts which, in time, became synonymous with Shanghai for us – or at least for our kids. Creamy, steamy deliciousness, cooked on site; it was tough to eat just one. So we usually managed a few, the boys even more.

We spotted the *Lillian Dàntà* stall in a food court in the basement of the building. But our parenting senses stepped in. "We first have to have some real food," Dale and I reasoned.

"Awww!" came the protest in unison.

We caved. Then towed back a bit, negotiating the deal to two per person before the "real meal." That seemed to work.

The enveloping aroma and rich flavor transported me to a very happy place. We did find a good meal in that same basement shopping mall, but the *Lillian Dàntà* stole the show, both before and after the "real food."

After some fun exploration – and growing confidence we could actually get ourselves around – it was time to head back to the apartment. I think the time out at People's Square gave us a sense we were not alone. How could we be, after all? We were in the third most populous city in the world!

Being different in a new place is both a humbling – and frequently energizing – experience. Humbling because you come to see how large and diverse the world is – and how tiny and insignificant you are. Energizing because you somehow, suddenly, are more aware of your interconnectedness with the larger swath of humanity.

Crowds can be alternately comforting and alienating to me. I love that feeling of blending in, when I know what to do and can sense a degree of competence in it, especially when I have to overcome linguistic and cultural hurdles. But the alienating aspect – namely, I don't *really* know what is going on because of differences in values, perspectives, experiences, culture, language and so on – can also arise within me when I am in a crowd. I become more the observer than the participant. I get lost in my own head.

We found ourselves in rush hour crowds as we waited for the Line 8 headed back to YZ's apartment. As the train neared, we aimed to keep our little band together. Doors opened, humanity poured out. We waited until we could push ourselves in, guiding the children in first amid the squash of people.

But before Dale and I could squeeze in ourselves, the doors shut! Our kids looked at us through the closed glass door with panic and dread. We had no Plan B! And we had no idea of whether or not our kids knew where to go, or what they would do.

This is the nightmare we hadn't seen coming. In a city of 23 million, our kids were hurtling through the dark subway tunnels without us. Sure, they weren't babies anymore, but they knew little language, had no money, no cell phones and no mom or dad with them. Immediate panic swelled up within us. But then calmness flushed first over my husband, and eventually me. (It usually happens in that order!) *Breathe.*

As we waited for the next train, we threw up a prayer. And then we began to discuss the range of possible scenarios. Our older two, especially, tended to be quite rational in their approach to a wide range of situations, we reasoned. This was a case of "What would Justin – or Erika – do?"

It's at a moment like this that a parent relies on his or her instincts and experiences with each particular child. We figured they would either get off at the next station. Or they would actually remember the correct station and get off there.

When we boarded that next train, we couldn't get on fast enough. With heightened senses, we pulled into the next station. Scanning the platform with eagle eyes, we decided to get off, just in case they had moved forward in the train and were further up on the platform.

Crestfallen, they weren't there. So we had to catch the next one and try a different strategy. Maybe they really *did* know the name of our final station. We began to think along those lines. So, even though we scanned each platform every time we hit a new station, we continued on until Huangxing Park. The ride seemed to take forever, much longer than it had when we headed out earlier.

But there, waiting for us at our "home" stop, were our three kids! When the doors opened, we burst out and several of us were crying. The uncertainty made it feel like we had been separated for days. The embraces felt *so* good at that moment! And we learned some valuable lessons through it all.

First, always have a Plan B (or C) if you're moving as a group. You never know when something like *that* will happen. Second, make sure your child(ren) know the "home" subway station.

Our kids are smart. Later we learned that, after some initial panic, Justin recognized his role as the oldest meant he needed to gain composure and attempt to calm the other two down. He remembered we had said it would be five stops to our station. So they got off at the correct station. But when we weren't on the next train passing through, Justin began to get nervous. Then Erika took the lead: "We just need to wait here until Mom and Dad come," she announced.

And the third lesson: chill. As with so many situations, you will be more effective with a clear head; panic only stresses and clouds your thinking. Being in a different culture adds a particular layer of challenge, perhaps. But remember, also – your kids often stand out as "different." And for you, at such a moment, that tends to work to your advantage.

11 | Learning the art of *'Bù yào!'*

"Most of my important lessons about life have come from recognizing how others from a different culture view things."
— Edgar H. Schein
Former MIT Professor in Organizational Development and Author,
Humble Inquiry: The Gentle Art of Asking Instead of Telling

The next day, about five days into our Shanghai stretch, we met YZ's friend, Andy. He had finished his exams and now was available to help us out.

While YZ remained our six-and-a-half-foot guardian angel even though an ocean away, Andy became our lifesaver. When he showed up at YZ's apartment one morning, we weren't quite sure if he'd be coming at all. We had heard from YZ about this imaginary Andy, and we knew he existed somewhere, out there.

But he became real first through the intercom at our apartment complex, and then with a knock on the door. When Andy stepped into this first chapter of our life in China, we all sighed a collective "Hallelujah!"

Unpretentious but friendly, Andy had just wrapped up his exams and would be headed to South Korea for the next stage of his business studies. Although Korean language study was occupying a large portion of his cranial capacity at the moment, his English skills remained quite strong, too. A relief!

Together, we soldiered out to Walmart (沃尔玛 – *Wò'ērmǎ*) for our first adventure with Andy. Being there felt quite surreal, with bins of live frogs and scampering scorpions among more recognizable fare. Then there were the rows and rows of eggs of all kinds ready for purchase.

Here's something to know about eggs in China. The variety is dizzying. The Chinese really know how to use an egg! Of course there are the white and brown chicken eggs common in the States. But they are often prepared in many creative forms. Perhaps the best known outside of China is the thousand year-old eggs (皮蛋 – *pídàn*), traditionally prepared by burying eggs in compost for three months.

And it's not limited to just chickens. The Chinese have tapped into both the dietary and medicinal values of eggs ranging from quail eggs (鹌鹑蛋 – *ānchún dàn*) to preying mantis eggs (螵蛸 – *piāo shāo*), as well as pre-laid eggs removed from the gut of butchered chickens. You name it! It's all fair game (no pun intended) for the Chinese.

Andy helped us identify items we never could have imagined as well as those we could. He also led us to a number of non-ramen food items we could easily prepare at the apartment. We left Walmart with a few heavy bags and boarded the subway home.

Next day, well rested and fed, we went back to *Yùyuán* (豫园) with Andy. It was that day we mastered the most valuable phrase in the Chinese language: *Bù yào!* (不要, literally "don't want" but really "I don't want it!"). As hawkers swirled around us, trying to sell us everything from fake Swatch watches to green laser flashlights to scorpion pendants to stuffed pandas, we became experts of the *Bù yào!*

Andy taught us we should not approach a vendor unless we are really thinking about buying an item. This was hard for those of us who like to browse and get a lay of the land. "Don't make eye contact," he cautioned.

And if you really want something? "You should ask the price, then walk away from the vendor as if you're not interested. They will offer a price lower than their given price. You turn around and offer them something absurd – very low, maybe a tenth of their original asking price. They will look shocked and act like there is no way. You signal you're still not interested by walking away. And then they'll lower again. Repeat this a few times until you've got a price you're willing to pay. Don't let them get you!"

"And, whatever you do, unless you're really good at Chinese, act like you don't know anything at all. You'll seem like the foreigner who knows nothing. They won't expect you can bargain so well. But you can," he offered with a wink and twinkle in his eye.

Dale decided he'd try it for a Chinese calligraphy stamp, or "chop," he'd been eyeing. In fact, we had hopes we could buy a chop for each of us with our name in Chinese characters. We thought it would be a fun item for us to have as we began our year in China.

Dale followed Andy's advice to a T. And yes, it worked, especially when he added in an additional bargaining point. Namely, Dale told the vendor he wanted five chops. This raised the stakes for the vendor if he lost the sale. In the end, Dale negotiated a 75 % reduction per chop, with a sizeable quantity discount on top of that.

Eight-year-old Luke wrote a blog post about his bargaining experience in Shanghai.

Luke's Voice: ~~~~~~~~~~~~~~~~~~~

China is a very hard place to get adjusted to. Like instead of $ there are yuan. That's Chinese $.

One of my favorite things is bargaining. I got a necklace for my mom and a scorpion named Freddy by bargaining in a park in Shanghai. I bargained the pure jade necklace down from 180 yuan ($27) to 30 yuan ($4). I bargained the scorpion down from 480 yuan to 50 yuan. It's fun to bargain!

~~~~~~~~~~~~~~~~~~~

All this is pretty hard for most Westerners since we don't have this practice of street haggling. Discussing this later with Andy as we attempted to decipher our meal at a cafeteria-style eatery, we came to an ironic realization. Americans bargain for large-ticket items – cars and houses – whereas Chinese focus on the smaller street items. "We would never think to question the price of a car or house in China," Andy informed us.

It was later this day we landed in the teahouse. Yes, Andy was with us. But it somehow seemed a point of arrival for our family. Thanks to Andy's help, a week's worth of our bodies catching up to our location, and a mental sharpening to the new world around us, the teahouse in *Yùyuán* marked one of the first turning points in our one-year adventure abroad as a family.

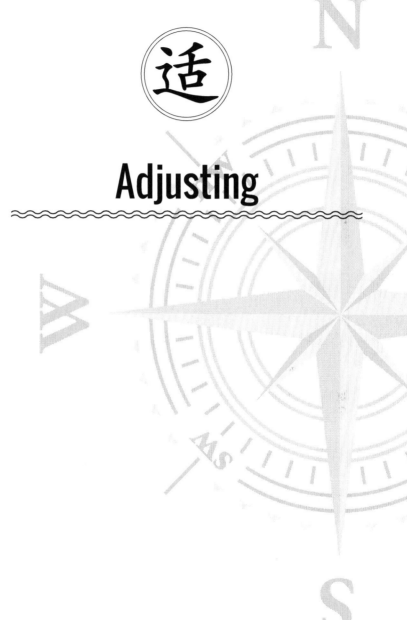

Adjusting

12 | Onwards to Ningbo!

"[The ocean] seems big enough to contain everything anyone could ever feel."
— Anthony Doerr
American Author, *All the Light We Cannot See*

We had crossed an ocean. But the ocean remained in our view. We needed to get to the other side of Hangzhou Bay (杭州湾 – *Hángzhōu Wān*) where our new home, Ningbo (宁波 – *Níngbō*), was located.

Oh, how we were ready to reach our new home and unpack our bags! We had been communicating via email with Ellen while recuperating from jet lag in Shanghai. Ten days later, Ellen sent a driver and her administrative assistant from Ningbo University (宁波大学 – *Níngbō Dàxué*) to come pick us up.

Two hours south of Shanghai by train or bus, Ningbo is a mid-sized or "second-tier" city with a population of 3.5 million in the six urban districts comprising the city proper. Including the outlying districts, the total rises to close to 8 million – a veritable urban sprawl. While 8 million is a huge number, it pales in comparison with top-tier cities like Shanghai (24M, the largest city proper in the world), Beijing (21.7M), Tianjin (15M), Guangzhou (13M) and Shenzhen (10.4M).

Previously, the only way to get to Ningbo was by train *around* Hangzhou Bay. But now there was a shiny, new and more direct route across the bay via the Xihoumen Bridge (西堠门大桥 – *Xihòumén Dàqiáo*). The bridge first opened in 2007 (with an expansion added later) and was, at the time, the world's longest suspension bridge, a source of pride for the Chinese. And yes, it stretched on and on. So much so, it boasts a rest stop midway. Of course, stopping there was part of the experience.

Rows and rows of travel snacks beckoned us. More familiar items included shelled sunflower seeds, crackers and chips (usually with an Asian food flavoring). They stood alongside more uniquely Chinese snack staples: stinky tofu (臭豆腐 – *Chòu dòufu*), hot and sour noodles (酸辣粉 – *Suān làfěn*), candied gourd (糖葫芦 – *Tánghúlu*), steamed small buns (小笼包 – *Xiǎo lóng bāo*), lamb skewers (羊肉串 – *Yángròu chuàn*) and Chinese breakfast "pancake" (煎饼 – *Jiānbing*).

One of these items bears exploring more here. That is the phenomenon of stinky tofu. First appearing in Chinese culture some 300 years ago, this pungent fermented bean curd fried golden brown either entices or repels both Chinese and foreigners alike. But regardless of whether you like it or not, the pungent aroma characterizes Chinese street markets, food stands and night markets like no other. Once you smell it, you'll never forget it.

As we entered Ningbo midday, we noticed all the industry and activity. No question, we weren't going to experience the Chinese countryside here! But we became pleasantly surprised as we passed through the gates of Ningbo University and discovered rows and rows of tree-lined streets and lanes, and large swaths of green grass. It was almost as if the university was aiming to soak up all the nasty CO_2 and other pollutants clogging up the air and offer it a blast back of oxygen. Ah, an oasis! Dale and I looked at each other and smiled.

Evidently Justin also appreciated the green before him. Not much later, he contributed this brief perspective on our family blog.

Justin's voice:

Ningbo stretches far and wide, with tall buildings looming everywhere. While compared to Shanghai, Ningbo is small; its streets still seem to go on forever. In the Ningbo University Campus, on the other hand, there is a lot of green and it differs quite a lot from downtown Ningbo. There are paths that run beneath tunnels of trees and lots of small shops and restaurants that make it a friendly place. We live in an apartment that looks quite dirty and ugly from

*the outside, but when we get inside, it feels nice and has everything
necessary for us to live. Coming to Ningbo has awakened my feeling
that, while things feel like necessities at the time, the petty possessions
that we see as large part of our lives aren't really that meaningful in
the long run.*

〰〰〰〰〰〰〰〰〰〰〰〰〰〰〰〰〰〰〰〰〰

Like our hometown of Monterey, California, Ningbo also lies on
the coastline. But this is where the similarities end, both in terms of
size (no comparison) and geography. Contrary to Monterey's pristine,
protected coastline, Ningbo is *industrial* coast. In fact, Ningbo is a
productive engine for the world.

As China's second-largest port after Shanghai, and its largest
deep-water port by volume, the Port of Ningbo is the exit point for the
region's largest industry, textiles. Chances are you are either wearing
something right now that has been produced in Ningbo, or you'll
easily find garments hanging in your closet that have been. "Made in
China" on clothes often means "Made in Ningbo."

In addition to the textile and garment industries, the city is also
a mass producer of home electrical appliances, plastic machinery,
moulds and auto parts. Rising industries include IT, electronics,
semiconductors, photo-electronics and new materials. And the staple
industries of petrochemical, steel and paper keep the Port of Ningbo
thriving. In fact, Ningbo even holds the distinct moniker, "Stationery
Capital of China."

It's no wonder that Ningbo's prominence in paper production
even from centuries ago led to the establishment of China's oldest
public library, Tian Yi Pavillion (天一阁 – *Tiānyī Gé*). The library once
boasted over 70,000 books in its collection, an impressive number
in its Ming Dynasty heyday (1368–1644) . The luxuriant grounds of
this magical place, an oasis of calm in the midst of this bustling city,
proved a place of solace and reflection for us more than once. And, of
course, it turned out to be a happy coincidence for the bibliophiles in
our group as well.

13 | Inside the gate(s)

*"Be grateful for the home you have, knowing that at this moment,
all you have is all you need."*
— Sarah Ban Breathnach, Author, Philanthropist & Public Speaker

After passing through the university's main gate, our first stop was Ningbo's Department of Education, where we met our Foreign Affairs Officer, Ellen. We were eager to meet this person who had become a virtual lifeline for us.

Slightly awkward, with a round face adorned with glasses, Ellen welcomed us with a warm, shy smile. We pushed through convention and both gave her big hugs. Those hugs may have taken her aback, but later she told us she really liked them, and it affirmed her choice of us. We felt that way, too.

Ellen wanted to give us a tour of the building at that moment; but we sensed our kids, especially, needed to arrive at our new home first. We were sensitive to how the kids were taking it all in. Even with the internet challenge and, especially, the shutdown of Facebook, at this point all seemed quite optimistic and rolling with the punches. We wanted to give them the smoothest landing into their new life as possible.

We got our first glimpse of what real life for a year would be like when we saw our new residence, a rather unremarkable three-story apartment in a residential section of campus. To get there, we needed to pass through a checkpoint gate. The guard in the booth tipped his head and acknowledged our passing group in the van ever so slightly.

We passed through another gate, the roads lined with red banners sporting white character messages. We later learned these were propaganda slogans, such as "Long live the great Communist Party of China!" (长寿中国伟大的共产党! – *Chángshòu zhōngguó wěidà de gòngchǎndǎng!*) and "Sing a folk song for the Party." (为民歌唱歌。 – *Wèi mínge chànggē.*)

Then we ran into an unexpected treat: a small pond, rock and grassy area with a bench and a couple pieces of exercise equipment alongside our route to our apartment compound. It was a small gift nestled into our otherwise concrete living environment. It would become, we discovered, a little gem of solace whenever everything seemed too industrial around us.

At the entry to the apartment building, Ellen called on Mr. Chun. He and his wife, a jolly, weathered couple who appeared to be in their sixties or even early seventies, emerged from a tiny house. The two spoke with each other, cryptic expressions shooting back and forth, and then Mr. Chun turned to us with a wide, alternately toothless smile, "Hallo!"

That was the extent of his English, we discovered. But his friendliness seemed genuine. Ellen told us Mr. Chun and his wife lived here, in two tiny buildings guarding our apartment. They would keep us safe. She also told us they don't speak any English. "They're part of the old generation who would never learn English because it was prohibited then," she shared flatly. "But I think you can communicate through gestures."

Mr. Chun offered a "hallo" to each of our children, and took a special liking to Luke. He muttered something to Ellen. She turned to us and said, "He thinks Luke is probably a naughty boy! Is it true?"

Here's a phrase we would encounter again and again over the year. Apparently, boys who are between 7–10 years old, or thereabouts, are routinely called "naughty." The Chinese word is *tiáopí* (调皮). At first, we took this as an affront. "Of course he isn't naughty," we reasoned to ourselves. "We are raising him well." Over time, we came to see this as a term of affection. And, if we were honest with ourselves, we could see some of that playful "naughtiness" in our eight year old at the time!

So we answered as diplomatically as we could at the moment, without real cultural insight: "Well, at times! But we try to teach him properly." Luke scowled a bit as those backpedaling words trickled out of our mouths.

More mysterious interchange ensued between Ellen and Mr. Chun. Ellen seemed to be giving Mr. Chun some instructions. "Ah, ah," Mr. Chun acknowledged by nodding. He smiled again.

Later I learned, after asking Ellen, they weren't speaking standard Mandarin Chinese (普通话 – *Pǔtōnghuà*), at all! Rather, they were communicating in Ningbo dialect (宁波话 – *Níngbōhuà*). It was a completely different set of words and sounds – rough and gritty, with sharp endings, at least to us.

We marched up a narrow concrete stairwell to the second floor with our first set of suitcases, on the heels of Ellen and Mr. Chun. She told us we actually had two apartments. They were the only second-floor apartments on this side of the building and they faced door-to-door. Apparently there was another set of apartments off the east stairwell, so we shared the second floor with the occupants of those two other living spaces.

Mr. Chun unlocked the larger apartment first. It was more spacious than we had imagined, but not huge. The formica tile floor and clunky red-hued furniture would be our mainstay. This apartment had a long main room, with one larger bedroom and attached bath, as well as a tiny laundry area and patio off the bedroom. It also had another modest bedroom off the living room, the size of a generous walk-in closet in the States. We planned on that one for Erika. Last came the narrow kitchen, much like an alley where about two people could stand, jutting off the living room.

Everything looked clean, better than we had expected. We smiled our approval.

"This apartment has a heater and A/C," Ellen noted. "Most of the living spaces on campus, especially the dormitories, do not have one. Here, let me show you how it works."

The unit stood in the corner of the living room. Directions proved fairly straightforward, aided by the standard "red is hot, blue is cold" symbols. Because it was hot and sticky, we couldn't wait to cool the air in the room so, once set, we kept the A/C going for a bit. Little did we know then how vital the other function of this upright "modern" machine would become just a few months from now.

The kids were getting antsy. "What about us?" Luke asked.

We went across the hall. The apartment there sported a smaller front room and tiny kitchen off of it, with an ample bedroom and attached bathroom, but no patio. The desk area on the far side of the room faced a window. And the room had several built-in bookshelves. We had planned to turn that room into the boy's bedroom. But Erika expressed – strongly – how much she wanted it, and we needed to rethink how all that would work. In the end, we decided to turn the smaller front room into a shared space for the boys. But we faced a challenge – no bed, only a couch. We wondered aloud how we were going to work that one out, and so did our boys.

"Don't worry," Dale piped up. "We'll find you a bunk bed set like back at home." The boys seemed content with that option. Still, I could see a bit of concern rise up in Luke's eyes. The two heavy apartment doors and small stairwell hallway separating our littlest from his parents was something he – and we – definitely weren't expecting.

We turned towards Ellen and asked if she knew where we could find a bunk bed. "A what?" she responded. This proved a novel concept. As we explained, she nodded her head, and the idea started to become clear. This was our first limit-pushing request, really. There would be more down the line.

We made a plan to go shopping with Ellen for bunk beds the next day. Meanwhile, the boys slept in the double bed in the tiny bedroom on our side. Everyone seemed okay with that.

Erika was eager to have her own space. In fact, once her stuff was all in, she practically turned into a decorating machine for hours, transforming the bare room into her personal haven. This, we realized, was Erika's way of coping with the transition, the jarring changes she already was facing in a life so far shielded from much change.

The boys, on the other hand, fell onto the couch in the living room and took out books and toys, as well as one of the laptops we had brought loaded with several games, kind of in a daze. They didn't know what to do or where to put their stuff. We helped them to put their main bags in what would become their room, and just bring in the needed items to the "temporary" space.

At this point, Ellen pulled out a map of the university campus and oriented us.

"There's a market nearby." She proceeded to explain how to get to it. "It's called *Jiā Jiā Lè* (家家乐), or Carrefour. Maybe you know that last name?" (Actually, we didn't. Carrefour is a French company.) This would be the place, just a five-minute walk away, where we could get almost any item we need, she assured us.

Jiā Jiā Lè was one of two larger markets on a campus flanked by extensive shopping alleys. These areas boasted shops and restaurants of all kinds, frequented by students, professors, staff and others who made their livelihood on the Ningbo University campus.

One additional place Ellen pointed out was Jack's. "It is the restaurant on campus offering not just Western, but all types of other food in addition to regular Chinese dishes," she explained. "I suggest you try this place for dinner. I think the kids will like it."

We bid Ellen goodbye after arranging a time the next morning to meet at her office and finish off some paperwork. Thankfully, she recognized our need to rest, set up and explore a little bit.

Dale and I told the kids we'd be back in about an hour. They all preferred to stay back – Erika, proceeding with her decorating project, the boys chilling out on familiar computer games. We could've pushed it and required them to come with us, but we chose not to. After all, they had just been on a long van ride to the campus and were still adjusting. "Give them some space to find their way," we agreed.

14 | Small language victories & Jack's burgers

"Earth is a small town with many neighborhoods
in a very big universe."
— Ronald J. Garan Jr., NASA Astronaut

With map in hand, Dale and I made our way to the closer shopping alley. Passing by a school, our Japanese character knowledge told us it was an elementary school. Maybe this would be where Luke would attend, we wondered. We then spotted *Jiā Jiā Lè,* went inside and explored the aisles. "Yes, this would work," we exclaimed exuberantly to one another. A post office stood next door as well as a pharmacy, places we could decipher.

Our greatest discovery that first day on our initial foray was the Farmer's Market. Now, before you start thinking "trendy, upscale, produce mixed with creative ethnic clothing and other goods" type of farmer's market, think again. This market was all about real farmers and food. Think farm-to-table of the most basic kind. And yes, it was fresh, as in just-arrived, "bearing the manure-y smell of the field" type of freshness. And the market sprawled over a large area.

We wondered why Ellen hadn't mentioned it. Perhaps it was unremarkable to her? For us, though, the market proved a treasure trove not only of goods, but also a linguistic, cultural and experiential gold mine! We were thrilled!

Much of the market was indoors, under a semi-permanent roof, and the cacophony, especially at this late hour of the afternoon, was almost deafening, in a good sort of "this-is-the-real-thing" kind of way. We loved it!

And many of the vendors looked up and smiled at us. Most were nonplussed. They had seen our type before. After all, we were just a couple of *wàiguórén* (外国人 – foreigners), and this was a university after all. And, when it comes down to it, most all of the *wàiguórén* look the same to them anyway, we reasoned. It wasn't until several days later, when we went there with our children, that we'd stand out. While most of the produce was marked with prices, some was not. We decided to purchase a few items. *Duōshǎo qián?* (多少钱 – "How much does it cost?"), we'd ask in our best Mandarin. We had certainly mastered this most necessary of phrases in Shanghai, if not from long ago. But now we were about to put it to use for real-life stuff!

This moment was exhilarating, in a personal way. We were crossing the language divide because these people *couldn't* come in our direction. In fact, we learned, most of these farmers and their helpers, communicated with one another and with the locals in *Níngbōhuà*, but they easily switched over to *Pǔtōnghuà* with us. We never met a single one who tried even a word in English with us. This was fertile territory for us to make some linguistic advances unencumbered by our mother tongue. We were alternately scared and delighted. Who knows what we might discover?

A cherubic but disheveled little girl, no older than five, helped her mother count out heads of lettuce and other similar produce. She looked up at us with wary eyes, but her mother smiled widely at us. A welcoming sign.

Nǐ de niūer ma? (你的妞儿吗 – "Is this your daughter?") I asked.

Duì ya, (对呀 – "Yes, yeah!") she responded.

Wǒ yě yǒu niūer! (我也有妞儿 – "I also have a daughter!")

Zhēn de ma? (真的吗 – "Really?")

Dui ya, I mimicked. I knew I was getting to the edge of my Chinese language skills.

Nǐ de niūer zài nǎ? (你的妞儿在哪 – "Where is your daughter?") I stumbled, then thought. For a moment. *Wǒ de niūer zài jiā.* (我的妞儿在家 – "My daughter's at home.")

Ah, ah! (啊啊, "Ah, I see.")

This is where it ended. Only later did I realize she thought I had meant back in the U.S., or wherever I was from. Several days later, when I brought my daughter with me and introduced her, she seemed surprised, though I couldn't understand what she was saying at all. Although I did understand one thing she said: *Nǐ de niúer hěn piàoliang.* (你的妞儿很漂亮 – "Your daughter is pretty.") Yes, she was pretty cute, in that middle-school sort of way. (Now she's quite striking.)

We explored more of the campus, trying to cover the perimeter – the East, South and West gates. There was no North Gate because the university bordered a river on that side.

We found modernesque-style buildings, along with standard block-like structures, reminiscent of pictures we'd see of Soviet Communist-era structures. Oddly, few people were on the streets at this time of day. Later we would learn this was because school had not started just yet. But the lack of people in otherwise-crowded China, combined with the stark structures and slate grey sky overhead, gave the campus a type of surreal, even eerie, ambiance.

The heat of this rather long day was subsiding, and now, at dusk, we knew we needed to return. Along the tree-lined pathway to the center of campus, through the shopping streets near our home, past the street vendors offering a quick bite (of what, we didn't quite know yet), past *Jiā Jiā Lè* and the elementary school, through the guarded gate, past the small pond and grassy area, past Mr. Chun, up the concrete steps two flights, we returned to our new home.

Kids were hungry.

They were ready to get out.

So we took Ellen's advice and went to Jack's, the nearby restaurant offering "foreign food." The proprietor, a taller, hefty man who happens to go by the name Jack but really is a Liu in disguise, greeted us with a wide grin. He spoke a few words of English, but then quickly fell into Chinese, or probably, *Níngbōhuà*.

Jack directed us up to the second floor of the eatery. Up the narrow metal staircase we went. The most distinct feature of the restaurant's decor were the two whiteboard walls. Visitors far and near had made their marks by expressing their thoughts in Chinese, English, Japanese, Korean, Russian, German and a host of other languages. Some did so through pictures, others through poetry, some with graphic flair, others in a messy hurry. This looked like a fun, open-minded place.

The menu was a veritable cornucopia of cuisines: schnitzel, udon, french fries, kimchee, caesar salad. And lots of American foods the kids recognized! The boys ordered burgers, Erika ordered spaghetti and meatballs, and Dale and I each went for something a bit more Asian. The food arrived in no time, and it was consumed in less, especially by those boys. We would come to learn very soon that one entree wasn't enough for our 14-year-old son. He had become an eating machine.

And the burgers tasted like burgers! And the spaghetti like spaghetti! Just a bit off from the "real thing" in the U.S., but not by much. Jack had nailed it – and he had never stepped out of his country!

We slipped in desserts for the kids this time, so I think Justin got filled up enough. Everyone left satisfied. Dale and I sent a little "thank you" up to God for Jack and his special restaurant. It would become a haven for us – and especially for our kids – when we simply needed a taste of home.

Everyone went to bed that night pretty early, tired and content. Even the boys, who managed to sleep together in the double bed in the tiny bedroom, seemed to get themselves a deep sleep.

We had arrived. Again.

15 | Unexpected visitors & a warning

*"We were meant to survive because of our mind's ability to reason,
our ability to live with frustration in order to maintain our virtue.
We wore smiling masks while dying inside."*
— Anchee Min, Chinese-American Author

One morning some unexpected visitors knocked on our door. Opening it, we found five students, all male.

"Mr. DePalatis?" asked the one in front, tall with close-cropped hair and thick-rimmed black glasses.

"Yes, that's me," Dale responded, intrigued.

"I'm Russell, and the former teacher here, Taylor, told me to come meet you."

Dale invited them in, pulled out chairs and they all sat down after a few greetings with both of us and nods to our children.

Russell spoke up. "We're here because Taylor told us he's pretty sure you guys are Christian believers. Is it true?"

Dale and I shot each other glances, and he responded with a smile, "Why, yes!"

Russell broke out into a smile, visibly relieved. The other guys seemed to relax as well.

"We were studying Bible with Taylor every week. We were sad when he had to return back to the U.S. But then we learned about you and your family. And we were excited to know you might be able to meet with us, too."

Then Russell's voice became very low, almost inaudible but still clear to Dale: "We always need to be careful how we talk. I hope you understand. We just never know how much others can hear."

Russell went on, with a louder voice now. "I also know of some girls who would like to meet and study with your wife. Will that work?"

I responded, "Of course!"

Russell arranged to meet Dale in front of *Jiā Jiā Lè* the following Monday evening for dinner.

After that, the conversation's tone changed. We spent time getting to know these surprise visitors to our new home. We didn't have much to offer them but managed to boil some water for tea and bring out a few decent snacks left over from our Shanghai days.

Most of these guys were juniors or seniors at Ningbo University. They were studying a range of subjects, many of them technical. Their facility with English proved wide-ranging. In this context, Russell, an English major, emerged as their natural leader.

The guys left about 20 minutes later, with many of our questions unanswered. How did they know when we were coming? What was Dale supposed to prepare, if anything? Where would they meet? And what about the women – how would they connect with Caroline?

Still, we found the whole experience to be another slightly surreal moment in a string of surreal moments during that first month of arriving in China. We knew we had been called to this place by the way the doors opened up. But we suspected it wouldn't all be smooth sailing.

As the time approached for the meeting with Ellen's boss, Mrs. Li, it became clear only one of us would be able to make it. The kids needed food and, if possible, a little exploring outside. And, after a successful outing with Ellen the day before, we were expecting a bunk bed delivery anytime after 3 pm. So we decided I'd head to the meeting and Dale would stick with the kids and make sure everything got installed properly.

Around the conference room table sat seven other *wàiguórén* teachers, three men plus a couple from the U.S., one young guy from Canada, and one woman from Korea.

Our cohort of teachers included Jonah, a recent UC Berkeley grad with a serious demeanor, and Canadian Andrew – playful, outgoing, with the air of a college frat boy. Both would teach in our department. They seemed to strike up an instant friendship in spite of their very different characters.

Middle-aged, robust and an engineer by trade, Bruce came next. He told of how he burned out on engineering and began the English teaching circuit, working his way through Japan, Korea and now China. He would be working with Ningbo University's School of Technology.

Rounding out the single men was Parker, a Brown University economics graduate with an aloof nature who would teach at Ningbo's Business School. Joining him at the business school were a couple probably in their late 50's, Jerry and Ellen. With grown kids, they had been living abroad for the last dozen years or so, teaching English, mostly in Asia.

Finally we met Soo-jin from South Korea. We learned she lived directly above us with her two young boys. Her husband had to remain back home because of his job. Soo-jin had been hired to help start up a Korean language program at the school with a Ningbo University Chinese teacher of Korean.

All of us were new hires and were living in the same building, but we hadn't met one another yet. We all were friendly with one another, but when the meeting began, the mood in the room became distinctly somber.

Mrs. Li stepped in, along with an assistant and Ellen, both who took seats on the sides of the room.

"Good afternoon," she began, with a smile I'd come to associate with a slight increase in my stress level every time. "And welcome. We are glad to have you here and hope you are settling in well."

Her English was clear, strong and impeccable.

"I hope you've introduced yourself to one another. There will be many opportunities for you to get to know each other over the coming year. Today we want to orient you to Ningbo University and talk with you about some of the university policies."

Most of her "orientation" involved practical matters for our everyday living. But then she paused and continued with a tone of gravitas.

"As you know, China is an open and free country now. Our government allows for four religions to exist in our country

– Buddhism, Islam, Catholicism and Protestantism. However, we have had some problems with past teachers spreading their beliefs and ideological views both inside and outside the classrooms. This is not allowed."

In a single breath, it seemed, she was contradicting herself. "Free and open?" "The government allows?" "Outside the classroom...not allowed?" All these questions – and more – were spinning around in my mind. *This* shed even more light on our surprise visitors just that morning.

16 | First glimpses of our teaching life

"In the beginning there was only a small amount of injustice abroad
in the world, but everyone who came afterwards added their portion,
always thinking it was very small and unimportant,
and look where we have ended up today."
— Paulo Coelho, Brazilian Novelist, *The Devil and Miss Prym*

A few steps remained for us to get settled in our new environs. First, Dale and I needed to meet the staff, administrators and other teachers in the School of Education. Ellen arranged for that to happen the following day. Jonah and Andrew joined us. This meeting is where we *thought* we'd learn about our schedule and the classes we would be teaching.

We entered the cavernous lobby of the School of Education ready to meet a bunch of new faces and make every attempt we could to get names into our heads. This was a tough task, we found. Fortunately, our years of working with international students and, for Dale, with high school students, had helped us develop some techniques, often using mnemonics, to put these names in our head and, we'd hope, keep them there.

But with Chinese, we found, this proved much more difficult than we had imagined.

Settling in around the large wood conference room table, with Ellen sitting off to the side, the 14 other attendees nodded and smiled slightly towards all of us before the department chair, a man named Liu Bao, took his position at the head of the table and opened the meeting.

Mr. Liu's Chinese was fast, and although I could pick up a few isolated sounds, I had no idea what he was saying. But then we heard our sort-of-garbled names, and everyone stared at Dale and me. After that, a nod to Jonah and Andrew. And then a woman stepped to the front.

Mrs. Dang was the top teacher in the School of Ed. Wearing thick-rimmed glasses, with greying hair pulled up tight in a bun, she seemed both harsh and refined all together. She spoke with excellent, though accented, English to our group.

"Mr. and Mrs. DePalatis, Mr. Moreno and Mr. Pike, we are pleased to have you with us in Ningbo University's School of Education. We hope your experience here will be positive and the students will learn many things from you as native English speakers."

She paused.

"I know you have all been through the Orientation in the Foreign Affairs Office. So we won't cover what they have done. All we ask is that you be fair graders and mind the code of conduct in our school."

I felt, at this point, she looked more pointedly at the two young men, but still I'm not sure. I don't think she was worried about us. At least not yet.

She motioned towards her assistant, standing on the side.

"We have prepared for you a draft schedule for classes beginning next Monday. Please understand, the classes are just filling right now as students register, and we may need to make some adjustments before the start. But this is what we have now. Each one of you has about 15–18 hours in class. And then of course, we know you will spend the rest of the 40-hour work week planning and grading. Please let us know if you have any concerns."

We looked over our schedules. They were typed but some parts were scribbled out with handwritten additions.

With undergraduate and master's degrees in English Literature, and several years of high school teaching under his belt, Dale looked forward to a new teaching challenge with college-level literature students. Fortunately, the department had assigned him the higher level Literature courses rather than the conversational English classes the rest of us had. I know he wouldn't have been satisfied with anything less. Overall, he seemed pleased as he looked over the draft schedule: Three American Lit classes, one Practical Writing class, and one Advanced English Conversation class.

While I had taught before, I was not a certified teacher and teaching was not my main focus. But I had taught one-on-one and to small groups, worked with internationals for so long, was good in front of groups, and felt confident in my ability to plan and teach. I, too, was pleased with the classes they had sketched out for me: Two Intermediate Conversation classes, two Speech & Debate classes, and one Movie and Film class. "Hmmm," I thought. The last three especially intrigued me.

Then I piped up and asked a question.

"Excuse me. Could you please speak a little about grading? Is it a standard system – 90–100% is an A, 80–89% a B, and so on?"

"Yes, I'm glad you asked. Generally speaking, we try to give out A's here," she responded without missing a beat. "We believe the students have worked hard to get into our university, and we want them to be employable when they get out."

I was a bit shocked when I heard this. Did this mean we could only give them A's, even if a student didn't deserve it? I asked her about that.

"There will be times when a student does not do the work well enough to get an A. I understand that. And in such cases you may award him or her with a B. Such a grade may often be a warning for us to watch that student, however."

So, we realized then and there, there was no "so on."

This response shocked my sense of justice. And it was not the only issue in the Chinese university education system that would prove to do so.

17 | On being *wàiguórén*

"The world accommodates you for fitting in, but only rewards you for standing out."
— Matshona Dhliwayo, Zimbabwean-Canadian Author

We were not hired by Ningbo University to blend in and be the same as everyone else. No, we were hired because of our "differentness."

I believe the experience of being different from others – really sticking out – can be a valuable learning opportunity for anyone. It forces a person to recognize the variety of people in new ways. When most of the surrounding people have black hair, the finer details of a person's appearance, character and overall presence stand out more, leading to a new appreciation of others.

In my case, I became acutely aware of the challenge of sticking out wherever I went. Sometimes, I just didn't want to be noticed; I wished I could just blend in and get all those eyes off me. Other times, I was happily different, living in the alternate universe of my mind. And still, at other times, the differences added layers of nuance to my experience. I came to realize the many ways people approach this thing called life. At the same time, I became more appreciative of the common humanity we share on this planet.

I cannot deny it. As white, educated Americans, we were accepted outsiders. I don't want to minimize in any way the challenges people of color may face with regard to acceptance. Still, I believe this experience of being in the minority, although hard at times, can lead to growth as well.

I had experienced this before – and much moreso – as a foreigner

(外人 – *gaijin*) in Japan in the 1980's, especially in the more rural areas.. So this feeling was not new to me.

Dale and I realized our kids would experience this, perhaps in an even more acute way than we did, in China. While both Justin and Erika had been abroad before, Luke had not. And none of them had lived overseas, as Dale and I already had. So we aimed to monitor the impact of this "outsider factor" on their emotions and overall well-being.

Athough we wanted to make sure we gave our children all the attention they needed, we also had learned years earlier the importance of making time for ourselves as a couple. We had made it a point to take a weekly night out for ourselves from the earliest days of parenting. These date nights would range from the "WOW!" to the "What happened?" and everything in between. In fact, when the children were very young, we would be so tired we barely made it out on our date nights. But we managed to persevere, making it a priority, both in terms of time and finances.

We were determined not to let the year in Ningbo derail us from this practice.

One date night early on, being *wàiguórén* led to a funny cross-cultural communications experience over the meal. Dale wrote this piece on the experience afterwards:

Dale's voice:

We entered a restaurant that was a typical hole-in-the-wall establishment with a street-side buffet that stood in a narrow alley in the business district between the main Ningbo University Campus and the West Campus. As we sat at the rather cheap plastic table under the glaring fluorescent light hanging in the middle of the eight-table restaurant, a television hanging in the corner blared out the latest Chinese drama. The air was redolent of cooking oil, Chinese food, and the strange mixture of cigarette smoke, smog, and grime that characterizes quite a lot of the air in urban China.

The proprietor's husband, obviously interested in the wàiguórén who had ventured into their little shop, kept passing by and making small talk. While "Wǒ yào zhège" (我要这个 – "I want this") and

"*Xièxiè*" *(*谢谢 – "*Thank you*"*) are among the most basic Chinese expressions to know, success using these led us to further boldness as the meal progressed.*

And, even though we'd been in China for a relatively short time, we were beginning to move from the stage of understanding nothing, passing through the stage where we understood "is," "he," "I," "have," and "you" with an occasional "hello" in a mush of incomprehensible sound, to a new stage where we began to actually catch an idea now and then.

*The proprietor made a comment that sounded to me like he was asking where we were from. I promptly responded with a phrase we'd been learning in our Rosetta Stone studies: "Wǒ lái měiguó." (*我来 美国。 – "*I'm from America.*")

*We exchanged names, and then he asked us another question to which all we could say was "Tīng bù dǒng" (*听不懂 – "*I hear; I don't understand*"). *He asked something again, and this time we thought we heard a word that indicated he was interested in how long we've been here. We replied "Liǎng gè yuè" (*两个月 – *two months).*

*Another question was fairly unintelligible, but we guessed he was asking what we were doing in Ningbo, so we responded, "Wǒmen shì níngbō dàxué de lǎoshī." (*我们是宁波大学的老师。 – "*We are Ningbo University teachers.*")

The evening went on like this with much laughter and apologies for our bad Chinese, but we left feeling quite elated to have communicated more than basic greetings in the Chinese language.

*But in reality, from the perspective of the shop's proprietor, we wonder if the conversation really went more like the dialogue below. Imagine the following is all in Chinese. The proprietor of a shop is called a Laoban (*老板 – *lǎobǎn).*

Laoban: *So… are you enjoying your food? It must be different than in your country…*

Me: *We are Americans.*

Laoban: *You're from America, so isn't America a place where it takes a long time to start a business?*

Caroline: *What's your name?*

Laoban: *I'm Guo.*

Me: *I'm Dale.*

Laoban: *So don't you have a Chinese name?*

Me: *We don't understand.*

Laoban: *It… takes… a …long … time… to start… a business.. in America? (spoken slowly)*

Caroline: *We're here two fish. (She thinks she's saying "two months" but has the wrong tone.)*

Laoban: *You're here two fish?*

Me: *Young phoenix, uh, uh, moon. (another couple of attempts to say "yuè," but with incorrect tone)*

Laoban: *Ah, I see you've eaten two fish and there's a nice moon tonight. Hey honey (yelling to wife), these two are a bit looney!*

Caroline: *We are teachers at Ningbo Great Snow. ("Dà xué" is university; "dà xuě" with third tone on e means "great snow.")*

Laoban: *We don't usually get snow here…*

Me: *I'm eating well.*

Caroline: *I like spicy food.*

Laoban: *So, any ideas of how long it takes to start a business in America?*

Caroline and me: *Yes, yes. Thank you.*

Laoban: *Well, I hope you enjoyed your food. Would you like me to put what remains in a doggy bag?*

Me: *I'm eating well. Goodbye.*

Caroline: *Goodbye! Next time I want to speak more Chinese with you.*

Laoban: *Your Chinese is already very good.*

18 | How to feed a *wàiguórén* family

"Ask not what you can do for your country. Ask what's for lunch."
— *Orson Welles, American Actor & Film Director*

As *wàiguórén,* feeding our family proved an adventure in itself. We could get many of the packaged items we wanted at *Jiā Jiā Lè,* but we'd often have to guess what exactly we were getting. Pictures – and the occasional giveaway character – helped a lot. But if we wanted fresh fruits and vegetables – and even eggs and meat – we needed to make the Farmer's Market an almost daily part of our life.

Our refrigerator space was small, just a bit larger than those common in university dormitories in the States, making it difficult to stock up. But early on, we recognized that shopping in the market offered fertile language-learning ground; we couldn't resist.

Using the phrases *Wǒ yào zhè ge* (我要这个 – "I want this."), together with *Bù yào* (不要 – "I don't want this."), plus a command of the numbers, I could get by. But I found myself out in the market trying to challenge myself. Of course I'd ask the cost of something (*Duōshǎo qián?* 多少钱?) and express my surprise how expensive it was (太贵了! – *Tài guì le!*), but I also quickly sought to learn questions like, "Is it ripe?" (成熟了吗 – *Chéngshúle ma?*), "How do you eat it?" (怎么吃吗 – *Zěnme chī ma?*), "How do you cook it?" (怎么做饭吗 – *Zěnme zuò fàn ma?*) and so on. Sometimes I couldn't understand the response, but simply practicing the questions proved worthwhile.

Our little kitchen proved to be remarkably useful many days.

Narrow though it was, I learned how to whip together a quick meal using fresh ingredients purchased from the Farmer's Market. We did this especially when under a time crunch. But there were other options.

Restaurants lined the streets of the shopping areas on both sides of the university. There was a restaurant owned by a Muslim Uighur family from Lanzhou, in Gansu Province. There, everything was halal food – permissible meat, blessed by a Muslim cleric or imam. Closer to our apartment stood a pop-up eatery of sorts where you could eat pot stickers, or *jiǎozi* (饺子), for dirt cheap, but only when they chose to open (usually limited to the evenings). And then there was the ramen shop, a Chinese version of the Japanese national fast food. We stayed away from the ramen shop in those early days!

Here are some of Justin's early food thoughts in China.

Justin's voice:

There are both many fascinating restaurants and appealing marketplaces around our home. My dad and I went to one recently to get some fruit. The marketplace contained more than fruit and vegetables. Chickens walked around in small enclosures not knowing they would soon have their heads cut off and their bodies laid out on the wooden, unrefrigerated tables; and pig heads stared at us while they waited to be bought. To my sister, this was slightly disturbing.

There are also many interesting foods in China. Recently, at The Chicken Pot [a nearby restaurant], I ate a chicken foot, which looked like a little deformed hand. While we were there, we also ate quail eggs, bamboo, tofu, spam, and three different types of mushrooms. In Shanghai, I ate a bowl of frogs, which tasted like … frog.

Yet another option was street food. At first, we didn't frequent those vendors much, not knowing what type of bacteria might be lurking in their products. But, as time went on – and students helped us understand the foods better – we became more experimental and learned to rely on these places, with their student prices, for the occasional meal or two. I especially came to enjoy *jiānbǐng guǒzī* (煎饼馃子 – Chinese savory crepes) and *yángròu chuàn* (羊肉串 – lamb kebabs) when on the run.

Another favorite for the kids was jumping on bikes to get to a small refreshment stand. There we could buy *căoméi bīng shā* (草莓冰沙), strawberry smoothies for the equivalent of 25¢, to cool us off on those early humid days and into the cooler ones as well.

And the final option: the canteens.

Ningbo University had four canteens, or cafeterias, where we could eat. Three of them lined up on the first, second and third floors of a single building. They were designated for different groups: first floor for university staff, second for students, and third for faculty. And the variety and quality of the food – as well as the prices – increased as you moved up. The fourth canteen, in a separate building not far away, was strictly for students. It offered budget prices, similar to street food (but under a roof). All the canteens except the last one were open only Monday through Friday.

Ellen had encouraged us to use the faculty canteen with our family. "The food there is the best, no question. I think you and your family can eat well there." It was true. For approximately USD $3, all of us – even the boys – could get filled up!

One way of getting full – often too full – in China was the banquets. It seemed they happened all the time. First, there was the Welcome Banquet, as we all arrived. We attended one for all the foreign teachers, then one for our School of Ed, and then with the principals and teachers at each of our children's schools.

Chinese banquets. Lazy-Susan delivered delights of all shapes, colors, forms and sizes, floating around a table calling out to the guests on the periphery, "Try me." Well, they seemed to call out to everyone but eight-year-old Luke. Our family joke about the year is that Luke managed to survive on rice and the occasional Shanghai Lillian Danta. Although not true, sometimes it seems as if he came close. It was frustrating to us as parents that he'd be willing to try so little. But, then again, he was a "naughty boy" anyway. Guess his age got him off the hook.

I did wonder sometimes, however, if we were getting the proper nutrients into his little but growing body. Apparently, he managed. I worked hard in that tiny kitchen to prepare healthy meals to include cooked greens. I had always managed to do that back in the States. The Farmer's Market nearby helped, even if our space to cook was no larger than a small walk-in closet.

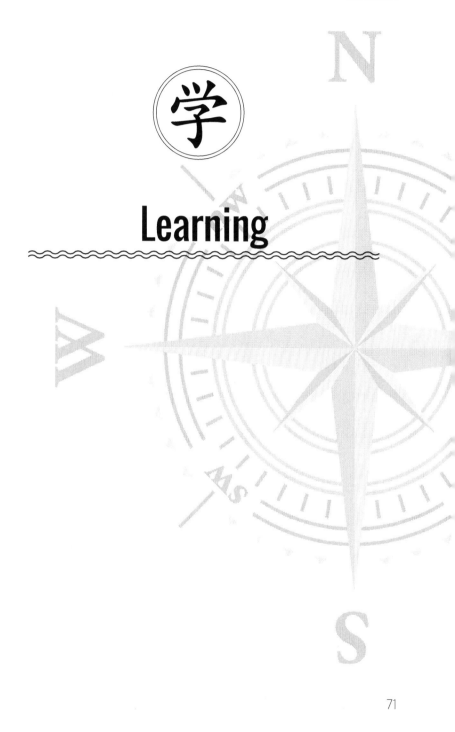

Learning

19 | Ningbo University wakes up

"Another fall, another turned page: there was something of jubilee in that annual autumnal beginning, as if last year's mistakes had been wiped clean by summer."
— Wallace Stegner, American Novelist

When Ningbo University opened up for its fall classes in early September, it was as if a sleeping giant awoke.

Nondescript restaurants and storefronts transformed into lively gathering spots as students pulling suitcases, purchasing bicycles and filling their dormitories with everything from bedding to cleaning supplies flooded the stores, streets and byways in our university town.

They gathered and laughed, shouted and giggled. I couldn't understand most of what they were saying, but I could sense their excitement and delight in reconnecting with friends after the summer. And then "Freshman Day" with all the new and nervous arrivals oftentimes flanked by their parents (父母 – *fùmǔ*), ever so proud... protective...relieved...reflective – *Where did that time go?*

I found myself thinking that very same thing as I watched them, remembering that day well over half a lifetime ago when I first stepped onto the Stanford campus as a new freshman – eager, invincible, yet apprehensive and wondering.... Where *did* that time go?

Ningbo University came alive this first week in September, and, in some ways, so did I.

Suddenly, I found myself with 160+ new people in my life – and more to come the following week, as I would meet two additional classes.

Suddenly, I wasn't simply a *wàiguórén* living in the Foreign Teacher's Building (外教大楼 – *Wàijià Dàlóu*). In an instant, I felt a burst of *reason* for being in China.

I was a *lǎoshī* (老师), a teacher, a respected role in this Asian society. I was a cultural ambassador. I was a light that wanted to shine – not just to represent my country, but to represent something larger and more meaningful. There was a *reason* to be here.

The few weeks we had for transitioning were exhilarating but also exhausting. Not until I finished my last class during the first week did I truly feel as if we had *finished* the transition and were now a part of the *living fabric* of this university community.

And in a larger sense, we are actually woven into the fabric of China this year, since we travelled around China's vast land during the course of our stay. We were indeed *wàiguórén* – and we'd continue to be on the outside because of limited language capabilities and our otherness, but we were on the path to becoming very much a part of what China was that year: a burgeoning land of growth.

As English teachers we had classes and students, lesson planning to do and papers to grade. We both had a full five-class, schedule (with a few extras thrown in) both semesters.

I remember my first class well – a 9:00 am Intermediate English Conversation class filled mostly with young women. They seemed to let out a collective "oooooH!" when I entered the room. I wasn't by myself. Lynn (her English name), from the School of Education, accompanied me. She shared what I imagined must be a few words of introduction – or instruction – and then gave the floor to me.

"Good Morning!" I exclaimed.

"Good Morning, Teacher!" they responded, almost in unison.

I smiled inside. You don't get this in the U.S. That's for sure!

"My name is Caroline DePalatis, or Mrs. DePalatis. It is a difficult name, so let me explain that to you…."

I spent time in each of my classes helping them understand not only *how* to pronounce my last name (*dee-pa-la-tis*), but also the origins of the name (Italian). I also told them the funny story of having a complicated maiden name (Del Gaudio, also Italian), and how I had always wanted to marry someone with a simple name, like Jones, or Smith, or...Chen?

Invariably, they would laugh at that.

Chinese don't have the custom of a woman changing her last name to her husband's last name upon marriage. And, although our customs are changing in the West – I let them know that – the standard name change remains in most cases. I wanted to make sure they knew that.

To further introduce myself, I used a bag full of items dear to me. Laying those object out before them, I then would ask them what they could figure out about me. A scarf. A book. A family picture. A set of colored pencils. I'd let them figure me out, rather than simply tell them. This proved an effective way to share about myself and let them use their English.

They engaged in the lesson, most with such eager eyes. Oh, yes – I'm sure there were at least a few who were fearful to be noticed, to look up, to be asked to speak. I could spot a handful in each class.

But the majority? Their enthusiasm proved contagious. I came to delight in my classroom time more than I would have imagined because these eager minds wanted to connect, learn, and grow.

Later, Dale told me he had experienced much the same response. And, not only did we find these students eager and ready to learn, but we found so many of them thoughtful, with lots of questions and the occasional insightful comment to blow us away.

~~~~~~~~~

Ningbo University, like the city itself, was deemed a "second-tier" university. These were not the students who got the top scores on China's infamous *gāokǎo*, or China's National Higher Education Entrance Examination. The Chinese characters, 高考, literally mean "top think(er) / test," and that's what the *gāokǎo* aims to do: pull out the "top thinkers" from the masses, rate the minds of China's high school seniors against one another. The top are siphoned off each year to a handful of select schools based solely upon their performance on the *gāokǎo*.

The test runs about nine hours over two grueling days. In most provinces all students take Chinese Literature, Mathematics, and a Foreign Language (English, Japanese, Russian or French) exam. They then have a choice of whether they will lean towards social sciences (文科倾向 – *wénkē qīngxiàng*) or natural science (理科倾向 – *lǐkē qīngxiàng*). If they lean towards social sciences, they will take an additional test on history, politics and geography (文综 – *wén zōng*); if the natural sciences, they'll take an additional test on physics, chemistry and biology (理综 – *lǐ zōng*).

Unlike the West, where factors beyond raw test scores will determine your educational – and likely professional – fate, in China the *gāokǎo* is king. It does have some modern-day detractors, but they have not been strong enough yet to topple the system.

Although as a Westerner I am prone to question the ultimate value of judging and determining the future with such finality for a 17 or 18 year old through an examination like the *gāokǎo*, one point I will concede. The Chinese government expects its young people to reach a level of knowledge and competency in a foreign language, and it tests them on it. From my perspective, I believe this is one area where China (and so many other countries) has set the bar far higher for its young people than has been done in the U.S. In this respect, it has created a system requiring its young people to look outward, and rewards those who do with a score that can help determine their future.

Of course, in the U.S., we have some standards for foreign-language learning as well. You cannot graduate a U.S. high school anymore without a minimum of two years of a foreign language. But there is no competency test at the end (unless a student wants to challenge an AP, or Advanced Placement, test).

The challenge in both environments, of course, is to present to the young student a *reason why* they should pursue a foreign language. Lacking that, it is easy to see the other language as only a textbook experience or a hoop to jump through in order to score well on a test. The challenge for the foreign language teacher is to make the language come alive, to empower his or her students to connect and communicate, and to provide reason why doing so makes sense.

So, as a second-tier university, I was not expecting to get "the best and the brightest" in my class. But the students I did have, on the whole, impressed me with their intellect, their curiosity, their commitment to communicate and learn. "If this is the 'second-tier,'" I thought, "I can only imagine how amazing the first-tier must be!"

20 | The new look of school for our children

*"If you aren't in over your head, how do you know
how tall you are?"*
— T.S. Elliot, Author

As we began classes with our students, we also were moving into new territory with our children, on two fronts.

First, we had set ourselves up to homeschool the kids for their basic grade requirements in the mornings, Monday through Friday. As public school kids, this would be as new to them as it was to us. And, as a professional educator, Dale was looking forward to it. Me, not so much.

My apprehension was grounded in fear, I'm sure. While I loved nurturing our kids' learning in an informal way, the idea of being responsible for their educations while also working full time appeared daunting, at least at first.

For Luke, the curriculum was straightforward. I was familiar with the material, especially because of my closeness to the educational process when the other two were in elementary school. I had volunteered a lot, so I didn't find his curriculum intimidating at all. The challenges would come later with his attitude – and his tendency to mimic big brother.

Erika's self-motivated and self-directed character meant the process was rather straightforward and easily achievable for her. She pretty much taught herself through 7th grade that year, with occasional check-ins and feedback from Dale and me. True to form, she knew what she had to do and simply went about it.

Justin proved the greatest challenge because we needed to make sure his study in China would count toward his freshman year in high school. The BYU curriculum he needed to follow for Freshman English, Geography, Algebra II and Biology, two elective classes, and a P.E. requirement, weren't difficult; in many cases they were not challenging enough for our bright son. Perhaps this lack of challenge led to diffused motivation. Some days he would nail the planned curriculum, finishing fast and on time. But on many other days, he dragged. And this would, of course, impact the plan for the afternoon. Justin's difficulties were not academic. Rather, changing hormones, coupled with being outside of his comfort zone in a foreign land far away from his peers, stuck in a relatively small apartment with mom, dad, kid sister and brother, made getting Justin through his freshman year homeschooling curriculum a constant challenge.

~~~~~~~~

Afternoons meant an entirely different plan. Ellen had arranged for our children to attend Chinese schools in the afternoons, at our request.

"Your children can begin their schools next Tuesday or Wednesday," she announced one late August day. First, we need to go to each school and meet their principals as well as the teachers responsible to discuss everything with them and have them meet your children."

This sounded reasonable.

Dale and I decided to begin homeschooling the children the following week, after a week of onboarding our children to their Chinese school experiences. The start of their homeschooling would then align with the start of our teaching.

What we didn't learn from that brief conversation with Ellen was that neither of these two schools had *ever* had a *wàiguórén* on their premises. Our kids, along with Soo-jin's little boys, aged 6 and 7, were the first ones ever at the nearby elementary school. But since those boys were Korean, they wouldn't stick out quite the same as Luke.

Family and friends back home had wondered why we didn't choose an international school for our children's education that year. There are three reasons: first, we wanted them to experience *Chinese* culture while there; second, the international school was far away; and third, we couldn't afford it. Most international schools have Western-style costs, and our modest teacher salaries wouldn't have made it. We thought the afternoon Chinese school experience would be good for each child.

The children were *not* going to these schools for subject matter or grades. They were going to learn and experience Chinese culture. And, we also hoped they would become cultural, linguistic, and even spiritual ambassadors to their Chinese peers.

A big piece of this experience would be the uniforms. As public school kids, this would be a new opportunity – and challenge.

Justin tended to run hot and through elementary and middle school had been obsessed with basketball wear – nylon shorts and sleeveless jersey. Although he was starting to grow out of that, he remained certain that wearing long pants was like serving time in prison. This was manageable in our temperate California home, but I wondered what this would look like as the weather got increasingly colder in our new locale. And Luke, of course, took his cues from Justin.

Thankfully, the late-summer uniforms for boys were white collared shirts with navy accents and, yes, shorts! This made it bearable – at least in the beginning – for the two boys.

Erika, on the other hand, was a completely different case. She seemed to find the uniforms cute. Or, at least, a novelty.

But the uniforms were just the beginning. We were in for surprises ahead as we navigated the Chinese educational piece for our children. And we ran into one of those the very next day when we headed with Ellen to Luke's new Chinese elementary school.

As an educator back home, Dale had numerous times taught non-native English speakers in his classroom. He had 504 plans for students with special needs, whether physical, emotional, mental or language/culture-based. He had learned how well, overall, our U.S. schools, at the district level, accommodate for "outsiders."

The U.S. approach is not perfect by any means. And a major debate lies along the faultline of the Bilingual Education vs. English Only divide. Do we mainstream non-native English speakers into regular classes immediately, or do we try to accommodate them with language help somehow, allowing for a soft-ramp to climb so they can be comfortable learning their subject matter in their own language while easing into English over time?

Dale admits he just assumed the Chinese schools welcoming their first *wàiguórén* would do the same. But nothing was in place. And, what we discovered, especially at the elementary level, was they didn't have any idea of what to do with Luke. In fact, after we got past the rehearsed introduction, it was almost as if he were an alien being.

21 | Luke: Stepping up to the plate

"The gem cannot be polished without friction,
nor man perfected without trials."
宝石不能磨擦没有摩擦，也没有人完美没有试验
(*Bǎoshí bùnéng mócā méiyǒu mócā,*
yě méiyǒu rén wánměi méiyǒu shìyàn.)
— Chinese Proverb

We traipsed over to the elementary school just five minutes from our home. We could envision Luke going there on his own after lunch each school day, Monday–Friday. Although they usually held school on Saturday mornings, we wanted him home with us on the weekends.

Ellen spoke briefly with the guard at the gate – *so many gates* – and they let us in. Our first impressions were of such a quiet place. Classes were on, so in the schoolyard it felt like a ghost town. But, just for a minute. As we headed up the stairs to the Principal's office, a bell pierced the silence. Immediately a cacophony of kid's voices and footsteps pounding along the hallways and stairwells enveloped us. The school kids looked at us with wonder as we passed. I knew this kind of attention wouldn't necessarily be easy for our eight year old.

The secretary welcomed and whisked us into the principal's waiting area. She brought all three of us some Chinese green tea and a small wrapped candy for Luke.

About ten minutes later, the Principal (校监 – *Xiàojiān*) stepped in. An energetic, middle-aged man, he seemed slightly nervous meeting us. After exchanging greetings, Ellen served as interpreter.

"He is happy to have you here," she interpreted for us. "He hopes this will be a good experience for your son...it is a new experience for the school, so please be patient."

The meeting lasted about 10 minutes. And then Ellen whisked us out.

Next we met Teacher Gao (高老师 – *Gāo Lǎoshī*), the woman assigned to be Luke's 4th grade teacher. A shy, diminutive woman designated the 4th grade English teacher, she actually spoke rather limited English but was willing to try having Luke in class.

She pushed through some of the basics (with a little help from Ellen) and established the pattern for Luke each day.

Luke would arrive after lunch, at 12:30, and she would make a place for him in the classroom. For the first 30 minutes of class, he would pay attention and try to pick up sounds he heard and piece together what was going on, keeping track as he used the Lego watch we had purchased him in Shanghai. After that, Luke would be allowed to read a book from home in the back of the class. *Gāo Lǎoshī* agreed she would try to include Luke in activities, especially physical play.

How was Luke processing all this? He seemed to be doing well, not whining, complaining or showing a sense of fear or boredom. He just went with the flow.

Just as we were leaving the teacher's room, we met the 5th grade English teacher, Teacher Yang (养老师 – *Yǎng Lǎoshī*). Yang, a man, also led the P.E. classes. He sported a sweatsuit and a wide, welcoming smile. And his English was relatively strong and confident.

"Ah, so nice to meet you!" he exclaimed. "I heard you were coming. And this...must be Luke. Hi Luke! I'm Yang. Welcome to our school!"

Wow, this guy impressed me. I wondered to myself if he might be able to be Luke's teacher instead. I made a mental note to follow up on this with Ellen. But for now we simply established a connection. I think Yang's friendliness eased Luke's heart just a little bit.

Then Teacher Gao took us up to her room. The kids, sitting at shared 2x2 desks, looked up as we entered, with a sound of "wooahhh" breaking the hush of kids studying. Then, chatter. And lots of whispering. A buzz of noise blanketed the room as we headed to the front.

Teacher Gao quieted the group of close to 40 students, saying a few things to them in Chinese. An occasional word or phrase triggered some faint point of recognition in my brain, mingling with context and assumption, but the message remained unclear. Then she shifted over to English.

"We have a new student. This is Luke. He is from America. He will be with our 4th grade class in the afternoons this school year. Please welcome him."

I'm not sure the kids understood much of what she had said. I felt it failed to register on most of their faces. So, when she sensed that, she repeated herself in Mandarin.

One child started a clap, and all the others clapped. Then Teacher Gao pointed to one of the boys and he stood up.

He had clearly rehearsed his part.

"Hello, Luke. Nice to meet you. My name is Jang Jirui. I want to be your friend. Welcome!" Then he sat down.

Then a girl stood up. Same thing.

"Hello, Luke. Nice to meet you. My name is Meng Xiaoli. I want to be your friend. Welcome!" Meng sat down.

A faint smile arose on Luke. We were happy, too. At least we could see they were trying.

Teacher Gao had cleared a space at a desk next to a girl about two-thirds of the way back on the far side of the room. We asked Teacher Gao if we could remain in the back for just a little while before saying goodbye to Luke. She said it would be fine.

Luke sat down tentatively. The girl next to him smiled shyly. I hoped, at least, Luke would learn her name today. It would be a start.

Just as quickly as English had interrupted the classroom that day, it scurried away. Chinese came flooding back, as the children scrambled to pull out their history textbooks.

We had given Luke a notebook for him to write down sounds he heard and any Chinese characters he might discover. And, perhaps, to doodle in. But, other than that, we had told him to keep an eye on his watch and wait for 30 minutes before pulling out his book.

We didn't see it then, but the children were passing around a "map" of their classroom desks, writing their names in both Chinese characters and phonetics (拼音 – *Pīnyīn*) for Luke to take home that day.

Luke had told us he would *try* – that he was going to be brave, even all on his own. He glanced back once or twice, mainly to check if we were still there. We could tell he was doing his best to focus, listen and write down sounds, as we had asked.

But this is not an easy assignment for an eight-year-old boy. Fifteen minutes into the session, we elected to leave. We had told Luke we'd come pick him up about 2 hours later, when school ended. And we slipped out of the classroom. As we did, I caught a glimpse of his brave little face, his lower lip protruding with a can-do spirit. But in those eyes, I could see his fear.

22 | Justin & Erika: Middling up

"Whatever is good to know is difficult to learn."
– Greek Proverb

The Chinese school piece for our older two children proved an entirely different adventure. Early the following week, Ellen took all of us, minus Luke, to Justin and Erika's new school, *Lixīngǔè* Middle School (李新股恶中学 – *Lixīngǔè Zhōngxué*).

Middle school in China is 7th, 8th and 9th grade. High school is 10th, 11th and 12th grades. So, Justin as a 9th grader and Erika as a 7th grader meant they'd at least be at the same school. Although we knew *Lixīngǔè* wouldn't be as close as Luke's five-minute jaunt, we never expected the next piece of news.

Ellen told us we'd need to travel over 45 minutes one way to *Lixīngǔè*. In fact, the school was almost on the other side of the city proper of 3.5 million! We wondered, "How could this be? And why?"

Ellen explained to us Ningbo University had a *relationship* with *Lixīngǔè*. This meant our kids would need to take three different buses and then, when dropped off at the closest bus stop, walk for another 15 minutes to the school each day, reversing on the way home. Adding the 10 minutes it took for the kids to leave our apartment to get to the bus stop in front of Ningbo University, we were talking about a one hour fifteen minutes each way. And that's hitting the buses right!

Justin and Erika had never done anything like this before. Learning this news right as we piled into the van contributed to a lot of pondering about what this would mean for their day-to-day lives as we plied through Ningbo's traffic.

Although Ellen showed us a map as we started out, we really had no sense of orientation as the university van careened along the boulevards and jetted through narrow streets on its way to *Lixīngǜe*.

After we passed through the gate with the obligatory stern guardsman and pulled up to the front, an affable and quite lovely woman stepped forward and, in excellent English, greeted us. "I am Li Xiaoling. Please call me Mrs. Li. Or, if you want, you can call me *Li Lǎoshī* (李老师). I am your daughter's teacher." She held out her hand, we shook, and then she turned to Erika. "Our students are so excited to meet you, Erika!"

Teacher Li led us up to the principal's office, and we sat down in a waiting room. When the door opened, out came a woman who appeared poised and in charge. Her slim appearance coupled with hair pulled up into a tight bun, red lipstick and high heels, projected an air of confidence.

"Welcome," she bellowed. "I'm Principal Deng. It is nice to meet you." We shook hands and all sat around a conference table adjacent to her small office.

She shifted into Chinese. Teacher Liu interpreted for us. "Principal Deng is very happy to have you here. She hopes you will enjoy our school and its students, and that it will be a mutually beneficial year for us all."

And then Teacher Li went on. "We are waiting for two other teachers to arrive. They should be here shortly."

First Teacher Chen (陈老师 – *Chén Lǎoshī*) appeared. She would be Justin's teacher. Teacher Chen had just returned from a three-month study abroad program in Australia. While on the program, not only was she improving her English, but she also was learning techniques for teaching her own language to foreigners. It turned out Justin would be her practicum. Indeed, Teacher Chen would become Justin's lifeline, not only to the school, but also to his overall experience in China.

Teacher Chen was also confident in her command of English. And it became clear as we got to know her, Justin wasn't just an "experiment." She really had a heart to help him succeed. We are so grateful for Teacher Chen, Teacher Li and a handful of other people at *Lixīngǜe* who helped our older children experience a degree of success in their Chinese culture, language and schooling experiences that year.

Principal Deng excused herself. But as she did, she looked at us while speaking in Chinese, then shifted her eyes over to Teacher Li.

"Principal Deng tells me she wants you to know that if anything difficult happens for you, please don't hesitate to let her office know. This is something new for *Lixīngǔè*. So we know it won't always be easy for you here. But she believes – and *we all believe* – this can be a successful year for all of us."

We never saw Principal Deng again.

Unlike the elementary school, both Teachers Li and Chen suggested they take our children from there and guaranteed us they'd take good care of them. So we bid our goodbyes, and knew we'd be waiting for a few hours before returning and learning how it went. Both children seemed to be taking all of it in quite well.

A few weeks later Erika wrote this blog post about her classroom experience and impressions.

Erika's voice: ∿∿∿∿∿∿∿∿∿∿∿∿∿∿∿∿∿

The room is cool, the desk is smooth, the discussion closed to my ears. Occasionally, I catch snippets of words, or sounds, or tones that sound familiar, like the ghost of a dream, meaning flitting just beyond my grasp. A few syllables I know. "Hao," "shi," "kan." The atmosphere has a dreamy quality to it, the hot breeze occasionally lapping through the open windows. My pencil scratches out dark lines on a piece of paper, copying Chinese characters, practicing, practicing.

The classroom is rather lacking of character, but the view isn't. Rows of apartments, each the height of the fifth-floor classroom I sit in or higher, rise up a little ways away, pale faces distorted by grimy streaks, from...rainwater? Drying clothes flap like thousands of multi-colored flags from protruding clotheslines in every window. Directly below is a plunge into a small decorative lake, or a large decorative pond, that dominates the front of the school grounds.

I glance around the room. My classmates are all black-haired, all with Chinese almond-shaped eyes. They all understand what the teacher, what the Lǎoshī, is saying. They all understand the muttered jokes their neighbors whisper to them, the yellow writing covering the black chalkboard, looking like some complex scientific or mathematical equation to me. The walls are nearly bare, pale white, with a lonely poster or two in grey with black Chinese numbering, writing I cannot comprehend.

But just outside is a riot of color, an explosion of mismatched marketing stalls, bicycles, laundry on clotheslines, old men sweeping the gritty sidewalk with straw brooms, entire families improbably perching on a single motorcycle, buses honking – perhaps unnecessarily – like foghorns, little toddlers picking up bottle caps from the side of the road in delight, sure they have found some great treasure, signs translated into simple, and sometimes inaccurate, English, that say, for instance, "East Yillage Hair and Beauty Chin," butterflies and dragonflies fluttering or buzzing through the air. There is also heat outside, humid, almost oppressive heat, smothering heat. It is such a strange place, strange, terrible, but wonderful, and so different – so different! – from home.

The class period ends, and I struggle to communicate – half in sign language, half in English, half in a tiny bit of broken Chinese. A few people speak enough English, so together we manage to make a bit of sense, although I find myself saying often, in a confused, apologetic tone, "I don't understand... I don't understand what you're saying..." with a half-smiling look on my face.

One person, a girl named Gong Qin Lu, or "Cherry" (her English name) translates for me. She has a round, cheerful face, an honest face. Her English is excellent – much better than my Chinese – for a person of her age. She smiles and laughs at our communication. For some reason, laughter is a universal language.

There is lots of laughter in the room – it is noisy now, now at the break between classes. Chinese sweeps by me as quickly as, I imagine, my casual, fast English would sound to them. I am careful to speak slowly when I am speaking in English, but nevertheless there are still a few confusing moments. I feel as if I am looking out through a window at the scene – and yet it is so like scenes in the USA at school, and if English words were inserted into their rapidly chatting mouths, I am sure there would be hardly any difference. So alike, yet so different – that is China.

~~~~~~

While waiting for Justin and Erika on that first day, we spent a few hours with Ellen at a nearby coffee shop, getting to know her better.

As we ate lunch and took some tea afterwards, we learned Ellen had been to Europe in the last year, on a special delegate trip for Ningbo University, developing a sister-university relationship. We also learned she was engaged to be married and hoped to have more than one child someday. "China is changing, you know," she asserted. "I think my fiancé and I will be among the ones who will benefit."

Years later, as we've kept in touch, I can attest: she was right.

After we picked Justin and Erika up, not only did we get our first taste of rush hour traffic in Ningbo, but our drive back to campus also came complete with bonus drama. As our driver jockeyed for position, honking to gain the upper hand, we still weren't making much progress.

After several minutes, we saw why.

In the opposing lane of traffic was a city bus turned sideways with a dumptruck embedded in its side. The truck must have been traveling at least 50 miles per hour (80 km/hour) in order to be able to push itself so fully into the body of the bus.

Dale later wrote the following blog post about this incident.

Dale's voice:

Living in Ningbo, China for a year, we didn't own a car. That forced us to use public transportation, so we often found ourselves on the streets of Ningbo as pedestrians or waiting for a bus. This gave us ample time to observe the driving habits of the people.

It wasn't too many years ago that few cars could be seen on the streets of China; instead, people rode bicycles. Urban streets would be choked with bicycles, leaving little room for cars or trucks to maneuver.

But with the growth of the Chinese economy, the number of automobiles increased astronomically. With this increase, the Chinese have developed their own style of driving.

I've found that Chinese drive the way they stand in line. They nudge and jockey for position. They dart through any opening, cutting off the next guy without an apology.

The big guy goes wherever he wants as exemplified by the way the buses in China turn right.

Pedestrian crosswalk? What pedestrian crosswalk?

And yet there is a kind of gracefulness in the whole process. The cars sidle up to each other, subtly reading signals as they weave from lane to lane, responding to the slightest wiggle of the other cars.

Horns communicate with a wide variety of meanings from the gentle "I'm here" tap honk to the blaring "I'm bigger than you – outtamyway!" honk.

Even the bus turning right that scatters pedestrians like leaves seems to have the ability to stop inches from a bicyclist's back wheel without touching it, then use a wake of air to push the bicycle on its way.

Maybe this is a metaphor for modern China.

Ancient China was a slow-paced, erudite nation with all the pomp and circumstance of an imperial system.

Modern China, on the other hand, is a brash, newly technologized country that has burst onto the economic stage of the world with cheap labor and a centralized communist government able to focus all the country's resources on the goal of modernizing and developing Chinese business and finance.

China awkwardly nudges and jockeys itself into the limelight with an Olympics that amounts to a giant infomercial glorifying China.

It darts into any business opportunity that becomes available, uses its weight to shove smaller players out of the way, and yet does it with a certain amount of Asian sensibility and relational sensitivity.

This isn't always a recipe for success, however. Early in our Ningbo stay, we found ourselves tangled in the knot of a traffic slowdown resulting from a collision between a city bus and a dump truck. From our vantage point in a university van, we could not tell the human cost. But the mesh of steel, concrete, glass and wire gave us a pretty good scare.

There can be drawbacks to this getouttamyway *approach....*

23 | Encountering the language dragon

"The limits of my language are the limits of my world."
–Ludwig Wittgenstein, Austrian-British Philosopher

Being a *wàiguórén* and being an English teacher – not to mention being a homeschooling teacher for our three kids – might have given us a pass on trying to learn the Chinese language during our year abroad. I know there are many who would decide not to even cross that bridge.

But for Dale and me, we both love learning other languages, so we knew we wanted to try.

When it came to pre-trip Chinese language study in the spring, all dreams of family language study seemed to evaporate as schoolwork, jobs and other responsibilities kept everyone going at regular high speed. Even when the summer came, aside from a few intentional sessions around the dinner table, the Chinese language remained largely shrouded in mystery.

Unlike the children, Dale and I had a bit of an edge, however, for two reasons. First, this would be our second time to China. Our first was back in 1988, with a group of American university friends, long before our kids were ever on the scene. During this earlier experience in China, three Chinese teachers led our group in vocabulary, grammar and practice dialogues for three hours every morning, five days a week, for four weeks. Fifteen heads all bobbing in sync with each tone change, along with occasional "air writing" for further emphasis, made for a humorous setting each morning.

In the afternoons we were matched up with university students eager to improve their English. My two students, *Liú* (刘) and Zhào (赵), took me all over the city, to the market places, museums, parks and eateries, showing me their city all the while speaking English and helping me along with my fledgling Chinese. In retrospect, I realize not only did those times help me linguistically, but they also became my first post-college experiences intensively relating with university international students. Well, sort of!

Even though so many years had passed, we still could draw upon many of the phrases we had tucked in our memories.

But perhaps more helpful was our experience in Japan and with the Japanese language. My experiences studying it at university, living abroad as an exchange student for six months, followed by two years living and working in Hokkaido, Japan shortly after Dale and I married, helped a good deal. Dale had also developed the ability to converse with ease in most day-to-day situations and read simple Japanese during that time.

This meant the Chinese characters were not alien to either of us. In fact, I loved (and continue to appreciate) them! I view them as a creative, artistic, fascinating and integral facet of both languages. To only learn "conversational" Japanese or Chinese, without the characters, seems to me as if it strips both languages of their unique beauty.

In fact, having been to China before and being familiar with Chinese characters via Japanese, spending the year in China didn't seem such a stretch. But, of course, for the children, the story was different.

～～～～～

For when it comes to languages, no question – Chinese is more foreign than most to a native English speaker. For one, the use of pictograms rather than a phonetic alphabet requires a different approach to the language itself. Most of the characters, originally created to represent an object or idea, hold meaning in and of themselves.

And then there are the infamous four tones – one up, one flat, one down-up and one down. The tone often differentiates a word. Most famous is má 麻 (generic name for hemp, or to feel numb), mā 妈 (mom), mǎ 蚂 (grasshopper), and mǎ 马 (horse). There's also a neutral, non-tonal sound, such as ma 吗 (like the ? at the end of a question).

So, one might reason, you need to be careful not to call your mom a horse or grasshopper. In reality, these words would almost never get confused because of context, even if for some reason the tone is just off a bit. This of course never happens with native Chinese language speakers but happens all the time with foreigners. But most times, people make it a bigger issue than it really is.

The best way to learn a tonal language, or really any language, is to try to mimic native speakers, especially those who are willing to slow down and talk with you clearly. Putting too much emphasis on the tones in the beginning, I believe, will distract a learner from ever venturing out to speak.

So, where does the Chinese language come from? Mandarin Chinese (普通话中文 – *Pǔtōnghuà Zhōngwén*), derives from the Sino-Tibetan linguistic group. Yet its origins still remain a subject of scholarly debate. It has no real linguistic connection with either Japanese or Korean languages.

The only connection are the characters, which the Japanese (and Koreans) "borrowed." And the languages do have many cognates that provide some lateral understanding. But beyond that, the Japanese and Korean languages are about as different from Chinese as Finnish is from English.

Because Dale and I were coming from a different perspective than most Americans, knowing Japanese already, we had a head start. But, besides some similar characters and cognates, as well as a few memorized phrases from years ago, this only took us so far. Still, we were determined to master what we could.

This began with Rosetta Stone. We had purchased it over the summer before leaving and tried our best to do a lesson or two a day. It was helpful and foundational. But the language in Rosetta Stone is staid and, in most cases, not too motivating. I mean, how often are you going to get to talk about "the book sitting on top of the table in the living room?"

Still, it helped. And we continued on with it as best as we could, encouraging our kids to make progress with it as well. We'd have our occasional language victories along the way. Erika shared in a November blog post about one of those.

Erika's voice:

It's always gratifying when you manage to communicate in Chinese. I enjoy the simple experience of going to the fruit and vegetable market to buy lettuce, tomatoes, beans, mushrooms, apples, and so on. The surge of energy and delight when I realize I have just made sense of a little of the Chinese gobbledygook that frequently surrounds me is invigorating. When a vegetable seller, after weighing a bag of potatoes that I've selected from his wares, says, "Liang quai wu," I am gratified when I realize that he's actually saying, "2.5 quai." (Quai is the English equivalent of buck – a sort of slang way of saying yuan).

It seems as though I am actually making sense of the language, and I'm proud of myself for it. It's so weird to think that these people have totally different set of sounds and words, but they still communicate in the same way we do. And the funniest thing is, I'm actually starting to comprehend this Chinese language, this strange, foreign mixture of tones and sounds and words. Odd.

All of us made progress, to some extent.

But, once we settled in, Dale and I realized we needed to give our Chinese language learning a boost. Being English teachers, almost everyone we had contact with wanted to speak with us in English. And, in most cases, their English was well beyond our painfully basic Chinese. And even though the Farmer's Market offered ample opportunity to practice, you can only shop for fruits and vegetables for so long!

So we sought out a Chinese teacher and eventually found one in *Wáng Lǎoshī* (王老师). Teacher Wang, a business professor at the university, had spent time abroad in Australia with his family. He had taught previous foreign English teachers at Ningbo University. So we arranged for a weekly lesson with him together as a couple. It was our little "haven" of language study and focus, almost every Saturday at Ningbo University's coffee shop.

Soft spoken and patient, *Wáng Lǎoshī* helped us better understand the complexities of his language. He also helped us realize those who claim Chinese doesn't have any grammar (and there are many!) are fooling themselves. Indeed, Chinese *does* have right and wrong ways of building sentences. Thanks to *Wáng Lǎoshī*, we understood that process much better.

Nevertheless, it wasn't enough. We had been spoiled through earlier language-learning experiences abroad (for Dale, in Italy and Germany, for me and him, in Japan) where we had time to really dedicate to learning and memorizing, and then using, the respective languages. In China, it was the reverse: Hear, use, then often, learn. With our concerns for the children, keeping the household running, and full loads of classes – not to mention communicating with friends and family back home – our language-learning during the year was much more haphazard than we would have wished.

I feel learning a foreign language as an adult is a bit like walking on a tightrope. The tightrope artist (and language learner) needs to trust her instincts and just go for it. Look straight ahead. Block out the noise, the naysayers who are mostly in the head. The tension the artist feels is mirrored only by the tautness of the rope. If it's not taut, it won't hold her. She takes the next step. She can't look backwards or to the side, for this will distract and throw her off balance. She must keep focused. And, if possible, have humor. By simply stepping on the rope, she is taking a risk. By moving forward, she is demonstrating she wants to make progress. When she gets to the other side, she has been successful reaching a milestone. But there are always other longer, higher tightropes to walk. The language learner must train her mind to master them with skill.

Of course, the analogy ends there. For the tightrope artist, a slip and step in the wrong place could result in a disastrous, and perhaps life-threatening, fall. For the language learner, not so. It is rare elementary language skills will lead to a disaster (though it *can* happen), much less a life-threatening situation. Still, the tension and tenuousness of both experiences bear noting.

Discovery

24 | Sirens, screams, remembrance & respect

*The living owe it to those who no longer can speak
to tell their story for them.*
– Czesław Miłosz, Polish Poet

As the sweltering heat of the summer months melted into the fall, we began to feel as if we, too, began to melt into the Ningbo University community.

We could feel the subtle day-by-day cooling in the weather – at times almost imperceptibly – as we started to develop a rhythm to our days: Wake up, pray together, ready ourselves and begin our homeschool day, prepare and eat lunch, send kids off to school and take off for our classes.

~~~~~~~~~~~

One day in September, during my last class of the last day of the week, something unexpected happened. After a full week, and running through the same lesson plan with two other classes, I was feeling confident in the flow of this class, riding on a wave of energy. All 82 eyes were on me – engaged and alert. Quite remarkable at the 16:00 hour, especially on a Friday.

And then the sirens began to wail. "What's going on?" I wondered. Everyone else knew; it took none of them by surprise. Presuming it might be a fire drill or something like that, I asked them, "Is this at Ningbo University? Do we need to leave the classroom?"

One of the three young men in the class spoke up. "No, this is all in China." I was confused and attempted to clarify. "You mean, this siren alarm is going off all over China?" The answer, obvious to them since they had known for their whole lives, was nothing less than a major cross-cultural experience for me.

Another student spoke up. "This is the day when we remember the start of the war with Japan." In other words, WWII. This day is known as *Jiǔ Yībā Shìbiàn* (九一八事变) or simply Jiuyiba, the "9-1-8, or 9/18 Incident," referring to the the Mukden or Manchurian Railway Incident of 18th September 1931, used by the Japanese as a pretext to annex Manchuria.

But what fascinated me was the simple fact that *everyone* in China – or, at least almost everyone – was hearing the three three-minute long sirens going off during that hour.

I cannot imagine *anything* like that in the States. There is nothing that universal or sacred or historical or…*coordinated* in the U.S. Perhaps Independence Day comes close. But it is a *celebration* – *not* a commemoration. Even though 9/11 still burns in the hearts of many Americans, there is no pan-U.S. moment of silence, reflection or reverence for the deeper meaning of that day.

The moment the first siren ended, I felt this overwhelming sense of how, in spite of its minority groups and dissensions and all the tumultuous change taking place, China's group culture impacts its people so thoroughly.

I also wondered what this meant for real, lasting healing between China and Japan. Could they both forgive *and* forget? Or was this nationwide memorial meant to keep the sentiment of mistrust alive and well for generations that have not actually known the horror of the moment?

We sat quietly for each of those three-minute siren rings. It just seemed the proper and respectful thing to do. Each time following the alarm, we resumed – laughter, interaction, discussion, and so forth. But for those few silent minutes, I stepped into the wounds of a culture. And I came to understand something much deeper and more complex about the Chinese people I was interacting with every day.

One breezy September night, after we had settled in, a sharp scream shattered the silence. First came the frantic sounds of a loud, angry voice spewing undecipherable chatter. After came a quieter voice, apparently trying to calm the angry one down.

Although we were now settled in our foreign teacher housing and getting on with our new lives in Ningbo, the horrible nocturnal screaming was quite a contrast from the polite reception we'd received from Ellen and many of the others earlier.

The next day we discovered the yelling was coming from the third floor of a building next to us where an old man who had dementia lived. His family lived with him there, and he would regularly come out on the balcony and scream out his thoughts and frustrations to the world. Over our year in China, his voice was a backdrop and regular source of interrupted sleep.

We learned later this man had been a respected professor at the university, but he had fallen out with some of the leadership as he spiraled downward into dementia. The school needed to find a reasonable solution to both care for him and contain him. Students were paying attention and some of his outbursts were causing division throughout the school. The solution they decided upon was to allow him to remain in his apartment rent-free, as long as he could have a family member or caregiver with him 24/7.

As I recall this situation, I'll be honest; over the year we lived in Ningbo, that man's screaming and ranting irritated us a lot. Selfishly, we felt like someone should put him in a home somewhere rather than have him disrupting people's sleep.

Now, after many years of reflection – and an interesting conversation we had with some Brazilian friends more recently – I believe the "screaming man" situation represents yet one more example of the respect and care Asian families give to their elderly. His relatives bore with the dementia with patience because this man was family and had lived a full and valuable life worthy of respect and compassion.

Fast forward a half dozen years. Now back in California, we were sitting at a table after going berry picking, enjoying some fresh berry pie and talking with Luiz and Gabriela, a delightful couple from Brazil, who were preparing to return to their country after a couple of years studying in America. Their two-year-old daughter Ana played with some rocks nearby as we talked.

"How are you feeling about going back home?" I asked Gabriela. "My feelings are mixed," she admitted. "I will miss this place and my friends here, but my family in Brazil is waiting. And so is my job." As we talked about family, the discussion moved into the issue of aging parents.

"What do you do in Brazil when your parents get old and need help?" Dale queried.

Luiz replied, "Usually one sibling will be responsible to take care of them. That doesn't mean we live with them necessarily, but usually one of the children will live near the parents and make sure they are doing well."

He continued, "In my case, when I was young, every day after lunch my mother would go to my grandmother's house nearby and spend the whole afternoon. I learned to love the time with Grandma. She had so many great stories."

"In America, so often I feel like we waste the wonderful resource of our elderly parents by putting them into rest homes rather than keeping them near us to hear their stories," Dale shared wistfully.

"Yes, I was the kind of kid who loved to talk with elderly people and hear their stories. It let me experience what life was like for them and taught me a lot of wisdom," Luiz continued.

We shared with Luiz and Gabriela about the "screaming man" experience in China and how the Chinese often live with their parents and grandparents in one home. This happens in so many other cultures as well. We talked about how, while there can be great benefits for young parents to have grandparents living in the same house for taking care of young children, sometimes having to live under the dictates of the patriarch or matriarch might be problematic for some young people.

We discovered that both the Chinese and Brazilian cultures have figured out ways, although imperfect, to deal with their elderly parents, giving them a sense of value and respect. Although the Chinese model doesn't seem to fit well with America's individualistic society, I wondered if perhaps the Brazilian model would make more sense.

If children in America understood that one sibling would take the responsibility to live near the parents, the others could probably help that sibling financially to deal with the added costs (including the opportunity cost) of helping the elderly parent. Or, finding an alternative living environment nearby, one of the siblings might work as well. Of course, sometimes this does happen in the U.S.

But since there is no societal pattern that most people follow, the issue of how to deal with elderly parents is often confusing to Americans. This makes me wonder what we can learn from other cultures as diverse as Brazil and China to help us do a better job in our own families.

25 | The elderly & the Chinese spirit

老吾老，以及人之老；幼吾幼，以及人之幼。
Lǎo wú lǎo, yǐ jí rén zhī lǎo, yòu wú yòu, yǐ jí rén zhī yòu.

"In supporting and showing deference to the elderly, we must not neglect those who are not in our family; in nurturing and educating our children, we must not neglect those with whom we're not blood-related."

– Mencius, Chinese Philosopher

Indeed, with a population aging rapidly, the elderly seem to be everywhere in China: riding ancient rusty bicycles along the city streets, sweeping the campus with twig brooms, or even washing clothes in the pond near our apartment.

Another person we would see regularly was an old lady who often sat on some rock steps that led down to the torpid green water of the pond near our apartment building.

Sometimes she had her laundry with her and a wooden stick with which she beat the clothes clean. She was dressed in nondescript, black pants and a vaguely Chinese-cut shift. Sometimes she had vegetables that she washed in the scummy water, and sometimes she just sat and watched the old men with their fishing poles who often lined the pond fishing for… garbage? I certainly never saw any of them catch a fish. Once I saw a turtle swimming in the opaque green water, but I don't think any of the fishermen are fishing for turtles.

I wondered about the old lady. Does beating the wash with a stick really get it clean when it's rinsed in that slimy water? Does her family suffer from intestinal cramps from the microorganisms present in the food she washes?

Has anyone ever told her that is not a very healthy practice? Has she tried washing her vegetables in the sink in her child's house with cleaner water and just felt that they weren't getting clean and therefore needed to be washed outside?

What goes through the head of a person who was born in what was essentially feudal China and has been catapulted into the 21st century over a period of just 70 years?

When she was born (in perhaps 1940?), China was in turmoil.

She saw years of civil war as well as war with the Japanese. She saw Máo declaring the beginning of the People's Republic of China. She saw the first Five Year Plan and the Great Leap Forward and the Cultural Revolution.

She saw the reforms of *Dèng XiǎoPíng* (邓小平), and the movement toward capitalism and free markets (even if it was called "Communism with Chinese characteristics").

She saw families saving for years in order to buy a bicycle, and she saw the rise of consumerism where many families could afford cars, homes, and cell phones.

She saw the destruction of entire neighborhoods of traditional *hútòng* (胡同 – alley) homes and the construction of highrise buildings, construction cranes raising over the landscape like flocks of long-necked egrets.

Was she an intellectual in the Cultural Revolution who was forced to the country to be re-educated? Or was she a farmer at that time who was brought to the city to run a company without any experience or education?

Maybe she used to be professor at Ningbo University, but now spends her days taking care of her children's laundry.

The language barrier prevented me from asking her these questions, but in her mystery she seemed symbolic of so much of current Chinese character.

Indeed, Chinese character is tremendously diverse. We experienced that first-hand in the fall, when Ellen arranged for Dale and me, along with three international students, to "train" for a cultural performance in early October where we would sing a Uyghur folk song from one of China's many ethnic groups. Dale's reflections on that experience shed some light on yet another element of Chinese society.

Dale's voice:

The sound man was the epitome of "cool." His hair was pulled back in a ponytail with a stylish cap turned backward on his head. As he prepared to help us record a song, he moved the fingers on one hand deftly over the soundboard while his other hand held a neglected cigarette. The built-up ash begged for an ashtray.

Chen manipulated the various tracks that he'd just recorded of the waiguoren singing the Chinese Uighur song.

"They don't sound very good," he muttered in Chinese, "but they are foreigners after all. They don't have to be perfect."

Two German international students, Hermann and Marcus, stood to my left. While they pronounced the words better than I did, they had a hard time carrying the tune. So I struggled to block out their off-pitch attempts in an attempt to keep the melody going.

We stood in a soundproof room complete with professional mics and headphones. This arrangement allowed us to hear every sound coming from each other and the sound man.

Chen had ratcheted up the tempo to twice the normal speed. This made smooth pronunciation of the words nearly impossible.

But, after about 20 attempts, we managed to get enough snippets of sound for Chen to cobble together one full verse. This would suffice for our lip-synching Uyghur dance at the China's upcoming National Day celebrations.

"Xiānqǐ nǐ de gàitou lái, ràng wǒ kàn kàn nǐ de méi…" (掀起你的盖头来，让我看看你的眉 – *"Lift your veil, let me look at your eyebrow…") The traditional wedding song from the Western province of Xinjiang celebrates the joy of the couple as the man lifts the veil and looks on his bride's face for the first time.*

After the men were done, Caroline and a Zimbabwean student named Fiona proceeded to collaborate on a nicely blended rendition of their verse in about five tries.

"Nǐ de yǎnjīng jīngming youliàng ya…" (你的眼睛精明油亮呀 – *"Your eyes are shiny and bright…") The wife rejoices at the joy on*

her husband's face.

Afterwards, we met the director of the show. He had joined his chain-smoking sound man to further pollute the air. We drank green tea together and listened to the finished recording. And then we met a lively little man who took us to another room to show us some of the Uyghur dance steps.

"Xiānqǐ nǐ de gàitou lái…" the verse echoed in our heads as we left the recording studio.

Little did we know then, but a powerful approaching rainstorm would cancel the outdoor performance. This meant we would not have to face the embarrassment of dressing up in Tang Dynasty costumes and dancing in front of hundreds of people! And yet, there was something symbolic about the whole experience.

Western-style director, choreographer, sound man, recording studio but with Chinese song, dance, costumes – the Chinese desire to have certain things from the West without losing their Chinese identity. Along with the western trappings, however, come western values that sometimes clash with eastern ideas.

I wonder if the Uyghur man is ever surprised by what he finds under the veil? "Xiānqǐ nǐ de gàitou lái…"

26 | America & China: The odd couple

"The custom and fashion of today will be the awkwardness and outrage of tomorrow - so arbitrary are these transient laws."
— Alexandre Dumas, French Writer

Over the first several weekends in Ningbo whenever we explored the city as a family, Dale, in particular, was on a mission.

Back home, Justin had taken up the cello and was now heading into his fourth year with the instrument, playing in the middle school orchestra. He is a naturally gifted musician, always carrying a tune and beat in his head. He gets the musical skills from Dale's side of the family, no question. Dale himself is also skilled with several instruments and has developed his vocal skills through various singing groups over the years.

So Dale, sympathetic to the cause and heart of the musician, and wanting to encourage a love of music in our children, saw an opportunity to find Justin an excellent cello while in China, at a price we could afford. A friend had tipped my husband off to the high quality and excellent prices of many musical instruments in China. So, after a variety of disappointing false leads, analysis of the quality of instruments at a variety of stores, and some bargaining help from a friend, we came back with a finely crafted *dàtíqín* (大提琴) for about US $225. (We later estimated a similar instrument to cost about $2000 in the U.S.) This cello remains a close companion of my son's even today.

On another foray into the city, we headed to *Tiānyī Guǎngchǎng* (天一广场), the central square in Ningbo. The many stores lining the square – most quite modern – alternately beckoned and repelled us with a range of unusual sights, sounds and smells. Michael Jackson's *Thriller* music video flashed across the monster screen on one end of the square. A man-made lake occupied a central position at the west end. Our kids were thrilled when they saw the floating bubble capsules; both Erika and Luke immediately wanted to try them.

So we let them each have a "ride" in a plastic bubble on the water for a mere 10 yuan (about $1.40) each. The ballasts on the bottom of the bubble prevented them from spinning too much. For the child inside, it was an exercise in balance. Erika and Luke were older and coordinated enough to master this feat within seconds, but some of the little kids were rolling around all over!

After a quick lunch at an American-themed hamburger joint, we all had a bit of a sugar craving. One of Dale's students had told us about a doughnut shop we shouldn't miss: Big Apple Doughnuts. Boasting a New York-styled theme and offering a host of neatly displayed confections, we ordered several and then satisfied our collective sweet tooth.

That afternoon we indulged ourselves with a taste of America. But it was "America with Chinese characteristics." I mean, after all, how often do you connect Jujube (date) paste (棗泥 – *zǎo ní*) with the word "doughnut" in America?

〜〜〜〜〜

This juxtaposition – old intermingled with new, foreign influences woven throughout society – is the China of the 21st century. So American doughnuts with Chinese characteristics were not such an oddity. But they rattled our senses a bit.

To give this some context, understanding China's journey over the last 30–40 years helps. Under *Dèng XiǎoPíng's* leadership (1978– 1989) following *Máo Zédōng's* (毛泽东) death, the term "Socialism with Chinese Characteristics" emerged. Boiled down, it means taking the core principles of socialism – common ownership of the core means of production of an economy, free access to products for consumption, central rule, a classless and stateless populous – and adapting them for the needs of the Chinese people.

As the architect of modern China as we know it today, *Dèng's* approach was to foster and harness the productive power of the people to create material wealth. A primary goal was to eliminate scarcity. By doing so, the theory goes, the creative energies of the people are harnessed to produce a more robust and fruitful shared prosperity. *Dèng* advocated a more "open-market" approach to doing so, but emphasized that China was still on its Communist journey, just at the earliest stages of its development (socialism).

Of course, from a Western market-oriented, capitalist perspective, it's natural to presume this "opening up" of China over the last 30–40 years has been all about "freeing" individuals to privately own their means of production. Really, just a Chinese version of capitalism – or "Capitalism with Chinese characteristics." And some scholars and politicians within China argue this version.

But regardless, one point is clear. China is trying to find its way. It's (still) trying to find out what it is and what it is to become. We found the Chinese we encountered to be particularly interested in China's role and relationship to the U.S. We often encountered the question, "How did the U.S., with its short history, become so successful so fast?"

The background to this question, of course, lies in a truth every Chinese knows: China, at 5000 years old and counting, is the oldest continuous civilization on earth (rivaled only by Afghanistan). The fact that a relative newcomer like the United States has had such universal cultural and economic influence, as well as has played such a major role in geopolitics, both intrigues and frustrates the Chinese. This situation has produced both a reverence and, for some, a disdain for the U.S. This awkward, love-hate tension in U.S.-China relations for several decades seemed to both capture the imagination and preoccupy the thoughts of Chinese at all levels of society.

From doughnuts to politics. All part of the experience, right?

27 | The PRC celebrates 60 & we join in

"It takes ten years to grow trees but a hundred years
to raise people."
十年树木,百年树人(*shí nián shù mù, bǎi nián shù rén*)
– Chinese Proverb

When we left the U.S., we had not done the math. In 2009, China would be marking the 60th anniversary of the founding of the People's Republic of China. And we would be there to celebrate.

A week before the October 1st celebration, Ellen approached us to see if we could share a family musical performance at a special university event to commemorate the occasion. She was aware we were a musical family and knew about our purchase of a cello for Justin.

We decided to sing two songs: *Amazing Grace* and another lesser-known worship song with lyrics Dale altered to share about our Ningbo University experience.

Ellen had told us she didn't want us to sing Christian songs, but "Amazing Grace" was okay since it was a well known tune and it wouldn't be considered offensive. "No one will care," she assured us.

The celebration was filled with food, drink, people and performances, many of them by students and teachers. A few professional groups added to the singing, dancing, musical performances and poem recitations. Red, the traditional color of both celebration and the Communist party, dominated the large hall.

Then the emcees called us up. We sang our two songs loud and clear and explained, in English, just a bit about each song. We made sure they knew the meanings of the words of the rewritten song so they could enjoy its particular relevance to life in Ningbo. At the end of the evening, cameras flashed picture after picture – us posing with so many we did not know – until we were about to collapse.

Before all the performances ended, I happened to be in the lobby returning from the restroom when a young woman approached me. *Nǐ huì shuō Zhōngwén ma?* (你会说中文吗 – "Do you speak Chinese?"), she inquired.

Yī diǎn diǎn (一点点。 – "Just a little."), I responded.

She started speaking much faster than I could handle. I really had no idea what she was saying. So I told her *Tīng bù dǒng* (听不懂 – "I don't understand"). She scratched her head for a moment.

Then I realized she wasn't Chinese at all; rather, she was an international student from Korea, studying in Ningbo. Immediately I thought of Soo-jin. I asked her, *Nǐ zhīdào Hánguó lǎoshī ma?* (你知道韩国老师吗? – "Do you know the Korean teacher?"). She didn't.

By then Dale had come up. And in the next few minutes this Korean woman – who told us in Chinese her name was Sarah – also, then began using only the hand gestures of playing music, a heart, opening a book, making a cross, and patting her heart and then pointing up – conveyed to us that she is also a Christian. She smiled widely.

We exchanged phone numbers and email. I had a sense she knew a few words in English. I would either text or email her and invite her to our place. But I had no idea how we'd really communicate. It was clear her Chinese language was much stronger than ours, but because we didn't speak each other's native tongues, I'll admit – I was a bit stymied how we'd proceed with the relationship.

Next day Sarah visited us and we invited Soo-jin to come down so the two could meet. Soo-jin's English was quite strong, so she became our linguistic bridge. As it turned out, Sarah and Soo-jin ended up developing a close relationship. In December Soo-jin came to tell us, with a glowing face, that she and her two sons decided to become followers of Jesus.

It seems our singing *Amazing Grace* that day had more impact than Ellen realized.

In other National Day action, we got glimpses of the 10,000

troop and multi-weaponry pageantry of Beijing's power via special programming on television. We intentionally did not have a TV back home in the States, so none of us had developed a television-watching habit. As a result, we had barely used the TV in our apartment since our arrival. But we felt the 60th Anniversary celebration might be worth watching.

This moment was China once again shouting out to the world, "Hey, notice me! Look at my finery and my power. Our great nation is on the rise!" This assertion of strength followed on the heels of China's Olympic hosting debut in 2008.

To celebrate its 60th birthday, the People's Republic of China ran 60 floats featuring themes such as "Beautiful Prosperous China" (美丽繁荣的中国 – *Měilì fánróng de Zhōngguó*) and "Progress of the Motherland" (祖国进步 – *Zǔguó jìnbù*) through Tiananmen Square. Over one hundred thousand people marched in the parade. One float displayed a giant portrait of Chairman *Máo,* founder of The People's Republic. Succeeding floats featured other respected leaders: *Dèng Xiǎopíng, Jiāng Zémín* and *Hú Jǐntāo.* Voice recordings of each of the leaders played through loudspeakers. There was even a float entitled "One World" (一个世界 – *Yīgè shìjiè*) featuring a host of foreigners from over 50 countries.

All in all, quite a spectacle.

The City of Ningbo also held its special ceremony and all of the foreign language teachers were invited. Since one of our kids was sick, last minute we decided I would be the only one attending on our behalf.

After the vast spread of food, the spectacular performance is what stood out. The music and drama all pointed to the central theme of the birth of the People's Republic. The colors and movement mesmerized me. I felt swept up in something much more emotionally powerful than I had expected.

Through this experience and talking with my students later, I came to better understand the place *Máo* plays not just in the propaganda of the government, but in the hearts and minds of all Chinese, even the youngest members of society. In spite of the great loss of life resulting from his sometimes miscalculated (and some would contend nefarious) leadership, the Chinese people view *Máo* as the one who finally liberated China from colonial and occupational powers. He is revered because, in the mind of most living Chinese today, he is *the one* who restored dignity and pride to the Motherland. Most Chinese overlook his sins or aren't aware of them.

This night at Ningbo's 60th Anniversary Celebration marked a starting point for me in my understanding the Chinese mindset from a new perspective. In some ways, that experience allowed me to step inside the collective psyche of China.

28 | Mooncakes, lanterns, Máo & memories

"Every festival, the yearning for one's family doubles."
每逢佳节倍思亲。*(Měi féng jiā jié bèi sī qīn.)*
– Chinese Mid-Autumn Festival Saying

That fall the Mid-Autumn Festival 中秋节 (*Zhōngqiū Jié*) fell just a couple days after the 60th Anniversary. So it was a week of holidays for the Chinese – and for us as well – celebrating both a more modern event (the start of the PRC) right alongside an ancient tradition dating back over 3000 years.

Dubbed an "intangible cultural heritage" by the Chinese government, the Mid-Autumn Festival – also sometimes known as the Harvest Festival or Moon Festival – has its origins in the agrarian society of the Shang Dynasty (c. 1600–1046 BC). Some experts point to the celebration arising among the Hakka people when they'd go to worship their Mountain Gods after the harvest was completed. It only gained widespread popularity during the early Tang Dynasty (618–907 AD).

The Mid-Autumn Festival's precise timing varies every year because it revolves around the full moon. Specifically, the 15th day of the 8th lunar month – usually late September or early October each year.

Traditionally, the Festival celebrated the successful reaping of rice and other grains, pairing them with food offerings to the Lady Chang'é (a goddess), embodied in the moon. While today much of that meaning has been lost, especially among urban Chinese, the occasion remains an opportunity for family and friends to come together, eat mooncakes and watch the full moon, a symbol of harmony and unity.

The celebration varies by region as well.

The mooncake (月饼 – *yuè bǐng*) is the symbolic food of the season. Around this time, we found ourselves suddenly "swimming" in mooncake gifts from students, other teachers, Ellen, *Wáng Lǎoshī*, the kid's teachers – everybody!

Even with the influx of Chinese to the West, for us the mooncake was a relatively new experience. A Chinese pastry, with thin dough, mooncakes are filled with a variety of dense pastes or jellies, usually slightly sweet. Some even contain a full egg yolk at the center to symbolize the full moon. They are usually imprinted with the Chinese character for longevity (寿 – *shòu*) or harmony (和 – hé), or a picture of Lady Chang'é on the moon, flowers, vines or a rabbit (a symbol of the moon).

All of this is round because, in Chinese culture, the circular shape symbolizes completeness and reunion. So the sharing and eating of round mooncakes with those whom you care about is meant to signify unity and completeness among the family, friendship group, or even among business partners.

Ningbo even had its own version of the mooncake, and a few friends introduced us to that. Unlike most of the mooncakes we received, the Ningbo mooncake fell more on the salty-savory side, filled with either seaweed or ham. We tried to like these ones but, I'll confess, we preferred the sweeter versions.

With several days free from school, we took our first trip all together by plane out of the area, to Hong Kong via Guangzhou.

Luke's eight-year-old perspective focused on the travel.

Luke's voice:

I had to go with my family to Hong Kong 7 days ago. We were having a rough time traveling because we had to take so many vehicles to get there. After we left, we called a taxi. Tisk tisk. 45 minutes. When we got to the airport we boarded the plane but had to wait 2 hours to get on it! After that we took a bus to the border station and had to sign some health notes. Then we thought we would ride a fairy [sic] but we decided not to. Instead we took another bus! It took a while. But we got to have a good time and the seats were comfortable. So I guess it wasn't so bad.

~~~~~~

My Mandarin-speaking American college roommate, Emily, lives in Hong Kong with her Mainland Chinese husband (now a U.S. citizen), Kai, and their three sons. These two are an amazing match, and their story of how they met could fill another book. Both well-educated, they also held high-profile jobs – hers in executive recruitment and his as an editor-in-chief of a top Hong Kong financial newspaper.

They both work long hours and Emily's job requires constant travel in and out of the Mainland. They are fortunate to have Filipina helpers for their children and their home, but work-life balance proves a constant battle, Emily confessed. "The landscape," she told me, "is constantly changing." That's true not just about their lives, but also about the economic and political future of Hong Kong, especially since it was handed over to China in 1997.

Emily and Kai have hearts of gold. They are generous spirits, curious, and globally minded. They took us into their home and treated us lavishly.

It was neat for our kids to interact with Emily and Kai's three boys, The oldest was prospecting colleges; the younger two were early elementary, miracle kids after a string of miscarriages attributed to mercury poisoning from fish they had eaten. These were hard experiences that, in the end, have made Emily more appreciative, resilient, sensitive and spiritually strong.

Our boys especially enjoyed the two little ones. Lots of Lego and Star Wars play ensued.

We enjoyed the time at their club, a magical 10-minute walk from their home on one of Hong Kong's many hills. While together, we caught up with our friends. It had been too long. And yet, it was almost as if no time at all had passed.

The kids loved the facility and, in time, were challenging jumps from the high-dive. Lots of splashes and play: moments of refreshment in the midst of the still balmy autumn air. One night we took the tram to the top of Victoria Peak and skipped along a trail. Emily had brought some pop-out lanterns, candles and matches. We became like the many locals and tourists, celebrating the Mid-Autumn Festival with glowing lanterns against the enveloping darkness. A moment of pure magic.

Kai and Emily took us to a famous noodle restaurant that evening, where we got to watch the chef pull noodles right in front of us. We were all entranced by his speed and dexterity, and then the realization we'd actually be eating those long strands in minutes.

On another day, Kai took Dale and Justin to a movie about *Máo* playing in a local theater over the holidays, presumably to promote respect towards *Máo* among the Hong Kong people. A rosy-hued propaganda extravaganza, the movie portrayed *Máo* alternately walking through fields of daisies with groups of young children riding on his back, to shots of *Máo* dressed as a tough revolutionary urging fighters on to new feats of bravery. To Dale and Justin it seemed humorous, over-the-top propaganda, but Kai later told Dale that even though he felt it was exaggerated, he also believed there was a lot of truth in the film. *Máo* had torn down traditional Chinese ways in order to build them up in a new way that was more competitive for a new world. Dale expressed how he found it interesting the way our cultural narratives affect how we view various aspects of life.

For me, personally, Hong Kong means my dear friend, Emily. We got some tea together and caught up. This friend has been through so much; she is an amazing woman of fortitude and persistence, hard work and empathy. The miscarriage losses softened Emily's heart and helped shape her into the thoughtful, hope-filled and yet driven person she is today. I simply love this woman beyond what words can express.

As we sipped tea, I examined her face (as she must've been examining mine). A few more wrinkles, especially around the eyes. But those eyes were full of smiles and brimming with warmth. It had been 25 years since we said goodbye to our time at Stanford. But what a gift when those 25 years seemed to fade away in a few seconds and we could take up from where we had left off. Yes, our lives had followed different trajectories, but much remained the same.

This time in Hong Kong, as well as a few other visits that followed, always felt so refreshing to me, like falling into an oasis of calm in the midst of a crazy, chaotic city.

29 | Reuniting with our angel

*"Move to a new country and you quickly see that visiting a place as
a tourist, and actually moving there for good,
are two very different things."*
– Tahir Shah, British author, journalist & documentary maker

Late October found us back in Shanghai to meet up with YZ. A denial of his OPT (Optional Practical Training) visa by the U.S. government brought him back to China, perhaps to his dismay but to our delight.

So we packed up, hailed a taxi outside the Ningbo University gate, and told the driver we wanted to go the central train station in Ningbo (宁波火车站 – *Níngbō huǒchēzhàn*).

But doing this as a family of five proved challenging.

You see, technically the driver was only to supposed to take four of us. Squeezing four people in the back was not allowed, but it happened all the time. We would often try to "hide" little Luke a bit, hoping we could get him in.

Some of the taxi drivers hardly would notice, especially as Dale or I would plant ourselves in the front. That would sometimes take the driver by surprise; they weren't quite sure how they'd communicate with us. But we always made sure we knew how to say where we wanted to go before taking any trip out of the university.

By now we had learned basic directional language to say things like "go straight" (一直走 – *yìzhí zǒu*), "turn right / left" (右转 – *yòu zhuǎn* / 左转 – *zuǒ zhuǎn*), and the all important, "STOP!" (停止 – *tíngzhǐ*)! We also picked up the Ningbo-*hua* for these expressions as well, since that's how most of our taxi drivers communicated. Some of the taxi drivers weren't too keen on all five of us getting in one taxi. I remember we'd often tell Luke to "be small" whenever a taxi was approaching. It became a bit of a game, in a way. Usually we were able to swing it, telling the driver, *Zhège háizi hěn xiǎo a!* (这个孩子很小啊! – "This kid is small, you know!"). I've heard from Chinese friends more recently this no longer works; taxi and other drivers now face a stiff penalty if they break the nationwide law. Probably for good reason!

Then, of course, we wanted our small troupe to remain together whenever possible. Somehow this gave us a sense of safety even when the taxi driver would career along the streets, sometimes at what seemed like breakneck speed, winding in and out around other cars. And they almost always did that. I found myself praying for safe arrival at my destination a lot.

Still, taxis were such a deal! We could get our family to Ningbo's central train station, a 45-minute trip in regular traffic, for about USD $5. Can't beat that – even if you're risking your life!

Riding in taxis was also a great place to practice Chinese and get in touch with what was happening in China. One time Dale successfully communicated with a driver a simple conversation:

Dale: "Where are you from?" (你的家里在哪? – *Nǐ de jiālǐ zài nǎ?*)

Driver: "Anhui province." (安徽省。– *Ānhuī shěng.*)

Dale: "Is your family still in Anhui." (你的家人还在安徽省吗? – *Nǐ de jiārén hái zài ānhuī shěng ma?*)

Driver: "Yes." (对。– *Duì.*)

Dale: "How much do you make as a taxi driver?" (你作为出租车司机赚多少钱? – *Nǐ zuòwéi chū zū chē sī jī zhuàn duō shǎo qián?*) Note: This is not an offensive question in China.

Driver: "I can make 1000 yuan in a good week." (我可以在一个星期内赚1000元。– *Wǒ kěyǐ zài yīgè xīngqí nèi zhuàn 1000 yuán.*)

Dale: "How much does your father make?" (你父亲做了多少? – *Nǐ fùqīn zuòle duōshǎo?*)

Driver: "He's a farmer. He only makes 10 yuan a week." (他是一个农民他每周只赚10元。 — *Tā shì yīgè nóngmín. Tā měi zhōu zhǐ zhuàn 10 yuán.*)

Dale was learning firsthand about the massive migration of Chinese from the countryside to the eastern cities where they could make 100 times as much as their parents. Although this is a great economic opportunity, it has also led to families being split, grandparents raising the children, and an increase in the gap between rich and poor that continues to have profound consequences in 21st-century China.

That day we headed to Shanghai we found the train fast, clean and comfortable. This was the case for almost all of our train-riding experiences. Train stations were overflowing with people, almost all the time. Chinese seemed to be on the move constantly, but I suspect this constant stream of people is a result of China's massive population as well as the constant migration between country and city. Being in these huge crowds can be a shock to the system at first. And then it becomes normal.

As we pulled up to Shanghai South Train Station, (上海南站 — *Shànghǎi Nánzhàn*), we anticipated the weekend ahead. This time we had made plans to stay at a hostel since YZ had arrived home. Not only would we spend time with him, but we had also been in touch with a few other recent returnees from America – one student, two scholars who were university professors – now located in Shanghai.

We had not expected YZ to meet us at the station. But he did! There was our six-and-a-half-foot angel, beaming ear to ear. It was a joyful reunion, as if we had known one another for years! So much to catch up on. We headed to a central shopping mall just off *Rénmín Guǎngchǎng* (人民广场 — People's Square) to grab lunch.

We probably wouldn't have discovered the 7th-floor eateries on our own. But we were so glad YZ knew where to take us. We ended up in a food plaza offering an array of delicious– and sometimes peculiar – fare. We could all find things we wanted to eat, and this put everyone in an upbeat mood.

30 | Levi's story

"Every single moment of a person's life, both of the understanding and of the will, is a new beginning."
– Emanuel Swedenborg, Swedish scientist & inventor

Through email we had arranged to meet up with Levi and Weston, Chinese professors at two different Shanghai universities. We had developed a lively email correspondence with these friends of one of our International Student, Inc. co-workers and were eager to meet them.

It turns out YZ already knew both of these men, so he was happy to join us as we toured Levi's campus. As we walked along, we asked them to share their stories.

Originally from rural Anhui Province, Levi grew up with a Christian mother who would tell him the stories from the Bible. So, when he learned during his U.S. stay that many around him were followers of Jesus, he became interested and desired to study the Bible. "I found it totally made sense, and it fit quite well with my understanding of the world," he remarked. "And, when I first went to church I felt some type of peace. I can't exactly describe it, but I feel as if I had come home."

"Before I felt as if my life was aimless," Levi admitted. " But since I decided to believe in Jesus," he told us, "my life has changed dramatically. I have hope now and I know what I should do next." He went on to share that he used to be obsessed with the need to make a huge mark in his field. "Now I feel very differently," he confided. "I want to do well and honor God. But I don't need to get the recognition for recognition's sake." It wasn't until *after* returning home to China that he realized how much he had changed.

"Before going to the U.S., I would often go out with colleagues to drink and would sometimes get very drunk," he shared. "But now I realize I can no longer participate in these type of activities."

"In fact, as a Christian, I cannot make any cheating thing, but sometimes I am pressed to do things that may be questionable." Levi went on to say, "In China, many people have two faces. I have definitely had to deal with this in the workplace." Then he told us he often asks God for a right heart to not fall into wrong behavior.

"After I returned to China, I really longed to be back in the U.S. It seemed like I could be a Christian there so much more easily." But now, he told us, he finds himself at peace with his choice to become a Christian even when surrounded by so many atheists, Buddhists, skeptics and others, especially in his workplace. Levi believes that it is Jesus who "gives me much peace."

When reintegrating with his culture, Levi found that his ideas about America had changed a lot. He used to think that the American family is just like all those messed-up families on American TV shows. But he was able to observe – and participate in – the life of several strong families while living in the U.S. He realized many of his impressions were incorrect.

Levi told us he feels the Chinese family too is experiencing many pressures in this fast-paced age, and that many people are too busy with their work. "The family in China is finding it increasingly difficult to stay together; so this gives me more determination to do so with my wife and a two-year-old daughter," he shared.

Upon return to China, Levi found that he was startled by the huge numbers of people in China as well as the crazy driving in his homeland. He wondered out loud why American drivers were so kind on the road and concluded it must be because they are so lonely, separated from others in their own homes, causing them to be kind to others when outside so that they can connect with them.

Overall, however, he came to realize that every culture has positive and negative points, and he is increasingly choosing to dwell on the positive in both cultures. He told us his faith gives him more power to do that.

"I have found a good house church to attend," Levi added. "Lots of young people. Maybe I am old there," he grinned. "But most of them have studied abroad, usually in the States. They want to keep their faith alive. It is difficult here, you know. I realize, being a little bit older, I can mentor them. This keeps my faith strong. I have to be strong so they can be strong."

31 | Perspectives on communism (& capitalism) in China

"We can complain because rose bushes have thorns,
or rejoice because thorns have roses."
– Jean-Baptiste Alphonse Karr, French Journalist and Novelist

As we moved along and settled at a café to cool down from the October warmth, we spent some time listening to Weston, or Wes, tell his story.

Wes made a choice to follow Jesus while in the U.S. because, as he told us, "I can tell the Bible is true. The story of Jesus is true. I'm a very logical, systematic person, and everything in the Bible made sense perfectly to me."

Then he went on. "But now that I'm back in China, I sometimes wonder whether Buddhism is right because I'm surrounded by people who are always going to the temple and talking about Buddha. You see, in China there is no freedom to talk for members of the Communist Party or someone with an important position. You have to be very careful with what you say."

This made us reflect on the question as to whether or not people really believed in communism anymore in China. In fact, one surprising development Dale and I ran into this time in China was that it appeared most people only gave lip service to communism, but no longer believed in it as a political system.

In 1988, when we spent six weeks in Tianjin and Beijing, we met quite a few ardent communists who wanted to find evidence of their system's superiority over American capitalism. They would ask us lots of questions about the gap between America's rich and poor and the violence they had heard so much about in the streets of America, hoping to validate their own understanding of the value of their own system.

At that time, we tried to honestly share what we considered to be the failures and struggles of the American system, but we questioned a system that depended so much on *guānxì* (关系 – loosely translated as "relationships") and the black market to allow people to get even basic goods.

The China in which we now found ourselves had undergone drastic changes. After the market reforms of *Dèng Xiǎopíng*, the economy took off, the populace became more prosperous, and the gap between rich and poor had become as pronounced as that in America, if not more so. It appeared to us as if the Chinese copied American capitalism, reaping the inherent problems of that system as well. Along with these changes, the ardent communists seemed to have disappeared.

Over our time in the café, we asked Wes if any of his fellow professors believed anymore in communism. His colleagues are all party members and are apologists for China's economic system.

Wes responded, "No one believes in communism these days. We just use our party membership to get what we want."

We were shocked. "No one! Don't you even have one or two people who believe in communist ideals?" we queried.

"Not one," he replied.

Later, one of my Ningbo University students explained it this way: "We put on communism like you put on a pair of clothes. When you go to an interview, it makes you look good and may help you get a job, but we just take it off when we get home." In fact, one of the professors at our school sounded almost dangerously anti-government when he said that the communists were not in touch with what the people wanted or needed.

This made us wonder, "How long can a system last if no one really believes in it?" In America, there are lots of cynics about whether our democratic system really works the way the founding fathers envisioned it. Yet a majority of the populace still seem to believe it's one of the best systems in the world, even with all its flaws. The design of checks and balances created by the architects of the U.S. Constitution remains critical to our functioning democracy, especially in tumultuous post-2016 election America.

32 | Travel trauma

"God put us here, on this carnival ride.
We close our eyes never knowing where it'll take us next."
– Carrie Underwood, Singer

Next day we met up with YZ late morning and visited *Yùyuán* (豫园) again. We were eager to do some shopping as well as take him to the tea house we had discovered the first time around. Street vendors eyed us and, in broken English, would call out, "You like watch? Twenty yuan, top quality."

Yeah, right! "Bù yào" (不要, "Don't want!"), we'd say with confidence. That day, we learned another phrase from YZ: *Jiǎ de* (假的, "Fake"). Clearly a Swatch would not be a cheap ¥20 (about USD $2.60 at the time).

We approached the tea house...only to find, it wasn't there! *How could that be?*

In its place stood a computer store, looking like it had been there all along. No traces of tea anywhere.

We lamented to YZ. He responded, "You know, this happens all the time. Things are changing so much in China now." He didn't seem a bit phased.

"But it was just two months ago!" we protested.

Indeed, we'd come to learn this lesson again and again. China was in the midst of unprecedented change. The disappearance of the tea shop proved to be just a tiny window for us into the scale of China's transformation.

One constant reminder of this change was the presence of dozens of cranes everywhere along the Shanghai and Ningbo skylines. China was building, up and out and in every direction. This stood in marked contrast to what we had observed in the U.S. Back home, you'd occasionally see a crane or two at a construction site, but not a half dozen or more.

After several hours hanging out with YZ, as well as meeting up with some of his friends and enjoying a delicious fish meal at a favorite restaurant of his, it was time for us to head back to Ningbo.

When we arrived at *Shànghǎi Nánzhàn* (上海南站 – Shanghai South Train Station), we checked the boards for a train to take us back to Ningbo but were dismayed to find out the seats were all sold out, and there didn't seem to be any other options! We should have secured something online. YZ felt terrible for us. "I should have known better and helped you," he announced.

We assured him it wasn't his fault. Really, we should have secured round trip tickets. But now we were in a dilemma.

"Let's check out the buses," he suggested. The stations are connected, right over there." He pointed.

There was a bus leaving in about an hour with space for five. But the price took us by surprise; it would be about double the train fare.

YZ wanted to help us find something cheaper, and he looked around. It never occurred to us that we had any other options. We stood there in a moment of panic, trying not to let it spread to our kids.

We sent up one of those arrow prayers: "Oh, God – Help!"

Moments later, YZ motioned for us to follow him. He took us outside of the terminal, to some buses parked much further away, on a corner.

He started haggling with a woman outside the bus. We had no clue what he was saying as he conversed fluently in Shanghai dialect.

He turned to us. "They can get you to Ningbo. It'll be ¥82 each." That was much better than the almost ¥200 the buses inside would have charged.

"Are you sure this bus will work?" Dale questioned.

"Yes, it should. Although I've never taken them myself. But they are going to Ningbo."

"Okay, we'll try it." Darkness was making its first intrusion into the day, and we realized our time to decide was short.

YZ haggled a bit more and brought the price for each of us down to ¥75. We paid our money, gave YZ our hugs goodbye (not something you see a lot of in China), and boarded the bus.

To Ningbo.

Or so we thought. From the moment we were on and YZ was out of sight, we realized something was amiss. One of the men with whom YZ had bargained came back to us and began trying to get us to pay more. His voice was threatening, but Dale repeatedly told him "No" until other passengers began to tell him to back off and he returned to the front of the bus.

The bus itself was filthy – sunflower seed shells littered the floor and a rancid odor hung over the cabin. Both Erika and I felt an immediate sense of queasiness. Both Dale and Justin seemed to fall into "protect my women (and son/little brother)" mode, almost as if a heightened vigilance took over in the moment.

We occupied three seat banks and, fortunately, nobody sat next to Dale, who was watching over all of us. The rickety seats made the prospect of a two or three-hour bus ride unsettling. I could feel a headache coming on, especially as the one mounted TV monitor (standard in most Chinese buses) began to broadcast some obnoxiously loud game show.

Our kids could have been whiny, but I feel as if they were both too tired and shocked to complain much. Indeed, I think we all just wondered if this bus would actually take us to Ningbo.

This got both Dale and me looking for signs all along the way, telling us we were headed in the right direction. But because we had never been that way before – going around Hangzhou Bay (杭州湾 – *Hángzhōu wān*) on the roads, not on a train – *and* because we could not recognize many of the Chinese characters on the signs, *and* because we didn't have a smart phone or anything like Google Maps at our disposal – this was a tough call.

Finally, we began to see signs for Hangzhou, so at least we knew we were headed south and going in the right direction.

But the bumpy, swervy ride was taking a toll. It was tough to get comfortable on seats with spring wires pressing through. The kids were pretty whiny now – and so were we!

I began praying silently, perhaps calling out to God more in desperation than anything else. But my underlying prayer was, "God, just get us home. Please!"

The one "light" in the whole experience was found in the wide eyes and sweet expression of a little baby sitting in front of us. Boy or girl, we could not tell. But that baby, held close to the mother but facing in our direction, kept our minds off of the hard moment we were in. Or, at least helped.

Still, this was one of those bus rides that seemed an eternity. Fortunately, slowly but surely, we began to see a few signs with Níngbo (宁波) on them. I cannot tell you how much that felt like a breath of fresh air in that stale bus!

But then, just as quickly as we seemed to get a fresh wind in our sails, the woman holding the baby in front of us threw up all over the floor. And boy, did it smell! We thought it had been bad up until this point, but we didn't realize how much worse it could get!

I felt sorry for her. Later, talking with YZ, I learned this type of thing happens all the time. A few people around her helped. The baby started to wail as another passenger snatched the child from the mother's arms in an attempt to help. Another passenger seemed to mysteriously come up with a rag to clean up some of the mess.

Finally, we began to see the lights of a city and soon we were certain urban was overtaking rural. Then the bus driver announced, "*Níngbō dào le.*" (宁波到了. – "We've arrived in Ningbo.") Those words were like a song to our ears.

We scrambled off the bus with our stuffed backpacks, and practically fell out onto the street.

"But, what street? Where were we, really?" we wondered.

Dale attempted to ask the simple question, "Is this really Ningbo?" but without the "really" because we didn't know how to say it yet. So it was more, "Is this Ningbo?" (这里宁波吗？ – *Zhèlǐ Níngbō ma?*)

The driver – who had already told us we were in Ningbo – looked at us as if we were a bit stupid. He spewed off something we couldn't understand, but we imagined it was something like, "Of course this is Ningbo! That's just what I said!"

But we recognized nothing.

In the end, we finally were able to hail two taxis – but it was hard because it was close to 11pm and, although we were in Ningbo, we discovered later we were only on its northern edge. Few cars passed by. It seemed the taxis were avoiding us. I mean, who wants to take a bunch of *wàiguórén* somewhere late at night?

Our ride on the "unofficial" bus had been a bit harrowing, but, in the end, we found a taxi and, when we got back to our apartment at Ningbo University around 1 a.m., we all fell deep into sleep within minutes.

Challenges & Celebrations

33 | The honeymoon ends

*"I have realized that whatever good comes to me, comes from God,
whatever bad comes to me, God has allowed it,
and I choose to be thankful for both."*
– Jeff Goins, Author
Wrecked: When A Broken World Slams Into Your Comfortable Life

As the novelty of being in China began to wear off, attending Chinese schools as the first and only *wàiguórén* (or, in Luke's case, the only Caucasian) grew more difficult.

For our older two, the commute back and forth proved formidable. Still, I was impressed by both Justin and Erika's initial attitudes; they approached it as an opportunity for growing their independence. They assured us they were up for the challenge after a week or so of practice runs with them.

Us? I'm grateful my husband gets this age group well. As a high school teacher, he's a man of keen insight into the teenage mind, especially when it comes to handling a teenager's growing desire for independence. But for me, this arrangement pushed me into new areas of trust. I needed to learn to begin letting go of my "babies."

As time wore on, the physical *and* emotional rigor of the schedule began to wear upon both older kids, but especially on Justin.

He began to find reasons not to go to Chinese school in the afternoon. Sometimes it seemed a general sense of hormonal malaise would wash over him, rendering him motionless. The first time this happened, we ended up sending Erika out on her own; for me this was terrifying. *"Would my little girl (who's just 12) be safe?"* I wondered.

But again, this "little girl" rose to the opportunity; indeed, she was almost *more* eager to take on the challenge herself. And she did fine. Eventually we asked around and learned about a driver we could hire at a reasonable rate to take the kids and pick them up afterwards two days each week. Later, Ellen corralled Dale and a few other Ningbo University Foreign English Teachers to give special classes to the *Lixīngŭè* students once a week. On those days, Justin and Erika joined Dale and the other teachers for the commute in a university van.

That meant the long bus commute to *Lixīngŭè* only happened twice a week as time went on.

Thanks to *Li Lăoshī,* Erika received a warm welcome in her 7th grade class. Overall, the classmates were kind and open, doing what they could to make her feel involved even though she remained a mysterious outsider to them.

Angel and Cherry, two girls in her class at *Lixīngŭè,* took Erika under their wings. More advanced in their English language abilities, they were the bridges Erika needed during this season. Of course, their English got better just as Erika's understanding of what was going on around her improved.

One special moment in the fall stands out for Erika. Led by *Li Lăoshī,* all the students brought little gifts to Erika on Halloween. My daughter was delighted, embarrassed, grateful and surprised, all at once.

"I think it's their idea of what we do on Halloween in the U.S.," she reflected. "Of course, Halloween is not a Chinese holiday, but I think they were trying to make me feel not so far from home. That was nice."

For Justin, it was *Chén Lăoshī* who proved to be the "glue" keeping him connected to the school. This woman bent over backwards for Justin. Every day he would show up, she gave up an hour of prep time to teach him Chinese one-on-one in her office. She designed lesson plans specifically for him. She seemed to possess an intuitive understanding of him and his struggles. But she was also determined, from the start, to turn him into a Chinese language speaker. *Chén*

Lǎoshī became one of Justin's trusted friends.

Still, even with *Chén Lǎoshī* and the commute accommodations, Justin struggled a lot as the fall wore on. From the perspective of a parent, we watched as Justin seemed to transform from the enthusiastic, optimistic adventurer at take off in San Francisco, to a somber, joyless, inward-focused soul. It seemed as if he was spiraling downward fast, caught up in something larger than himself. The lurking signs of depression alarmed us.

Among those developments were Justin's migration into the closet-like bedroom off of our living room even though we had worked hard to find a bunk bed so the boys could be together. Our eight-year-old was forced to adjust to sleeping in a room by himself for the first time.

At times, Justin would retreat into the tiny adopted room and lay on the bed, in complete darkness, for long stretches. It might even be daytime, but he'd pull the curtains and create night. When this happened, he seemed almost deaf and dumb to anything we would offer or say. We might get a grunt, or a faint "yes," "no" or "dunno."

Dale's foresight had evolved into our present reality; our oldest son was grappling with his newfound, but temporary, circumstances. Dale recalled how he, too, had struggled with depression around Justin's age. "The thing that pulled me out of that pit," he now shares, "was recognizing that Jesus was there at the bottom with me. I wasn't alone."

I observed one of the most amazing examples of selfless love in my husband during this time. Perhaps it was borne out of his own experiences, but even years later writing this, I get all choked up.

Dale would go into the room with Justin and simply sit with him. He'd sit on the bed, not lecturing him, not even gently telling him what to do. He would just sit for a *long* time and be present. He'd let Justin know by that very act, "I'm here. I care." Even with two other children, a wife and tons of prep to do and papers to grade, Dale would still do this. Again and again, sometimes for an hour or two. Eventually, as Dale sat with him, Justin would begin to open up, very slowly.

I'll admit, I tried it once or twice and found it brutally hard. I mean, I wanted to give that kid a piece of my mind. Or, if I couldn't do that, I wanted to at least utter a gentle, well-meaning, "mom-like" suggestion. I found how far short I fell when it came to patience. We began to swell with doubts. *"What if we were messing him up long-term?" "What if he became so depressed he would get suicidal?"* We even contemplated returning to the U.S. early for the sake of our son, if it would bring about a change. Justin would have nothing to do with that idea, though. For him, it would be failure.

Instead, together, as a couple, we prayed and prayed. And, through emails back home to our family and friends, we asked for prayer. We know others were lifting us up, and this helped so much.

~~~~~~~~~

Being eight, Luke looked up to his big brother who, until now, seemed to do no wrong. So, it wasn't surprising when Luke, too, started to show cracks in his "I can do it" determination, especially when it came to Chinese school. While it wasn't only the influence of his older brother, a large part of it was.

Imagine an eight-year-old proclaiming, "I'm soooo depresssssed!" We would retort, "Luke, you don't even know what that means!" But I think he was getting his first taste of learning what it meant. Even though his situation wasn't as critical as Justin's, it still was of concern.

I started helping out at Luke's school after talking with Ellen. She made arrangements for me to go over twice a week in the afternoon, during a scheduled music time, and offer English "classes." These were for Luke's 4th grade class. And the kids seemed to love it. Even more importantly, Luke seemed to love it. For once, he was in control.

Actually, he had claimed control in more ways than that. An unexpected outcome of our year in China was Luke's discovery of the joy of reading. Previously, he had been a rather reluctant reader. But the characters in the *Redwall* series of books – colorful forest animal characters – became some of Luke's closest companions that year. Over time, he moved into the *Narnia, Lord of the Rings,* and *Harry Potter* series, gobbling them all up.

These places – lands of adventure, chivalry and magic – became his "safe" place, where the world made sense. They became his "home away from home."

Truth is, the elementary school didn't really know what to do with Luke. They tried. But his classmates spoke only the most rudimentary

English ("My name is ---," "I like ---."). Unfortunately, we hadn't enough time nor expertise to help Luke gain ground with Chinese. And *Gāo Lǎoshī*, though well-intended, seemed intimidated whenever Dale or I were around.

A day came in mid-November when Luke came home quite dejected, crying. "My bike," he sobbed. "The air was taken out of my tires. I could not ride it home. I think that boy in my class did it!" Of course, we had no hard proof. So we went over to the school and picked up the bike and filled the tires with air. But it happened again and again. Finally we decided to bring the situation to Ellen.

"Oh, I'm sure they don't mean any harm. It is what naughty boys do," she replied.

Ellen did talk with the school about it, and they did apologize. But they also seemed to regard the act as harmless and "something boys this age – naughty boys – do." They didn't see what we believed were obvious signs of bullying.

One bright spot in all of this was Luke's 9th birthday in November. To celebrate, we left Justin and Erika back at the apartment and spent much of the day out with our new nine-year-old. We doted on him, took him to the local aquarium and a park, enjoyed a meal he would like, played games, laughed and soaked up the moment.

Nevertheless, the challenges added up. By the time we rolled into December, both of our boys were quite frayed.

34 | Living out our faith

"Jesus said 'Love...as I have loved you.' We cannot love too much."
– Amy Carmichael, American Protestant Missionary to India

Nurturing and growing our Christian faith personally and in our family has always been a priority. Yet when we arrived in Ningbo, we had no idea how we'd do that.

We knew we could pray, study the Bible and worship together as a family in our little apartment. Dale's guitar and now Justin's cello laid the foundation for lots of "joyful noises" emanating from our second-story apartment. I wonder to this day what Mr. Chun downstairs made of it all.

After Russell and his group visited us early on, they introduced me to Carissa, Sheryl, Cora and several other female Christian students.

At Russell's invitation, Dale began meeting weekly to study the Bible with a small group of guys. He would meet Russell each week, and they would then wend their way through various back alleys to a restaurant. They'd head to a private room in back that was filled with a spread of food and green tea, and at least seven or eight other guys. Together, they'd read and discuss a chapter in the book of Proverbs and then spend some time in prayer.

The people Dale would meet, the designated location, and the restaurant would change every week. By switching it up every time, the guys reasoned, it would be tough to track them gathering with the *wàiguórén* teacher. Apparently Taylor, the previous teacher, had become suspected by university officials of proselytizing. Some in the group had been reprimanded by the same officials.

It was all a bit of an adventure for my husband. But Dale went along with the flow, treasuring the moments with these guys. They looked to him to teach, encourage and build them up. Russell and a couple others acted as interpreters and made sure everyone understood what Dale had to say.

~~~~~~~~~~~~~

For me, it was a bit different. Perhaps I wasn't as suspect since there didn't seem to be a *wàiguórén* female teacher who had run afoul of the university; still some precautionary measures prevailed. "We need to be quiet when we go there," Carissa, my new friend, pointed out. "There" was a small apartment on the second floor of a university building. It was on the edge of campus, about a ten-minute walk from my home. We met on a consistent day and time, and in the same place. The goal was to not draw attention to ourselves.

We'd shuffle quietly up the steps to the second-story apartment and pack in. Most times at least ten would gather, often more. One woman, *Huáng* (黄), often brought the meeting to order. Quiet and composed, she was much older than the others and seemed to command their respect.

Later I learned directly from *Huáng* about her past, but not in English nor Chinese. Instead, we communicated in Japanese! *Huáng* had been an exchange student in Japan when some Christians befriended her and she encountered Jesus. We were able to communicate well and I found her story fascinating.

When *Huáng* returned to Ningbo University, she was dedicated to helping more people meet Jesus. So she began to share her faith with those who expressed interest, sometimes even in class. She did not abide by university code. A student reported this, and the university punished her.

Officials banned her from the classroom for a year. She was still allowed to conduct her research, but they warned her against contact with students. Her pay was reduced to a mere 25% of what it was, forcing her to rely upon her husband's salary. He, too, worked for the university but in its planning and site maintenance department. They lived in university housing.

When we arrived, *Huáng* was back in the classroom, taking a much more careful approach. Still, outside of the classroom, she endeavored to encourage Christian students, share her faith, and generally serve

her God in whatever ways she could. She had not been caught again...
yet.

As a group, we would study passages together and discuss them. Of course, I was on the outside most of the time linguistically. But Carissa and Cora, both excellent with their English, helped me understand whenever they could. They also would interpret for me. And, twice, when I was privileged to teach, they interpreted the whole thing, explaining it to their friends with passion and grace.

I really loved the prayer times. I could understand only a little of what was going on. Still, regardless of my limited understanding, a palpable sense of God's Spirit resided in that rather dingy, little apartment. I felt as if I had been invited into a very holy place.

Dale and I learned from the students about a few larger "house" churches filled with students meeting around the university. Carissa told me the one she attended had several hundred people gathering. I wondered where and how they did that, given the limited space in homes and the need to remain under the radar. She told me they gathered in halls and restaurants, so sometimes it didn't even look like a church was happening until the service started. I wanted to see.

But we also learned we really couldn't go with any of our new Christian friends. Doing so would put them and the church gathering in jeopardy because we'd draw attention. Keeping a low profile – or, *dīdiào* (低调) – was the way to go in such matters.

It was about halfway through our year in China when we learned about a church we could attend through Sarah, the Korean international student we met at the 60th Anniversary event. She told us about Ningbo International Christian Fellowship (NICF).

Sarah contacted NICF, and they arranged for a van on Sunday morning to pick us up. The church met in a home 45 minutes away.

This intrepid group of about 30–40 believers – with lots of little kids in tow – became a sweet lifeline during our remaining months in China. Started by one Taiwanese and one Korean couple (who communicated with each other through broken English), the church had grown to incorporate some Chinese returnees (who had become Christians while living abroad), Japanese, South Africans, Brits, Kenyans, Germans and one friend from Papua New Guinea.

We learned later we were in NICF's second year. It was very much a church plant in its earliest stages. (One year after leaving Ningbo, we returned on a short trip and found the church had more than tripled in size, meeting in a larger place, and welcoming a number of Ningbo University international students. This time, a large bus came to pick everyone up! The bus was full of other East Asian, Indonesian, African and European students. Amazing!)

When we entered the apartment the first time, we had no idea what to expect. Everyone was warm and friendly. Some of the women were at work in the kitchen preparing food. Several others were working with instruments and a simple sound system for the oversized living room. Although from the outside the apartment building seemed relatively nondescript, inside the story proved different – much fancier, with a spiral staircase to a second floor.

Chāng (張) and his wife, Jenny, met us. This was their home. Jenny, demure and warm, smiled broadly as we entered. Her dancing eyes spoke what she could not manage with words. *Chāng*, a friendly, bespectacled man who seemed in his mid-thirties, spoke excellent English.

"We are thrilled to have you with us today. Welcome, welcome! We're sorry it took so long before we found you!"

"Oh, we're excited to be here, too," Dale chimed back. Glancing over at our kids, I'm not sure they felt quite the same way. This was a completely different and stretching "church" experience for them. Still, they were game. We had promised them we would only return if everyone felt at home (as much as we could be) with it. We wouldn't force them to go. But we did expect them to try.

True, trying to make a "church" happen among a bunch of people from different nations who are new to one another in an apartment, and trying to be a bit discreet while doing so, can be, well, awkward. But, as we began to sing the first few songs, with words projected on the wall, that awkwardness melted away and a sense of deep connection began to flood the place.

As we moved further into the service, with a short (20 minute) teaching, a time of communion together and then a lunch meal, Dale and I knew we had found a special group of people we would get closer to in the coming months. On the way home the kids said they wanted to come back. This was good.

35 | Hard lessons, unexpected gifts

"The only real mistake is the one from which we learn nothing."
– John Powell, British-American Film Composer

Dale and I would take turns – and sometimes go together if the children were doing well – heading deep into the city by bus to do our grading. We did this because it proved quite difficult to do in our small apartment with the distraction of our kids. Plus, Dale and I had become coffee shop aficionados. Dale, in particular, had always found it difficult to concentrate on school work at home. He endeavored not to bring his work into his home life.

We were trying to find this option on campus. But we learned the only two places offering wifi were the library and the coffee shop. The former wasn't really an option because it was overflowing with students. We'd use the on-campus coffee shop from time to time, but the wifi wasn't entirely reliable.

So, what were our options?

Well, Starbucks, of course. At the time, Ningbo sported a handful of Starbucks stores. Their reliable wifi made them frequent haunts for us as we plied through our planning and papers.

Starbucks was – and is – on the march in China. For Chinese, Starbucks are upscale, trendy and western. But Starbucks, while maintaining brand consistency, does an excellent job catering to the Chinese palate, a preference for less sugary fare than in most western countries. The tactic certainly seems to work. As of the end of 2014, 823 shops of the iconic coffee maker had opened throughout China. In January 2016, the company announced a plan to open 2500 new stores over the next five years.

Evidently, the Chinese are drinking plenty of coffee.

So it must have been at least the tenth time I had been in the largest Starbucks in our city, a two-story circular structure in the middle of Tianyi Square (*Tiānyī Guǎngchǎng*). Modernesque in design, it was windowed all around, giving the interior a light, airy feel.

This Starbucks makes those in the U.S. look like cozy little rooms. While I'm not sure of the capacity of the *Tiānyī Guǎngchǎng* Starbucks, I'm certain it topped 200.

That day in mid-November I was working hard, ploughing through a set of papers the students had written. At Dale's suggestion, I took his laptop instead of mine. He needed my computer for something he was doing with the kids.

I lost track of the time as I read paper after paper, did my planning for the week ahead, and tried to respond to several emails. I was also downloading a video a friend had sent me, but it was taking some time.

Then I realized I needed to use the bathroom.

I had been to the bathroom at this Starbucks before. Down the stairs and all the way around to the other side, out the door and to the left. I figured I could go quickly and, since my computer was downloading something, I let it sit there.

A few minutes later, I returned up the stairs. My jaw dropped. The computer was...gone! I suddenly realized I had set myself up as the victim. I looked around in shock. Didn't anyone *see* that?!? *"But it's mine, you know!"* I felt like screaming.

As I registered the reality – my laptop had been stolen, in clear view, in broad daylight, and nobody else cared – I felt my stomach drop. How stupid could I have been?!? Somehow, I thought that because I was *downloading* something, my computer was anchored to something permanent and couldn't be moved. How wrong I was!

My head could barely think in English, much less in Chinese. What was I going to do? I turned to a couple sitting a little ways away and mustered up some very broken Mandarin.

Wǒ diànnǎo bù zhèlǐ. Nǐ kànjiàn le ma? (我电脑不这里。你看见了吗? "My computer isn't here. Did you see it?") I didn't know how to say "stolen" so I worked around it.

The couple told me they didn't see anything. I asked another person. He told me he remembered a woman walking by with a shopping bag. Most likely, she was the one.

One of the Starbucks employees could understand and speak a little English. She told me me not to worry and to show me where I had been sitting. Little did I know, I had chosen a table in the "blind spot" of two security cameras!

May, the Starbucks employee, seemed to feel my pain. "I am so sorry," she expressed. "I know my manager will be troubled to hear about this."

We went downstairs to her manager, and she explained the situation again. Meanwhile, the reality was sinking in. My computer was in some unscrupulous lady's shopping bag, probably well out of Tianyi Square. Hopes of ever recovering it were fading fast.

May told me, "We must report it to the police."

I wondered aloud. "Is there any chance it can be found?"

May looked wary. "I don't think there is much. But a little. Still, we should report."

I told her I wanted to take a moment to call my husband.

"Hey, what's up?"

"Well, I think you're gonna need to sit down for this one."

"Everything okay?"

"No, not exactly. Dale, I'm so sorry, but the computer got stolen!" There. I had said it.

There was a moment of silence. I could feel him thinking. He's so good about doing that.

"Where are you now?"

"I'm at the *Tiānyī Guǎngchǎng* Starbucks – the big one."

"I'm going to come there to see you, okay?"

"Yeah, I need you right now. Will you tell the kids?"

"Not yet. I'll just tell them Mom needs me and I'll be gone for a couple hours. It's a Saturday, so I think they're fine. They're all in pretty good shape today."

"Well, that's good. Because I'm not. Call or text me when you get close. The manager at Starbucks wants to take me to the police station in the square."

"Okay. I'll see you in about an hour then."

In the midst of my severe disappointment, mostly at myself but also at Chinese society in general for letting this happen, Dale's calm and uncritical response was a breath of fresh air. Another one of those many moments when I thanked God for giving me such an amazing man.

May, her manager and I went to the Tianyi Square Police Station and, with May's help, we filed a report. That moment I realized I was glad I took seriously the instruction to bring my passport with me everywhere. I needed it right then.

It was a rather nondescript place. We had to go to the second floor to meet the police officer in charge of such affairs. This man exuded an "I've seen it all" type of attitude, at least to me. I could read it in his body language, though I couldn't understand a word of what they were saying, because again, it was in Níngbō-*huà*, not standard Mandarin.

Reality was setting in. We were one computer short now. Our computer, presumably with much of our personal information on it, was out there in the world for anyone to see.

Dale met me at the front of the Starbucks just a little later. I was pretty down on myself at the moment. More than the physical loss of the computer was the anger I felt toward myself for being so careless. I had heard about incidents like this happening in China from my students and from others. Why had I so brazenly thought I would be exempt?

Dale just hugged me. He didn't say much at all, at first. I bawled on his shoulder, letting out sobs of grief and disappointment. Up until that moment, I had held much of the emotion inside, but it all came tumbling out on his sleeve as I heaved and tried to gain some composure.

"Are you hungry?" he asked.

I suddenly realized I was shaking and yes, quite hungry.

He pointed to a restaurant across the way.

"How about if we go there, get some food and talk about what just happened?" he suggested.

We did just that.

The food was not our focus, but I remember it was pretty good. Italian, actually.

And, playing in the background, I could hear Dido's 1999 song *Thank You*, reminding me *"it's not so bad, it's not so bad at all...I just want to thank you for giving me the best day of my life...Oh, just to be with you, is having the best day of my life...."*

An ironic twist that somehow was reminding me that the man sitting in front of me was what really mattered. It would be okay.

When Erika found out about the computer, she was the one most distressed because several poems she had written since arriving in Ningbo were sitting on that hard drive and nowhere else. I felt so bad about disappointing her like that!

After we talked it through, we realized there wasn't too much personal information on that computer. It was quite new as we had purchased it shortly before leaving the U.S. This was a small consolation, but at least it was something.

When we shared what happened with a friend back home by email, he suggested we look into our homeowner's insurance. I would have never thought of that given that we weren't even living at home right then.

But sure enough – our insurance company said they would replace 60% of the value of the computer! While this wasn't a perfect solution, we felt we could probably scramble the extra amount to purchase a replacement in time. We were grateful when our homeowner's insurance company processed the payment into our bank account back home for close to $800! That helped a lot.

36 | Sharing the heart of two American holidays

"We reveal to ourselves and others what is important to us by the way we celebrate."
– Nöel Piper, Author

With the approach of the American holiday of Thanksgiving, our daughter began to get nostalgic for apple pie. But, since China isn't much of a baking culture, the challenge of finding an apple pie, much less making one, proved formidable. Apples were easy to find in the market. But the spices? Nutmeg, cinnamon, and allspice, plus yeast for baking. We tracked them all down, but not without a good deal of cost and effort.

The last ingredient to make it work was...the toaster oven! We didn't have an oven in our apartment. We poked around some home appliance shops in the downtown area, and found them too expensive to justify. But we did discover an affordable toaster oven with directions in English!

Erika found a recipe online she could adapt to make a single, but really luscious, apple pie in a metal bowl. And from that time on, she became a bit of a toaster-oven-baking ninja. Some of our student friends even learned how to bake them alongside her.

Eager to share Thanksgiving with my Chinese university students, I attempted Erika's toaster-oven apple pie recipe and managed to make a version of her creation for each of my classes during Thanksgiving week. Even though each student only got a bite or two, sans vanilla ice cream, the reaction was overwhelmingly positive.

Of course, there's much more to Thanksgiving than apple pie! I decided to use drama to help them better understand the meaning and the traditional story. To make sure all students in each class could participate, I broke them into smaller "scene" groups and they would work their drama through, finding ways to acquire or make appropriate props a week in advance.

When the actual week arrived, we started rolling out the Thanksgiving dramas, class by class. I nearly burst with laughter when Eric, a funny young man with a penchant for garnering attention, played a Chinese Squanto. He did it well and had the rest of us caught up in alternating humor and drama.

After the dramas, I went on to tell them the story of the daily ration of five kernels of corn the Pilgrims purportedly lived on during their first winter. I tried to direct the students to the deep faith of many of the Pilgrims, how they were trusting a God they did not see but fervently believed in.

One student, Amanda, approached me after class. "Mrs. D," she started. "I don't really understand why God would make a difference for them. I mean, sometimes they prayed, but people still died. It didn't always go like they wanted."

"I know what you mean, Amanda," I responded. "But I think part of the act of praying is simply admitting you don't have all the answers and are turning to one you believe does. Remember, the answers aren't always what we expect, plan or want."

She paused. "You mean, God would want those people to die?" she queried.

"I think it depends upon what you believe about God. If you believe, as I do, that God is good and wants the very best for me, his child, as it says in several places in the Bible, then you trust that God's plan is unfolding exactly as He wills. And, actually, those people would have had to die at some point, right?"

I could see her wheels clicking. "Yes, I guess you're right."

"You know, when we pray, it *may* influence the outcome of a situation, or it may not. But I think prayer matters perhaps even more for what it does in us. It changes our hearts and perspectives. We humble ourselves before a power much greater. This may be the true value."

I could see her wheels spinning.

Another holiday not widely celebrated in China, Christmas, would be soon upon us as the days got shorter and darker. But our first snow in Ningbo lit the scenery up a little bit. It was a slight dusting, but enough to get everyone excited with a sense of change.

For our kids, this always brought a sense of anticipation and hope. Erika, especially, has always been into the traditions surrounding the holidays. So right after Thanksgiving concluded, she approached me with a proposal.

"I want to use some of the money I've saved to buy a sewing machine and then make Christmas stockings for us. Can I do that?"

Well, I didn't see why not. But I had no clue of where to find a sewing machine, much less fabric and thread. I had to turn to my students for that one.

Thankfully, one of them, Jean, grew up in Ningbo and had been a bit of a seamstress herself. She knew where we could go.

That next Saturday Erika, Jean and I took the bus to a department store I had never seen. Sure enough – they sold sewing machines, fabric, thread and yarn. We had given Jean a price range, and she proceeded to discuss the options with the sales clerk. In the end, I exited that department store with our treasure and a very happy 12-year-old girl.

Industrious, Erika got to work! And she recorded her thoughts on our family blog about it not too much later.

Erika's voice:

It's snowing in Ningbo! Well, in our apartment, that is. Over these past few weeks we've cut out paper snowflakes, strung together paper chains, purchased short lengths of shimmery tinsel and small colored lights at Tesco, even gotten a smallish fake tree and decorated it pretty nicely. We're getting ready for Christmas!

Christmas is my favorite time of the year. Usually, in the USA, we get a huge pine tree and spend a whole weekend decorating for Christmas with our twenty-odd boxes of decorations, ornaments, lights, a nativity scene, and even a train that we run around the base of the Christmas tree, with Christmas music playing loudly from our stereo. In China, however, things are a bit different. First of all, a good portion of our decorations are homemade – for example, Luke's paper snowman or the small clay nativity scene I made, plus the approximately 40 totally unique snowflakes and the several long paper chains hanging about. And of course there's the five red and green homemade stockings (made by me!) hanging on the wall.

This Christmas will definitely be different from all our past Christmases in the USA. For one thing, this is the first Christmas any of us kids have spent not at our house or one of our grandparents' houses. Another thing is that we probably won't have the customary Christmas goodies, like candy canes and gingerbread houses and so on. But despite all of that, we've got Christmas spirit, and I think that will make this Christmas in China very memorable for all of us.

And so, although we may have simple decorations, a very small nativity scene, and a fake Christmas tree along with the small bamboo plant we've wrapped in tinsel and Christmas lights, I can safely say this season is still "the most wonderful time of the year!"

Luke also had something to say about celebrating that year.

Luke's voice:

For Christmas at home, we usually go to either one of my grandparents' houses. When we go to my Mom's side of the family, we usually have a different kind of Christmas. The stockings are usually much more filled, and there are many more Christmas presents under the tree. Of course, grandmas make the best food in the world, so we'll miss Grandma Joan's Christmas dinner party. My Dad's side of the family lives in Alaska. We have a fun, snowy Christmas there. After we have a fun, little present opening, we usually go down to our cousins Trevor and Jessie's house. We usually play around on their Xbox and play with their dog and ferret. I'll miss that this year, too.

Even though we'll miss these things, we'll be able to open presents here, too. (And there are still lots of presents here, too.) We also have a bamboo Christmas tree, and we've had lots of fun making snowflakes, Christmas cookies, and paper snowmen. And we'll still be able to celebrate Jesus' birth.

Christmas is not a special day celebrated in China. It's just an ordinary day with classes and the like. Still, we were determined to share at least some of the truth of what that holiday is all about. We wanted to give our students a deep, balanced – and even nuanced – understanding of Christmas.

Of course, our students knew about the Santa Christmas. Indeed, years ago as China began to open more to the West, the commercial benefits of the Christmas holidays enticed merchants to make it a big deal. By now, most Chinese had a vague idea of Christmas as something special. Few, however, connected it with anything remotely religious.

We wanted to help our students understand the *whole* picture when it comes to Christmas. Even though we didn't mind mixing some Santa in, we wanted to expose them to the heart of the celebration, the birth of Baby Jesus.

Again, I decided to employ interactive drama since it had worked so well at Thanksgiving. I had written up a play, based upon the account of Jesus' birth in Luke 2:1–20. But I put the story in modern, simple words my students would understand. Plus I added a few twenty-first-century twists. My aim was to help the students grasp the historical depth but also the personal, modern-day relevance of this significant moment in history.

I split the class in two. They were two separate casts doing the same play. When they weren't performing, they would be the audience. The goal was for them to take the same basic story and spice it up a bit, adding some flourish to the already unusual perspectives I had added in.

Everyone had a role. There were lots of shepherds and angels. But mixed in were shoppers and Christmas carolers (an activity many found quite intriguing), bakers and elves. Even Santa showed up, but he wasn't the main dude. In each group, the role of baby Jesus fell to one of the young men. In most all of my classes the women outnumbered the men two or three to one.

I had a list of props they'd need to bring in for the final show. Some got so creative, especially with the scenery! They had fun, and they learned the true story at the same time!

"Mrs. D," Learner, one of my very enthusiastic students exclaimed. "I think I now understand why you celebrate Christmas. And we had a lot of fun learning. At least I did."

To be sure, focusing on the religious basis of Christmas is not all we did. We had another Christmas-focused class during that week. This time I took the class into pure Santa, watching one of my favorite Christmas movies, *Elf*. Will Ferrell, Zooey Deschanel, James Caan, Bob Newhart and the others do such a terrific job making me laugh and love more. How I hoped my students would feel some of that magic as well!

37 | A New Years unlike any other

"And now we welcome the new year.
Full of things that have never been."
– Rainer Maria Rilke, Bohemian-Austrian Poet & Novelist

Even though the traditional Chinese calendar is lunar based and does not match the Gregorian calendar, modern China celebrates the turn from December 31st to January 1st with pageantry as well, especially with fireworks.

Actually, we would hear fireworks all the time in China. As the inventor of gunpowder and fireworks, China has marked most rituals using explosives for at least a millennium or more. Some of my students told me how people would use firecrackers to scare out evil spirits when building or moving into a new home or opening a new businesses. Indeed, the sound of these explosions, along with horn honking and the screaming man, threaded through our one-year experience.

Incidentally, in more recent years, China's bad air has prompted local governments, pressed by environmental groups, to ban this practice, causing a clash between current reality and cultural traditions to ensue. Not everyone is happy.

But for China ringing in the 2010 New Year, the fireworks still took center stage. We got a chance to go downtown, in the chill of a frigid night, to watch Ningbo's fireworks shout out to the world *"Èrqiān shí nián dàodá"* (二千十年到达 – "2010 has arrived!") while most of the world was still asleep. The show proved a spectacular display, cascading over the intersection of the Yuyao River (余姚河 –

Yúyáo Hé) and the Fenghua River (奉化河 – *Fènghuà Hé*).

For us, the moment was especially thrilling because, back home in California, our city had terminated both New Year's and Independence Day fireworks to both save money and protect against fire in a time of drought.

We now had a new memory we could cherish and enjoy.

I might also say there is something thrilling about being among the first to step into a new year. Perhaps you'd never get this unless you're a Californian, Oregonian, Washingtonian, West Coast Canadian, Alaskan or Hawaiian, but being last for these things can be a just a tad lonely. Really!

Dale and I had lived in Japan before and had experienced New Years, or *Oshōgatsu* お正月. For Japanese, the New Year is perhaps the nation's largest celebration of the year. Schools, shops, government and everything is closed. We had experienced the lead-up to all this, with *Bōnenkai* 忘年会, or "Year-Forgetting" parties and Ōsōji 大掃除, literally "The Big Cleaning," as well as a host of traditions on New Year's eve and January 1st. These include special food known as *Osechi-ryōri* 御節料理, as well as "Cross-the-Year" noodles (*toshikoshi Soba* 年越しそば), listening to bells of a nearby temple ring 108 times (107 in the old year, one in the new, signifying the Buddhist idea of purification of sin), and visiting a local temple or shrine on January 1st with some Japanese friends, as is custom.

But for the Chinese, it is a bit different. Although they fete the passage into the new year according to the Gregorian calendar, it is a relatively low-key celebration. The Chinese New Year, often known as the Spring Festival or *Chūnjié* (春节) in late January or early February, is *the* real holiday in China.

Still, I knew that feeling of being among the first on the planet moving into a new year. It's a great feeling. And, being their first time ever, I think the kids found it a bit special, too.

No question, the most amazing experience for us was yet to come on New Year's Day. We didn't have classes that day, even though it was a Friday. And we had been invited by some of our Christian student friends to a very special gathering. They didn't give us many details, but they did ask us to prepare a few songs to share. "Just be ready to go at 10 am. We'll be taking two taxis from in front of the University Hotel," Carissa told me.

Carissa leaned into our taxi cab and told the driver where to go. Then she hopped in the other one with three friends. The cab spirited us away to an area of the city we hadn't been to before, not so far from Ningbo University, but in the opposite direction from our regular travels.

When the driver stopped on a side street filled with people, we got out to pay, but Carissa told us she had it covered. She and the others whisked us – along with Dale's guitar and Justin's cello – inside a large room.

What we saw and experienced over the next two hours at our first experience in an underground church service remains one of my sweetest memories of our year in China. New Year's Day 2010. A moment I can never forget.

At least 200 people had gathered in that room, and 400+ eyes suddenly were upon us. Under those eyes, dozens of smiles broke out, along with squeals of excitement from some of the little children. Some were simply curious and perhaps a bit shocked. To this day, I don't know if the congregation had been prepped about our participation or not.

Directed toward the front by friendly greeters, we made our way to our seats. Carissa, Cora and Sheryl sat among us and interpreted for us what was going on.

Up front, the pastor spoke to the group gathered. He exuded a compelling and genuine charisma. Although the room was quite cold, with temperatures close to freezing and no heating in the facility, Pastor Ren cultivated a growing warmth in the room. He was sharing about the need we have, as Christian believers, to "stand firm" in the face of trials, and to look to the New Year as a time to recommit ourselves to Jesus.

And then the place warmed up even more as bundled toddlers came up to the stage with their adult leader and sang a Christmas song. Then two women, one on the violin and the other flute, played a lovely rendition of "O Holy Night." And then...us!

Carissa asked us to introduce ourselves and then interpreted as we thanked them for including us in this special celebration. I told them the names and a little about the two songs we were going to sing for

them: "It is Good to Praise the Lord" and "In Christ Alone."
Despite cultural and linguistic differences, music always seems to communicate. After playing and singing our songs, we seemed to have crossed the cultural divide. Later, several of the members communicated their appreciation to us.

Once the service concluded, it was time to eat! We went to an outside courtyard, prayed together, and then gathered around a table with Carissa, Cora, Sheryl, Russell and several other guys and girls from our weekly group. Together, we began to enjoy the meal: hot pot, or *huǒguō* 火锅, a steaming soup cooking on a burner at the center of our table. That warmed us up despite the frigid air.

Chinese hot pot has a history of over 1000 years and is probably one of the most popular meals in China. While previously limited to winter, modern Chinese enjoy hot pot year round. It's a social meal where everyone gathers around a pot of steaming broth at the center of the table. People chat, eat, drink and have fun as they put their choices of the fresh vegetables, meats, tofu and other items stacked nearby into the pot. The ingredients simmer and soak up flavor and nutrients. According to the Chinese, eating hot pot in winter helps warm the body and improve circulation; doing so in summer helps people sweat and cool down.

The two most famous styles of hotpot are Sichuan Hotpot, with a spicy and numbing flavor, and Beijing Instant Boiled Mutton Hotpot. The latter is not spicy but savory. It is the one we were enjoying that New Year's Day.

The moment stood still for us, and we delighted in the connections with people we knew we'd never see again this side of heaven. It felt like such a privilege to be invited into their world and experience as Chinese believers. Although brief, we felt as if we got a glimpse into their lives as Christ followers in China.

This experience stood out because it seemed, in many ways, to mark a turning point for us as a family. The fall had been rough, especially with Justin's and Luke's struggles. As we turned into the new year, even though it was still cold and dark, a sense of light pulling us ahead began to permeate our days.

Interlude

38 | Fleeing the world's largest annual migration

"A change is as good as a rest."
— Stephen King, *Hearts in Atlantis*

For a few months now, we had been making plans for the seven-week semester break. This break coincides with the Chinese Lunar New Year, or Spring Festival *Chūnjié* (春节). *Chūnjié* begins in late-January or early February every year.

I'll confess, the name does baffle me some since the world in most of China is still frozen at this time. I'm wondering if dubbing it *Chūnjié,* as it has been known over the last 100 years, reflected more a desire to hasten the warmer season of spring?

Chūnjié officially stretches over a 40-day period known as *Chūnyùn* (春运). The second character in this word means "transport." It refers to increased passenger traffic on all modes of transportation during *Chūnjié.*

Often referred to as "the largest annual human migration," *Chūnjié* is not simply a Mainland Chinese phenomenon. Chinese throughout the world, as well as several other Asian cultures, celebrate this season as well. The 40-day stretch empties the populous eastern Chinese cities as people return to their hometowns in more rural areas. While some travel by air, most journey by bus, train and car, making already strained systems extra crowded. In 2015, Mainland Chinese made over 3.5 billion trips during *Chūnyùn*, an average of 2.5 for every Chinese man, woman and child!

Realizing all this, we decided to get out of China during the hectic *Chūnyùn* season. As much as we might want to "experience it" during our year abroad, we also felt as if it was time to explore other nearby countries.

We ended up planning three separate trips – the first to the Philippines, the second to Taiwan (via Hong Kong), and the last to Japan. In all cases, we flew in and out of Shanghai.

In 2009 and 2010, flights out of Shanghai to Taipei (and the reverse), referred to as Cross-Straits Charters (两岸包机 – *liǎng'àn bāojī)*, finally had become available to the average Chinese. People often booked these trips a year or more in advance. So, due to the season, we had to take the more circuitous route through Hong Kong.

Packing for this trip proved a daunting experience! We knew we'd be in warmer weather in the Philippines, but expected very cold weather in Shanghai, Japan and possibly Taiwan. So, how to manage it all?

At that moment, another "angel" arrived in our life. This time, she wasn't six-and-a-half feet tall, nor even Chinese.

Our friends Marielle & Roger in the States connected us with Lora, then a top-ranking executive with McDonald's (麦当劳 – *Màidānglǎo)* in China. The company housed her in an elegant high rise in the *Xīntiāndì* (新天地 – literally, "New-Heaven-Earth") District in Shanghai. This upscale neighborhood is known for its abundance of expats. Lora had come to China never expecting to rise in the ranks as she had nor stay so long; she was nine years in.

Lora lived in spacious, luxurious quarters on the 12th floor. Although the apartment wasn't huge by Western standards, it was more than ample for a single woman in China.

Sandy-haired, pragmatic and welcoming, Lora took us in from that point on every time we landed in Shanghai. We felt a bit invasive coming into her apartment and her life like that. But she had a very "unattached" attitude to her possessions. She wanted the place to be used. That, according to her, was what it was all about.

Our kids would sleep on the very comfortable couches in Lora's living room, while Dale and I slept in the guest bedroom. It seemed to work out fine. We even got to stay in her place once or twice when she was out of town.

Lora's place proved so helpful as we were going in and out of Shanghai for these trips, especially since we'd need such a variety of clothes to handle the different climates. Thanks to Lora, we could leave the heavy clothes at her place for a couple weeks as we headed off to Manila, and then switch out as needed – a huge gift to us!

As we arrived in Manila, the tropical heat immediately hit us, but so too did a compelling friendliness to match. Broad Filipino smiles greeted us, with the aromas of jasmine (*sampaguita*) and plumeria (*frangipani*) wafting from almost every direction.

The contrast between the cold of Mainland China (both the season and the more rigid way of life under communist rule) and the warm, laid-back approach to life in the Philippines struck us immediately.

Dale and I had been in the Philippines before, in 1988. And in 2006 Justin and I had spent 10 days on a short-term trip to the Philippines led by our pastor, so this wasn't such unfamiliar territory.

We replicated many parts of that 2006 trip during our two weeks in the Philippines. First came a few days in Dumaguete, on the southwest coast of the southern province of Negros. There, we stayed with Pastor Les and his wife, Celia, in a guest house on their property with a large wall surrounding the compound of about 12 buildings. I wondered aloud how being in a gated compound might affect the ability to connect with the local community. Pastor Les responded.

"We wish we didn't need to have a wall here. But in the Philippines, that's what you need. There have been so many robberies in our area. Not having the wall is opening yourself up to theft. Plain and simple."

Dale and I wanted to get out as we could, so we'd sneak out early in the morning to walk around the area as our children slept. Nearby, we discovered farmers out tilling their fields, readying for new planting as the weather would get warmer in February and March. We heard the pitched cry of dogs both in the distance and nearby. We ran into women. carrying hefty containers on their hips, as they headed to community wells. We found ourselves enmeshed among giggling school children on their way to another day of classroom learning.

People seemed friendly, but also curious and sometimes a bit cautious.

Openness and warmth, but also robbery, barred windows and walled compounds. In China, little fear of robbery or violence, but a lack of freedom of expression. I began to ponder the question, "Which land, the Philippines or China, was really the "freer" of the two?"

A few days later, we found ourselves on a rickety bus headed north to Bacolod, on the opposite side of the island. On the seven-hour trip, we'd encounter occasional traffic along the narrow roads, a steep wind up a mountain, and several stops along the way.

Our packed bus included goats and a few chickens. This was the same trip Justin and I had taken three years earlier. I remember the trip had been a bit trying for then 11-year-old Justin. I wondered how Luke, at nine, would do now.

Other than the verdant green overwhelming our senses, the crowds at various stations along the way hawking their wares, the braying of goats, and clucking of chickens, the trip – thankfully – went rather smoothly. No one got sick, although Luke complained of feeling dizzy at times. We chatted, read, ate, observed, got off for the potty stops, slept and otherwise enjoyed our "tour" across the lush island with its varied landscapes.

As we pulled into the northern town of Bacolod, Ed and a troupe of his kids were waiting for us at the busstop. The five kids with him, boys and girls ranging in age from 8 to 17, exuded energy and warmth, with wide smiles and sparkling eyes.

"*Maayon Hapon!*" "Good afternoon, or hello!" in Bisaya, the local dialect. Several of them could speak freely with us in English.

After that warm greeting, Ed piled us and our luggage into the oversized van and headed out of Bacolod City Central to the spot I had come to view as, quite possibly, "the happiest place on earth."

I know full well this is Disneyland's tagline. But my *happiest place on earth* became something very different three years earlier when our then-pastor had introduced Justin, me and the rest of our short-term team to this unexpected community nestled in the rice fields and rolling hills outside of Bacolod, Negros Province, in the Philippines.

39 | Songs of sorrow, songs of joy

"Every heart sings a song, incomplete, until another heart whispers back. Those who wish to sing always find a song."
– Plato

They were expecting us. Just like the welcome we had received three years ago, over 150 people, mostly small children, were waiting for us with posters, balloons and fanfare as our van pulled into the end of the long dirt driveway. Music played, commotion everywhere! We felt like celebrities, even though we were just an ordinary American family.

This is the Olivino family – Ed (Tata) and Susie (Nana) and their 150+ children! A retired marine but also a soft-hearted man of God, Ed offers just the right combination of leadership, discipline, joy and warmth to fill the place with nothing less than contagious energy, charisma and purpose. This couple responded to the call years ago to begin an orphanage in this Filipino city of half a million people. Only, it didn't turn out quite as they thought.

Over time, they had people literally giving them their children to raise. This was the case even when one or both parents were alive, not to mention when children were truly orphans without any family. After prayer and investigation, they realized that adopting one…then five…then 10…then 25 of the children was the better path to follow. So they did.

You might think that Ed and Susie have to be superheroes to do this. I mean, really – how can *anyone* care for and raise children in such huge numbers and keep going for so many years?

This is a case where, "With man, it is impossible, but with God, all things are possible," to quote Jesus (Mark 10:27). Ed and Susie are truly people of the Book; they live, breathe and walk their faith so fully. It's inspirational.

But, exactly, what *is* this place they created? It's a home for approximately 150 children, from infants to 18 year olds, as well as a host of "graduates" who help in a variety of ways. Some of the kids have special needs, but they are given dignity and a place in the family as much as any other child. It is also a school, a farm, a training ground, a small business, and a church – a holy place of worship and play.

Because of their large numbers, the Olivinos have elected to open their home on a regular basis – not just on Sundays, but on other days as well as a place for, in Ed's words, "in-gatherings."

"While we would love to do 'outreach' into our local community, we tried that for awhile but found it put so much stress on our family and was unsustainable. So we tried a different approach, inviting the community in. And it has worked!"

No question – the home itself is magical. Everywhere you go, there is art, scripture, song, and beauty. The children attend school in one of the four classrooms, taught by some of the "graduates" of the Olivino household. The children also learn how to work in the garden and fields, with animals, and make different types of handicrafts for sale.

The kids all have jobs in teams. Disciplined work is part of the training. A crew of 10 to 13-year-old boys was on cooking detail that night, along with a few of the regular cooks. Another crew of 6 to 9-year-old girls were setting up the tables, while the 6 to 9-year-old boys were on clean up. We spotted some of the older children attending to the special-needs kids nearby.

Little ones kept us entertained. Their smiling faces lit up the eating hall.

The meal, though simple, was nutritious and delicious.

Although we were weary from a day of travel, the food gave us a spike in energy. After we finished, one of the older helpers, Julia, approached us and offered to give a tour.

Julia showed us all areas of the grounds: The different sleeping rooms, where at least eight and often more children shared a space, as well as Tatay and Nana's room down the hall. She took us to the room where they made creative items they then sold for a small profit. These included all sorts of sewn and shell-crafted items. After that, she took us to see the classrooms.

Although I had seen many of the places before, I felt as if many of the rooms were in better shape than they had been just three years ago. I asked her about that.

"Yes," she responded, "You are right. We have made a number of improvements. Tatay believes we should always be working to make our home better and better – both the space we live in and the relationships we build. He says it glorifies God."

The classrooms were clean and airy, and they were set up for the different age groups: 3–5, 6–9, 10–13 and 14–18. Julia told us they maintained a pretty rigorous school schedule Monday through Friday. But they also got to go on field trips, and part of their curriculum involved working outside in the gardens and caring for the livestock.

We went to see that livestock next: three milk cows, 24 hens, a few roosters, two horses, and six goats for cheese. Even from the youngest ages, the children were involved in caring for the livestock, as well as milking the cows and goats and collecting the eggs.

They also took turns caring for and harvesting the fruits and vegetables in the garden. These children had a clear understanding of where their food came from.

But probably the biggest surprise to me was the addition of a large swimming pool on the property. I asked Julia about that.

"Some friends of Tatay and Nana back in the U.S. gave them money to build the pool. It is especially for our special needs brothers and sisters. We have 16 of them right now, and the pool can be like a therapy for them. We have some nurses who come work with them in the pool. It helps them feel better and gain movement."

On another day, we'd have time to play in the pool with a bunch of the kids. That, however, followed an intense water balloon fight outside all over the property. The kids seemed to really get into that, and the weather was just right.

Everyone played. The only exception was Susie's (Nana's) 85-year-old mother. Wheelchair-bound, they had brought her over from the States two years earlier. She was a spirited lady whose body just didn't want to keep up with her mind. Still, she was involved with the children and took great delight in them, and they her. "Granny" was a special presence around the otherwise youth-filled home.

And today Granny was smiling. Wide.

She was in the "off-limits" zone. No one was allowed to hit her with the water balloons. But boy, she seemed to really enjoy the fun!

I couldn't help but think, "This is the way old age *should* be. She gets to be around so many young people. It may not be keeping her body young, but her mind and spirit certainly benefit. The kids gained a great deal as they interacted with her too, learned from her, and grew in their patience towards an elderly presence in their midst.

[Postscript: Granny passed away in 2013 at the age of 88.]

Of course, it was not our intention to simply hang out at the Olivino's home. We also wanted to be of service. So we set out to help in any way we could – with clean up, in the kitchen, and even with a small painting job. Most of all, we just played with kids. As we did, we grew more and more in love with those little ones.

But one thing made this particular trip hard. It was Justin's continued struggle. He still was quite inward-focused. This meant, at times, all he wanted to do was remain in the room they had set apart for us, brooding. And, of course, little brother would want to follow suit. Dale and I felt troubled by that. I mean, after all, the Olivinos were opening up their place for us. We wanted to integrate as much as possible. But we had a teenager going through a tough stage, as well as a little brother copycat.

We pushed through it, though. Deep down, Justin realized when he interacted with the children, they weren't the only beneficiaries; it raised his own spirits a lot.

There was an office area in the Olivino's home where internet connection was available. We would occasionally check our email and Facebook there. One morning we opened up our email to find news that jolted us.

It was an email from Marisol, the mother of Jejomar, one of the children we supported and Justin's penpal. Three years earlier, when Justin and I were on that short-term trip, we actually had the opportunity to meet Jejomar and his family for the first time. Now we had a plan to connect with them again.

Marisol told us her husband, Hernando, had suffered a heart attack and passed away suddenly. We were due to see them in just a few days. After the initial shock wore off, the question arose – "What should we do?"

Dale and I prayed and discussed this. I wrote back to Marisol, telling her not to worry, we didn't want to bother them or be a burden in any way. We recognized this was a time for the family to be together and we didn't want to intrude.

What she wrote me back touched me deeply. And it blew my mind.

"Yes, it is difficult. But we have been looking forward to your visit for a long, long time. It would be much sadder for us if you *didn't* come. Please still come."

Then we shared the news with our children. They, too, shared in our shock and sadness. But they were as willing to go as before, perhaps moreso.

As we shared the news with Ed and Susie, they also confirmed we should go.

"You know, they will likely have the father's body in a coffin in the living room," Susie told us. "That is the custom so that people can pay their respects. You will need to decide if your kids are comfortable seeing the dead body. Just be aware of that."

We appreciated Susie's heads up.

She and Ed should know. Over the 25+ years they have been loving children in this tiny corner of the world, they have faced their share of hardship: deaths of children (and friends), illnesses, court battles, threats, financial hardships. But they have soldiered on, trusting in a God they cannot see but experience every day. He is present in that place.

40 | Presence, presents & coconuts: Reverential moments

"It isn't the size of the gift that matters, but the size of the heart that gives it."
– Eileen Elias Freeman, Author
The Little Angels' Instruction Book

When we touched down in Manila, Pastors Juni and Casama, whom Justin and I had met three years earlier, were there to meet us with a big jalopy known as a jeepney. Leftovers from the U.S. post-WWII occupation, these colorfully painted open-aired vehicles capture the lively spirit of the Philippines and are its most ubiquitous form of transportation. Our friends had one for their church.

Introductions and hugs overflowed. These two men sport ear-to-ear smiles and have effervescent personalities to match. The familiarity of these two immediately made Manila feel a very warm, welcoming place. We had an anchor in this otherwise chaotic city.

Casama, at the wheel, careened through the streets with skill. Nevertheless, as most who have spent time in a developing nation will attest, we had to develop a steely attitude to our inner-city transport, placing our full trust in the driver.

After a couple hours rest at our accommodations, a retreat "oasis" in the center of the city, Casama returned to pick us up to hang out with Pastor Juni's family at the church compound where they lived. As we arrived, we met Pastor Juni's graceful wife, Luna, his oldest son, Aaron, his daughter Naomi and their littlest, Blessy, just three.

The kids seemed to instantly connect as Justin and Aaron played chess and basketball, with Luke tagging along, and Naomi and Blessy inviting Erika to play in their room. Suddenly, it was just the adults. As we caught up, Casama and his wife Evi showed up, as did several others.

"You must be hungry," Luna offered. "Please, come, we've almost got the food all ready."

That was the moment those savory aromas became a flavor-filled adventure for us. At the long table spread before us were *lumpia* (spring rolls), *pancit palabok* (a savory noodle dish), *fish kinilaw* (fish dressed in palm coconut, vinegar, ginger, chili and other spices), pork barbeque, seasoned rice and an array of other items.

Magic seemed to set in. Kids enjoyed one another. The adults swapped stories. Culture, language and socioeconomic differences melted away. God's sweet spirit filled the place.

So did the mosquitoes. Next morning Erika and I were covered with bites! Seems those mosquitoes were quite selective, drawing only sweet blood. Dale and the boys had a few, but nothing like the two of us. We had forgotten the repellent!

This was the day we would visit Jejomar and his family, as well as his cousin, Malaya, Erika's pen pal. On the way, we'd stop and meet Danilo and his family, Luke's pen pal. These were our "sponsorship children" through Partners International.

A friendly driver, Luis, accompanied Edna, the head of the Philippine Partners' program. Justin and I had met Edna before. After introductions and a brief catch-up, we were on our way.

Edna, a warm lady in her late fifties, began to explain to us about Danilo. "He's a sweet boy who comes weekly to our programs. His father collects and sells coconuts for a living. His mom is home with several kids. They do not have a permanent home. They live alongside a road."

As we pulled up, we got a glimpse of several tarps draped over some wooden frames on the side of the road. It was a makeshift home, filled to the brim with scruffy, dusty kids with wide eyes, some smiling, some peering at us and our van with unbridled curiosity.

We got out, and Edna took the lead.

She rattled off a bunch of stuff we didn't understand and then introduced us to Jabol, Danilo's father. "He wants to thank you so much for your help with Danilo and their family," Edna interpreted for us. "It has made a difference because Danilo is now in the third grade. He is making it through regular school, thanks to your gifts."

Then she went on. "He says he is sorry he doesn't have any good gift to welcome us." We had not been expecting anything, of course. We asked Edna to tell him that.

We also met Danilo's mother, Isabel, who was sitting on the side nursing a baby. But when we came, she took the baby off her breast, passed him to one of the older girls there, and came over to greet us. There was a gentleness in her eyes, but also a sense of weariness.

I asked Edna if all these children were theirs. By now, quite a swarm surrounded us.

"Oh, no! Most of these belong to others, neighbors and such. But they have six children now. Danilo is the second oldest. Both he and his older sister participate in our programs."

The dad brought Danilo out to meet us. Luke towered over him, even though Danilo was just a year younger.

Clearly, Luke was taking it all in. I could tell he was thinking about how his own home back in the States compared to this. Economic disparities in our world seemed to register in his mind for the very first time.

"Please let Danilo know we have a small present for him," I requested.

Luke pulled the fuzzy panda out of the bag and handed it to Danilo. His eyes lit up. I'm not sure whether it was surprise, gratitude or confusion. Nevertheless, when Edna explained the gift – that we were visiting from China where pandas are a rare and special animal – Danilo erupted in a huge smile.

That panda looked quite funny there. It was a clean toy that fit more in a wealthy child's bedroom than in a shanty alongside a Filipino road. Still, it was something special this little boy now had, and he didn't let go of it the whole time we were there.

Then something we weren't expecting happened. Jabol and Isabel emerged with two large but beat up trays and six hulled coconuts with straws jutting out.

Edna spoke quickly with him and then turned to us. "These are his gifts of welcome to you. Coconut milk prepared in the Filipino way. Please enjoy."

Years later, Justin would write one of his college application essays about this experience.

Justin's voice:

Many things matter to me, from a soothing melody plucked out on a cheap guitar to the sweet succulence of a fresh summer strawberry, to the people I truly care about; all these things I hold dear within my heart. Perhaps mattering more than any of these, however, is a coconut, and the sour milk it produces.

Four years ago, my family and I spent two weeks in the Philippines, and we were able to visit the families of children my siblings and I had been sponsoring with gifts of 25 dollars per month. I had met my friend, Jejomar, a couple years previously, but when we met the boy named Danilo, with whom my little brother had been exchanging letters, and his family, I was shocked by the starkness of their lives. Their house consisted of a few pieces of plywood and scrap metal bound together with whatever was on hand, and they lived alongside a dusty highway, certain of their inevitable relocation at the hands of the government. As we came down from the edge of the road, Danilo's parents tearfully embraced us; though we had never met before in person, their gratefulness shone through our geographic separation. They welcomed us into their dilapidated living space and had us sit as they prepared several coconuts, complete with straws, and passed us the delicacies.

I tasted the milk and inwardly cringed, for it was incredibly sour. But I drank the milk anyways, for I realized that this coconut was worth more than any other gift; it was all they had. Within my heart, I yearned to somehow return the gift, but what could I give that could ever compare? Money? Gratitude? I am still searching for that elusive something, and I will likely spend much of my life ever searching, ever attempting to bring full circle what was given to me.

This is why the coconut matters to me. This is why the taste of sour milk is important. For relative to the giver's resources, that was the greatest gift any human has ever given me.

We bid Danilo and his family goodbye. As we did, we realized there was little hope of keeping in touch with the family. The father and mother were illiterate, and their makeshift housing meant they could be forced to move elsewhere at a moment's notice. Fortunately, Danilo would remain connected to the program a little longer. In the end, they remained pen pals for another few years, and then Danilo graduated out of the program.

With the echo of that intense experience reverberating through all of us, we headed over to the Ravillo's home, a mere 20-minute drive away. But it seemed in some ways like we had entered another world; the family's living conditions, though meager by American standards, were much higher. They lived in a *real* village, in a *real* home on *real* property.

As we approached, I recalled the first time three years ago when the two boys, 11 and 12, sat awkwardly as Edna, Marisol, Hernando and I, along with a few other adults, chatted. Eventually, Jejomar and Justin began playing chess, and this became a worthwhile connecting point, opening up the communication. Now, at 14 and 15, the boys were a bit more equipped to relate.

Since Erika's pen pal Malaya lived on the adjacent property, we'd be able to meet and spend time with both children and, of course, the families. But, no question – overshadowing the event was Hernando's recent death. Everything would be different this time.

Dale's voice: ~~~~~~~~~~~~~~~~

"What do we talk about?" I thought as we sat on the porch of the little concrete block home in the Philippines with a coffin nearby containing the body of the family's 53-year-old father who had died suddenly of a heart attack a few days before.

So here we were, six chairs for our family members and Edna, and a seventh for Marisol. We sat in the little entry porch with the casket inside the door with many extended family members, old and young, gathered around to pay their respects and support the family.

It was a strange thing to meet the eye of a new acquaintance, see the sadness there, but also glimpse a smile behind the pain. After expressing our condolences, we sat together, awkwardly at first. Slowly the stiffness melted away and conversation began to flow.

We talked of our life in China, of the Ravillo children, of father

171

Hernando, of kids' educations and job aspirations. We also spoke of heaven and of the mutual hope we had that Hernando was in a better place.

As time went on, Justin and Jejomar stood a little ways away, conversing on their own, while we took some photos and watched children play. Erika met Malaya, who took her off to show her home and the vegetable garden nearby. Luke was fascinated by the dogs and the chickens, and we all learned about a variety of Filipino plants around the house. Some women served us "ginataang halo-halo," a hot sweet mixture containing yam, ube (a type of root), and cassava.

After a time, the kids each decided to join Caroline and me as we paid our respects to Hernando. We stood before the open casket and looked at his body, then looked at the large photo of him in life that stood above the casket.

Not being used to open-casket wakes, we weren't sure how any of us would feel about this. As I looked at Hernando, I thought about how a dead body is truly just a container. The Hernando I could see in the photo was truly not there.

I also realized it is a valuable part of the grieving process to view the dead body of a loved one when possible. It gives the opportunity to say goodbye, and it confirms the fact that the loved one is no longer there. The spirit has gone elsewhere.

Having experienced the passing of my own father a few years earlier, I felt a connection with Hernando and Marisol's children. When dad died, I had thought I didn't need to see his body (he was cremated), but, now, I wonder if it would have been good for me.

I appreciated the way that, in Filipino culture (as in many developing nations of the world), the community surrounds the grieving family. In America, we tend to give a grieving family space, then go to the funeral or memorial to pay our respects, but having so many people, young and old, surrounding you is a tangible cushion of love. It is powerful.

The sudden passing of Hernando was a shock to all of us. For the Ravillo family who live, like so many in the Philippines, on the edge of poverty, it means increased struggle.

Marisol, however, is blessed to have five beautiful and intelligent children who will help her as she ages. They have a strong, supportive relationship with their mom and with one another.

I wish this family had been spared this grief, but pain draws people closer, and I believe it has created a bond between our families that will not easily break.

[Postscript: We have remained in close contact with Jejomar, Marisol and several of her other children over the years. Social media, especially Facebook, has helped. Very sadly, Marisol lost her eldest son, Christian, to cancer in early 2017. Still, the family remains confident the God they trust will carry them through.]

41 | A visit to the 'Other China'

"We are curious creatures, we Taiwanese. Orphans. Eventually,
orphans must choose their own names and write their own stories.
The beauty of orphanhood is the blank slate."
– Shawna Yang Ryan., Taiwanese-American Author

After an overnight at Lora's in Shanghai, coupled with a quick repacking, we were on our way to Taiwan via Hong Kong. As we arrived, the chilly but moist weather made us feel like we were still in Ningbo – quite a contrast to the past two weeks traveling around the Philippines.

Precisely because we had moved around so much there, we decided we'd spend the week located in one spot in central Taipei. This proved a smart move. We had secured two rooms online in an inexpensive but nicely equipped hostel.

All of us were pretty tired. We laid low, and Dale and I began to communicate with two of our Taiwanese friends who were "hosting" us during our stay. We couldn't wait to see them!

Next morning, Grace met us at the hostel, just after we had finished a breakfast of steamed buns and dried cereal we had packed from Lora's place. Maybe not too nutritious, but it would suffice.

Grace was a returnee from some of our earliest days working with international students in the U.S. A strong Christian believer, she has dedicated her life to working with kids, teaching them English. She was single, living with her parents in Taipei. But she was involved in a burgeoning relationship, trying to discern whether or not this boyfriend was "the one."

This would become the predominant topic of conversation as we set out to walk along a nearby river front. My first question to her was, "Are you compatible on the essentials?" These include fundamental values and beliefs, how each handles conflict, how their dreams fit together, how they each feel about children, and where they hope to live.

Then I asked two other, perhaps more abstract, questions: "Do you make each other better people?" and "Do you make others around you better?"

Grace seemed to appreciate using me as a sounding board as she thought over and answered these questions.

Grace really appreciated these insights. I still share them today.

[Postscript: At least some of Grace's answers to these questions must have been "no" or "unfavorable" because she is still single as of this writing. I hope I didn't derail her!]

The following day we met up with Selina, another Taiwanese returnee. Selina took the day off from work to spend it with us. She first took us on a few trains and a bus, leading us to a lush green park on the outskirts of Taipei, *Máokong* Mountain (茅洞山 – *Máo Dòngshān*).

Tropical and fragrant, we hiked along trails winding through forest groves and then opening up to gorgeous vistas of the city and beyond. Our kids seemed to enjoy getting out of the city and into the fresh air. The three of them kept one another entertained as we spent time catching up with Selina.

Indeed, this friend had been on an unusual journey. She had come to our home city in the U.S. to pursue a Master's degree in Translation & Interpretation for Chinese/English. But at the end of her two-year program, she bumped into a harsh reality.

It was a diagnosis that she had cancer of the tongue. Selina's tongue really mattered for her future career. "Why, God, why?" she wondered.

Selina had come to the U.S. from Taiwan as a recent convert to Christianity. But she was young in her faith.

Coming from a nominal Buddhist background, the Christian faith seemed to make sense, she reasoned, and the Christian friends she met all seemed to be prospering in their different spheres. "Maybe God gives you more blessings if you choose to be a Christian," she thought. Selina recalls those first months as a Christian as a real high time for her. Everything seemed to be falling into place. "This must be the key to luck," she thought.

But now – cancer of the tongue! What?!? Neither a smoker nor drinker, it just didn't make sense. What was she to do now? She had even received a good job offer so she could stay in the States for the coming year under an OPT (Optional Practical Training) agreement!

Those days were dark and lonely for Selina. She confided in me then that she couldn't see where God was in all this. She couldn't decide whether to remain in the U.S. for treatment or go back home, where she understood the system better. Eventually she concluded she should go back home. She said "no" to the job in the U.S. to be with her family.

At that moment, we said "goodbye," but not forever. Over the years, Selina became an excellent correspondent, both by regular mail and email.

About one year after the cancer discovery, she wrote us: "I'm in a great small group right now and have made many friends. My faith in Jesus has never been so firm and sure. I can feel the Holy Spirit dwelling in me every day! I believe there is something even better and more wonderful in the future. I'm glad that God has brought me back to my country and made me see what I can do for Him in this precious land. We have a group of dynamic, energetic, passionate people here at our church. We're eager to help more young people encounter God!"

A biopsy revealed that the cancer had remained localized. Selina ended up having that much-needed operation and lost a good portion of her tongue. She went through radiation and chemo as a backup. Over time, she was pronounced "cancer free!"

After extensive rehabilitation therapy to regain use of her tongue, she learned how to use this vital instrument in new ways. Eventually she could communicate well with others.

Through this ordeal, her parents and younger sister stood by her, supported her, loved her, and, in the process, became interested in her Christian faith.

Although a career in interpretation (oral) was no longer part of her future, Selina came to realize that *teaching* was her passion.

In time, a prominent university hired Selina to teach translation and interpretation. As she formed relationships with her students, she shared about her journey. She began to mentor them, not only academically and professionally, but spiritually and wholistically too.

Selina could see God's hand even through the struggles of her life, and the way He creatively used the hardships to grow her and impact others.

After the hike, we were hungry! Selina had arranged a place for lunch close to her university. Mark, Harry and Olivia – all Taiwanese we had known from years ago but who now were working in the military and marketplace – were there to greet us.

We ate, sipped and savored a smorgasbord of textures and flavors. I made a comment about my surprise at the wide variety of food set before us.

"You know, we think – of course – that Taipei has the greatest food culture in the world," Mark spoke up. "But I know we're biased. Still, people don't always recognize that. I think we get overlooked. But, that's okay. Then we get to enjoy it ourselves!"

Mark had come to the U.S. as a military student. He actually was in our city twice, once in the mid-1990's and again in the mid-2000's. In between, he and his wife raised their two children and he rose up the military ranks. He is ten years our senior and now retired. Crowned in white, he exuded the wisdom of his many years. And, in typical top military form, he pursued a post-retirement career. He was now the president of the Taiwanese Division of Toastmasters International, and continues to thrive in that position.

Next to him sat Harry, a lower-ranking officer when first in the U.S., now following in Mark's footsteps. Across the table sat Olivia. She told us she now runs her own business in marketing, creative writing, translation and interpretation. She passed us her card. All three, along with Selina, shared with us the challenges and discoveries they encountered as they returned to Taipei and reintegrated into their cultures.

After the meal, Selina suggested we head to Taipei 101, Taiwan's tallest building at 101 stories (+ five basement levels). Taipei 101 was the world's tallest structure from March 2004 – March 2010, when it was eclipsed by the Burj Khalifa in the United Arab Emirates (still the tallest as of this writing in 2017). Taipei 101 also retains the position as the world's highest "LEED-certified green" building.

It is a creative, memorable structure. The views from the top took my breath away. It was an unusually clear day; we could see well into the horizon, even the ocean in the distance. Taipei 101 houses the world's largest sundial and New Year's Eve countdown clock. In fact, the 101 floors, the number itself a palindrome, are meant to symbolize the cyclical nature of time.

[Postscript: We did not realize that day when saying goodbye to Selina it would be our last time to see her on this earth. Five years later she encountered cancer once again, this time a more aggressive type, and it took her life within a few months. We followed along with and contributed to the tribute Facebook page. She had impact!]

~~~~~~~~~~

During this one-week period, we connected with close to a dozen friends, many with powerful stories to share of their post-study-abroad life – challenges, trials, and victories. We visited the colorful night market – a whirlwind of sights, smells and sounds both tantalizing and repelling. We toured the old city another evening, encountering a vendor on the street holding a python while trying to entice people into his restaurant! And yet another evening we held a party at a restaurant to bring together several other friends.

Talking with these friends, I found it intriguing how every Taiwanese I had met in the U.S. distinguished themselves as coming from Taiwan, not China. Yes, they were Chinese, but their land stood separate and distinct from Mainland China. In contrast, all my students in China believed Taiwan was a renegade province of China and would eventually be reattached to the Mainland.

When I returned from this semester break and shared with my students about our experiences, I showed them Taiwanese money. One student was shocked people use different money in Taiwan. He insisted, "They *are* part of China, so they should use the money we use – with *Máo* on the face." It never occurred to him it was precisely that very man and his ascension to power that symbolized all that Taiwan had come to stand against.

42 | Layer upon layer: Return to Japan

*"Japan never considers time together as time wasted.
Rather, it is time invested."*
— Donald Richie, Author & Historian
A Lateral View: Essays on Culture and Style in Contemporary Japan

From Hong Kong to Shanghai, another quick and blurry overnight at Lora's, and then on we went to Japan. I simply couldn't wait to arrive; it had been 17 years since Dale and I had spent time living in the country.

We were riding the *Tōkaidō Shinkansen* (東海道新幹線), the renowned "bullet train," the oldest and most heavily trafficked express route of travel in the world. The trains, running from Tokyo to Osaka, reach speeds of 240–320 km/h (150–200 mph). Rides on the *Shinkansen* are clean, smooth, speedy, efficient, and incredibly scenic.

I spotted Mount Fuji on our way to Nagoya; it was a lucky day! Clear and captivating, I pointed out the iconic mountain to our kids. How I wanted to exit right then to explore!

Japan in February possesses a stark beauty. The green fields of spring and summer were now either grey or covered with patches of snow. Winter grips Japan like it grips the U.S. Northeast. The distinct four seasons form the basis for much of Japan's artistic and literary expression. In earlier times, I had passed through this same corridor during the spring, summer and fall. The contrasts were breathtaking!

The significance of this moment caught me. I had travelled the same route as a single college student. And then, again, as a young married woman. And now, with my three kids. Layer upon layer. And yet a sense of time collapsing, too.

My connection with Japan runs deep; my life has Japan running through it. When I was in high school, a string of college-aged students, many from Japan, staying with our family short term over the ensuing years. Nami was the first.

The 1st layer

We visited Nami in Nagoya (名古屋) midway through our two weeks in the country. I had seen her just once since those late-seventies homestay years. At that time, Dale and I wrestled with her twin preschoolers, a boy and girl. Now those kids were college-aged, soon to graduate.

The view from the top-floor restaurant over Nagoya, especially on this sparkling day, took my breath away. Yet spending that time with Nami, a journalist by training, exceeded that. Now into her early 50's, Nami was considering the last third of her life. What would it become for her? For her husband? What about her aging parents and emerging children? Years later, now finding myself in the same place, I understand better the swirling concerns.

After our visit to Nagoya, we hopped the *Shinkansen* to *Kyōto* (京都) as the day was drawing to a close. Although now Japan's ninth largest city (at 1.5 million), it once was the center of all culture, commerce and communications throughout Japan.

And to think, that could have been snuffed out in an instant.

It was Henry L. Stimson, Secretary of War first under President Taft (1911–13), then again under Presidents Roosevelt and Truman (1940–45), who spared Kyoto from the atomic bomb, selecting Nagasaki instead. It was originally one of the planned target sights.

But according to Otis Cary, Professor at Doshisha University in Kyoto, Stimson had visited Kyoto at least twice. He believes that the splendor of Kyoto first touched Stimson in 1926 during his first experience there, a five-day honeymoon stay. Cary was able to confirm the Stimson stay by checking registrations at the Miyako Hotel, where "nearly all foreigners stayed before the war."

Cary went on to write, "The glories of Kyoto in the fall, her gardens, temples and surrounding hills, evidently impressed Stimson, and the decisions he made two decades later prove that the memory of this visit remained vivid."

In fact, Kyoto was largely spared even the conventional bombing most of Japan's other large cities suffered. This means Kyoto is one of the few places in all of Japan where ancient architecture remains. In abundance.

Indeed, visiting Kyoto is like taking a step back in time. Of course, there is modern Kyoto – highrises, subways, traffic – but, coming out of Kyoto Station, it doesn't take long before one stumbles upon parks, temples and the Kyoto Imperial Palace. Whether it's the striking gold temple (*Kinkaku-ji* 金閣寺), the famous rock garden of *Ryōanji* (龍安寺), or the sprawling temple area of *Kiyomizu-dera* (清水寺) – or any number of other traditional sites – Kyoto captivates.

We walked through the *Higashiyama* (東山) district, where our little *ryokan* (旅館 – traditional inn) was nestled, up to Yasaka Shrine (八坂神社), meandering along the quaint streets of *Ninen-zaka* (二年坂 – "Two-Year Slope"), *Sannen-zaka* (三年坂 – "Three-Year Slope") and *Kiyomizu-zaka* (清水坂 – "Pure Water Slope"), before finally reaching the *Kiyomizu-dera* temple. The sharp air outside kept us moving. We heard a few groans from kids on occasion, but they were generally good sports. We promised them food at the top; that seemed to provide a good dose of motivation.

Along the way, we caught glimpses of fancifully clad Japanese women, donning the traditional kimono, obi (sash), swept up wig and painted white skin of the *maiko* (舞子), or apprentice *geisha* (芸者). These women are artists in training (the Chinese characters for *geisha* means "art person,"), performing songs and dances, and playing traditional Japanese instruments for guests at parties and events.

With their numbers dwindling into the couple thousands, modern maiko and geisha can rarely be seen on the streets. Rather, it is more common to see *maiko henshin* (舞妓変身), usually foreigners who pay to dress up as *maiko* and roam the Kyoto streets. My guess is that is probably what we were seeing.

We made it to the top, just before the temple entrance. Hungry and all a bit whiny by now, we ducked into a fragrant noodle shop and filled up on the warm broth. Happy again. The mood improved.

We milled around the temple grounds for a long time. Most tourist guides will tell you never to visit in the winter. Indeed, the views are much starker and less colorful. But, on the flip side, you have quieter streets, fewer lines and the gamut of choices for food and souvenirs.

During the low tourist season especially, the vendors are often quite open to the simple question, "Do you have any discounts?" (割引がありますか。– *Waribiki ga arimasu ka?*) This is the simple, inoffensive way to bargain (which generally doesn't happen in most places in Japan). If they say "no" (いいえ – *iie*), then you just drop it. But if they say "yes" (はい – *hai*), then get out a pen and paper and start writing numbers. Or let them suggest. The results may be surprising.

One delicacy I didn't want to miss sharing with our kids – not to mention enjoy myself – was the *Yatsuhashi* (八ツ橋). The name literally means "8 Bridges." *Yatsuhashi*, a triangle-shaped confection with a mochi-like consistency on the outside, filled with red bean paste on the inside, is a speciality of *Kiyomizu-dera*. Lightly dusted with cinnamon, they are a memorable treat; they proved a huge hit with everyone.

43 | Old – & not-so-perfect – Japan

*"The great thing about growing older is
you don't lose all the other ages you've been."*
– Madeleine L'Engle, Author

～～～～～ The 2nd layer ～～～～～

After three years of Japanese language study in college, I took the opportunity to head to Japan to try out what I had learned. That learning curve had been steep. The first year, with our Japanese textbook almost exclusively in *Rōmaji* (ローマ字 – Romanized writing of Japanese), I had no clue of the almost-180-degree difference between English and Japanese, not just in terms of grammar, but also in terms of mindset. In many ways, I approached it as I had high school Spanish.

But in the second year, when the textbook morphed into all Japanese, everything changed for me, almost from Day 1. Suddenly, my mind shifted and...it clicked! We had learned both syllabaries – Hiragana (ひらがな) and Katakana (カタカナ), as well as about 350 *Kanji*, or Chinese characters (漢字) – during that first year, but it wasn't until we were using them daily, interacting as they do, that it all made sense to me.

So off I headed for my first overseas living experience, in the southern prefecture of Yamaguchi (山口) Japan through an organization called Volunteers In Asia (VIA), run out of Stanford University. During those six months I stayed in two cities, Yamaguchi proper (the prefectural capital), and Ube (宇部市).

Chako stood waiting for us at Yamaguchi's relatively small train station. Now nearly 70, she still had a gleam of vivacity in her eyes. Digging back over 25 years, our friendship began through a series of contacts over many years.

For a very long time, Chako had been the proprietor of a family inn, *Fukuda Ryokan* (福田旅館), in the heart of Yamaguchi. She had also developed a friendship with the founder and executive director of VIA, Dwight Clark, a gentle Quaker man who is legend in my books.

Because of Dwight, numerous Stanford students or VIA "volunteers," had stayed in the Yamaguchi / Ube VIA post. We served as English teachers, editors, and in so many respects, "ambassadors" to Yamaguchi University (山口大学 – *Yamaguchi Daigaku* or *'Yama-Dai'*), both to students on the main campus in Yamaguchi, as well as to doctors at Yamaguchi Medical School (山口大学医学部 – *Yamaguchi Daigaku Igakubu*), in nearby Ube City.

My predecessor had introduced me to Chako.

And now she stood before us.

While the years had weathered her a bit, I felt so connected with this amazing woman.

We had last seen her 22 years ago, so it was quite a reunion.

But things had changed.

"My English isn't so good anymore," she spoke to us in English. I smiled. "I hope your Japanese is still strong."

We switched over. While I wouldn't say our Japanese was as strong as it once had been, both Dale and I could still understand and communicate well.

She greeted our children with much enthusiasm. In English, of course!

"Your mom sends me your Christmas card every year, so I feel like I know you. Hello, Justin, Erika and Luke!" Chako remained ebullient.

She turned to me and went off in Japanese. "You have done such a good job! Look at these beautiful children! And Erika! She is like you. I feel she will become as beautiful as her mama."

"How is everything, Chako? I mean, for you?"

We began to walk, pulling our bags behind us. At this moment, I was thankful we had limited our luggage to small suitcases with wheels. We weren't far from her place – she assured me – but we still had several blocks to walk. And many of the streets were cobblestoned. Old Japan. I love Yamaguchi!

"Well, you know, in these years my mother died. And then my sister-in-law from lung cancer. It was terrible. And then it was just my brother, Akane and me. But he passed away two years ago. I am Akane's chief caregiver now."

Akane must have been close to 30, at least. She is autistic.

I remember those years when Akane was smaller. She was different. But I couldn't understand why or what was wrong. Back then, knowledge was more limited and many disorders didn't have a name. But I do remember little Akane. Everyone had to keep an extra eye on her.

Now I understood. I briefly explained to my kids about Akane as we arrived at Chako's house. Chako called out for her. Akane appeared before us, but she didn't seem to register we were even there. For my children, this may have been rather startling, but they handled everything well, quietly observing.

"I think I told you in one of my letters, but we sold *Fukuda Ryokan* many years ago. It became too much for us to handle and we were losing money, especially in Japan's economic downturn."

She went on. "You will not stay with me because I don't have the space. I have made arrangements for you to stay with my friends who own a nice *ryokan* nearby. We'll head out for dinner all together. On the way, we'll go by the *ryokan* and drop your stuff off."

I took a sneak peek into the adjacent room. There stood Chako's *butsudan* (仏壇) or Buddhist altar, laden with offerings – fruits, candies and other items. Prominent pictures of her mother, sister-in-law and brother leaned on the shelf. A smell of incense hung in the air.

It was in this room that, according to tradition, the spirits of her ancestors resided. Most Japanese believe they need to keep those spirits happy through their regular offerings. Doing so will cause the ancestors to bring about favorable circumstances to those still "trapped" in the earthly realm.

Although she had been responsible for the day-to-day operations of *Fukuda Ryokan* in earlier days, her brother and sister-in-law had helped out so much, freeing her up for chunks of time for travel. She had traveled throughout Japan as well as in much of East and Southeast Asia. She had also explored Europe, Russia, Latin America, and the U.S. east coast.

My favorite story of hers involved her travels in Latin America.

"You know, those people think I look like them. Perhaps I do! One time I was sitting on a bench alongside a road in Mexico wearing a poncho and a hat. People would come up speaking to me in Español all the time. I could speak *así-así* (so-so), but I thought it was funny how I fooled them so!"

Chako was also a great lover of music. I remember her frequently playing the violin alongside taped recordings of great artists.

She had also hosted Dale's parents one time when they came and visited us during our newlywed stay in Hokkaido. After that time, they journeyed throughout Japan via train, and Chako's place, *Fukuda Ryokan*, was one of their lodgings. I remember that my in-laws and Chako really hit it off (my father-in-law especially was a classical music and opera lover). They managed to remain in contact by mail for several years afterwards.

Our experience in the *ryokan* that evening and the next was full of rest, fun and discovery. The unique feel and grassy smell of *tatami* (畳), woven floor mats, the comfort of *yukata* (浴衣), traditional bathrobe wraps usually found in *ryokan* or other lodgings in Japan, and the *ofuro* (お風呂), the uniquely designed Japanese bath tub, the whole bathing experience, catapulted us back to a time when Japanese life was once free of "foreign" influence.

This very traditional *ryokan* gave our kids an even better feel of Japanese traditional life.

Justin found many ways to entertain his younger brother with various *yukata* poses, and Luke was quick to join in. Younger sister Erika rolled her eyes at first but eventually broke down in laughter.

Although the kids had already experienced the Japanese-style bath, this one was much more spacious and hot! We emphasized to them – especially to the boys – that they clean themselves *outside* of the bath, in the tiled area with spigots, bowls and stools, and *then* enter the tub, completely clean. This is the Japanese way. Of course, they had done it this way all along during our time in Japan, or so we thought.

"Ah, gotcha!" Justin winked.

Not quite sure what that all meant. But, given the humor of that first evening, it could have meant anything!

Leaving Yamaguchi a couple days later proved wistful, especially for me. Given Chako's age, I wasn't sure if, and when, we'd ever meet again. And I knew how hard her life at this stage had become. We hugged each other for an unusually long time.

As we rode the train to Ube, my brain strained to remember the sights, sounds and sensations from almost 25 years ago. Every once and awhile a city name, train crossing or building would jump out at me, almost as if it were shouting, "Don't you remember me? You passed by me dozens of times! Why am I not in that memory of yours?"

Traveling through rural Japan, I began to grasp the scope of the changes since my earlier visits. First, the Japanese were now much more accustomed to seeing foreigners in their land. Back in the 1980's, it was hard to go anywhere but in the major cities without feeling conspicuously foreign. Painfully so at times! Though not a shy person, I remember how difficult I would find being out there on my own, the object of stares, points and comments almost everywhere I went.

But now, even as a family of five *gaijin* (外人 – foreigners), we seemed to turn only a few heads. It made me wonder if the fascination had worn off, the Japanese had somehow been "instructed" to not behave this way, or the reality that white Americans really aren't so special after all had set in. Whatever the case, I felt somewhat relieved – and encouraged – by the change.

Another change I noted was the lack of the economic vibrancy that had been so tangible 25 years earlier. In these areas, Japan seemed to feel tired, as if its vitality had been drained. Although I had gotten occasional hints of that in Tokyo and Kyoto, here it was much more pronounced. Japan's ageing society (高齢化社会 – *kōreika shakai*) was apparent in its infrastructure, activity and overall atmosphere. This made me a little sad.

We felt that *kōreika shakai* as we went into Ube City (宇部市) to meet up with Dr. Nagano, an opthamologist (眼科医者 – *ganka issha*) and VIA's direct contact in the area for many years. It was through him that Dwight Clark had established the teaching post I had served in.

"Welcome, you are here! And look at the family! Such beautiful children!" Although over two decades had passed, Dr. Nagano retained a spring in his step and a spritely manner. He was well into his seventies now.

"It is so good to see you after so long! What is it? At least 20 years, right?" I could tell Dr. Nagano was committed to using as much English with us as he could. "Thank you for your cards over the years," Dr. Nagano added. "I have been able to see your family grow."

When we met up with Dr. Nagano's wife, Kimiko, I could tell how old age had impacted them. She had suffered a stroke two years earlier and was still in therapy, regaining her ability to speak. One side of her face drooped, but she remained warm and gracious.

"Old age has come upon us, I'm afraid," Dr. Nagano announced. "I will retire my practice soon, and my son will take over completely. But I still walk an hour every morning to keep active. Sometimes Kimiko will join me, when she is feeling well enough. This is the way we are trying to beat back old age."

Being back in my old "stomping grounds" felt bizarre. When Dr. Nagano took us to my former apartment, Green Heights – or Guri-nu Heitsu (グリーヌハイツ) – I was struck by how very different it was from my memory of it.

But one tell-tale sign remained. It was a small metal box on the wall – or, perhaps, the shell of it – once containing the single pay phone available to all the occupants of the 10 apartments in the building. That device held meaningful memories for me and Dale.

Pre-cell phones. Back then, many in the building didn't even have their own landline in their apartments. Instead, most relied on the common payphone to keep in touch with family, friends and others. For me, I viewed it as a once-a-week lifeline to the man an ocean away I would eventually marry.

The exchange rate was so unfavorable then, it made a call to or from Japan cost a small fortune. Once each week for about 10 minutes was about all we could afford.

Pre-internet. We wrote *real letters* to each other almost every day for those six months. But the mail took close to a week to cross the ocean back then. So we were always a week behind in knowing what was going on with the other person, how they were feeling.

I tried to impress all that on our kids, but I think they could barely imagine it all, given the world of instantaneous global communications we take for granted now.

I had made a very close friend during my six months living in that drab apartment building. Hitomi was a medical student at Yamaguchi University Medical School (山口大学医学部 – *Yamaguchi Daigaku Igakubu*), and we became regular running buddies. We would often enjoy meals at one another's apartments, and even study together.

We got a chance to meet up with Hitomi and her husband, Jiro, in the city of Okayama (岡山), on our way back up and out of Japan. Still fit, she had become a marathon runner along with her doctor husband – a real power couple, although she confided in me that it helped relieve all their stress.

"We have two sons, I think you know. I am sorry they could not be here. My oldest, Daichi, is also working as a doctor, and he just could not take the time away. I am so sorry. And Atsuya, my youngest, well…." She trailed off. I could sense this was a bit of troubled territory.

"He wants to become an English teacher someday. Or, at least he thinks that right now. He is also interested in film. He might be considered a 'late bloomer,' I'm afraid." Hitomi looked downward, pushing up her glasses, a behavior of hers I remember well.

It is not easy for the child of two doctors to consider going in any different direction. Especially in a country like Japan.

Hitomi had suspected all along Atsuya might have a learning disability. "He's, well, 'different,'" she told me.

I'm not sure what that "different-ness" was, other than being painfully shy. But I learned later that, while he had tried university in Osaka, it just didn't work for him. He dropped out and returned home and lived with his parents for almost two years doing nothing.

"Except playing video games," Hitomi told us with a sense of dismay. "We could not do anything. Of course, we could not kick him out on the streets. He is our son. But he had no motivation for anything."

The journey Atsuya went on, especially those two years as an adult at home, is a phenomenon known in Japan as *hikikomori* (引きこもり) – namely, reclusive adults who withdraw from society. The Japanese government estimates there are approximately 700,000 *hikikomori* and an additional 1.55 million people on the verge of becoming one in Japan.

So when Atsuya eventually discovered English and got really excited, Hitomi and Jiro "wanted to encourage him as much as [they] could."

Some years later, Atsuya home stayed for two weeks with us in the U.S. He came to the U.S. to pursue his dream of really learning English. At 24, it was his first time out of Japan and in the U.S.

I could feel Hitomi's mother's heart when she contacted me by email to try to arrange something with us. And we did it! We set up a good plan with a local adult school, a bus pass and tried to get him as independent as possible in the time he was with us. Although he stayed with us most of the time, we even had arranged a hostel stay for a few days, to help him be independent even from us. And it worked!

Later that year, Atsuya joined a summer English program at UCLA. Now he is an English teacher in the Kobe-Osaka area and, according to Hitomi, enjoying what he's doing.

He might be a late bloomer, but it seems as if Atsuya finally bloomed!

44 | The layers interweave

"If we take care of the moments, the years will
take care of themselves."
– Maria Edgeworth, Anglo-English writer

～～～～ The 3rd layer ～～～～

Shortly after we married, Dale and I traveled two different *Shinkansen* lines, the *Tōhoku Shinkansen* (東北新幹線), heading north out of Tokyo, connecting with the *Hokkaidō Shinkansen* (北海道新幹線), and then a much smaller trunk line, to get to our new home in *Obihiro* (帯広), northern Japan. We would be English teachers for two years there.

Unfortunately, this time we wouldn't make it all the way up to Hokkaido. The 10 days we had in Japan made taking that trip with all five of us too difficult.

～～～～ The 4th layer ～～～～

While in Tokyo, we met up with our friend Saori who, in many respects, characterizes our *fourth layer*, the three years we lived in Dale's hometown of Anchorage, Alaska following our two-year stint in Asia.

We had gotten to know Saori during her time working as an attaché at the Japanese Consulate in Anchorage. We had hung out with Saori a lot, sharing good times and bad. We were all pretty young then, discovering life, struggling to define who we were. I think our friendship proved an important influence in Saori's life at the time. She saw a healthy relationship she admired. We gained a great deal of insight into Japanese culture through Saori and several other friends at the Japanese Consulate.

Saori had invited us to a restaurant owned by one of her friends. They had closed the restaurant that evening so we could have a party together. That itself proved amazing to me. Her friend, Kaz, was a sushi master. Sporting a mustache and neatly trimmed beard, Kaz bellowed out a hearty, *"Irrashyaimase"* (いっらしゃいませ! – Welcome!) when we entered, his eyes dancing.

The cozy, warm, inviting atmosphere of the tiny restaurant evoked a strong sense of *wabi-sabi* (侘び寂び), a "Japanese-ness" to it all. Essentially, this is a word to describe Japanese aesthetics, and a worldview acknowledging transience and imperfection. The concept derives from Buddhism, expressing the "three marks of existence": impermanence, suffering and emptiness.

Now, if this sounds depressing, take heart. The way this is often lived out is through austerity, asymmetry, simplicity, economy and modesty. You can see this in the designs of traditional buildings, life tools (pottery, for example), and societal structure. There are, indeed, many benefits of *wabi-sabi* people anywhere can apply to their lives.

When our eyes met Saori's, it felt as if the dozen years since our last meeting collapsed in a single minute. We were all older, more wrinkled perhaps, but Saori looked fit and trim. In fact, we learned later, windsurfing had become her passion.

Out popped dishes of salted edamame, miso soup and crunchy pickles. And then, within seconds, came two elegant plates of sushi. Luke, allergic to fish, enjoyed some rice and teriyaki chicken Kaz had prepared especially for him.

"Please make sure to know," he spoke rapidly in Japanese, "this is the appetizer. We'll have *oden* (御田 – Japanese-style hot pot) in a little bit."

We covered a lot of ground as we talked away during those few hours. Family, work, interests, hopes and dreams. Our connection over that time did more to strengthen our friendship than all those years of sending Christmas cards and *nengajyo* (年賀状), traditional New Year's greetings, to one another.

Meanwhile, the hot *oden* braced us for the frigid weather we'd encounter later as we stepped outside after gushing goodbyes.

The 5th layer

Our *fifth layer* of Japan coincides with our lives over a twenty-year period spanning from my entrance to a California graduate school and into our years of parenting. Most of our contacts were a result of our involvement with international students.

It was within that context we met Sonja, a vibrant, young American woman who came to our city to begin a graduate degree in TFL (Teaching A Foreign Language). Her language? French.

Her decision to pursue this degree was an intriguing choice since Sonja was an aviator – a commercial pilot – with five years of experience under her belt. The daughter of a commercial pilot, she has pictures of herself in a cockpit when she was two or three years old. It was simply part of her upbringing. And it stuck.

Now she was a French-language-teaching commercial pilot! (And, ironically, she is now married to our six-and-a-half-foot angel, YZ! But that's another story, indeed! At this point, however, she wasn't even aware he existed.)

Because of her flying experience and privileges, it proved easier and less expensive for her to hop on a plane to meet us in Japan. So, she did and accompanied us for about two-thirds of the time there, while we met up with a number of returnee friends in and around Tokyo, and then soaked up the ambiance of Kyoto.

One of those friends we met up with was Ryōhei. We had arranged to rendezvous in *Harajuku* (原宿), the very heart of Japanese teenage rebellion. *Harajuku's* ascendency to that defiant reputation was in the 1980's. At that time, it stood out against the more rigid lines of Japanese culture. I remember that time. But now it felt as if the rebellion was well-worn, even forced. Somehow, the 1980's spike-haired dancing kids filling the streets of Harajuku no longer seemed as disruptive and disarming.

It didn't take but a minute after we exited the subway station to recognize Ryōhei waiting for us. While his face was more creased and his hair thinner than 15 years ago, his eyes sparkled with genuine warmth.

His perky wife, Nozomi, and their two rambunctious little boys scrambled around them. Nozomi immediately introduced herself in flawless English.

"It's almost noon. You must be getting hungry, right?" she asked. "We have a sushi place we like nearby. Is everyone okay with that?"

Well, again, we had the fish problem with Luke. So we brought that up.

"Oh, don't worry," Ryōhei chimed in. "They will have tofu, noodles, rice, *tonkatsu* and things like that as well. He can choose something besides fish."

They led us to a restaurant a couple blocks down the bustling street. Lots of colors, movement, and shiny objects to distract. The sushi bar we entered was what's known as conveyor belt bushi, *kaiten-zushi* (回転寿司), or the more colloquial, onomatopoeiac version, *kuru-kuru-zushi* (くるくる寿司) – small plates of sushi and other items on a conveyor belt (or sometimes a water moat) moving around a sushi bar.

I love the presentation at these type of establishments – always fresh and fanciful. Our kids also loved it.

The items passing by sit on different color plates, each indicating a value, usually ranging from ¥100–500. The number and color of the plates determine the final bill. And choices are not limited to sushi and sashimi (raw fish without rice) alone; you can also get many cooked items as well.

As we caught up with Ryōhei in a combination of English and Japanese (or, as it's called in Japanese, *champon* – チャンポン), we learned more about his career as well as how, as a Christian, he had been getting along as part of the one-percent minority in Japan..

"It's difficult here," he began. "Working life, especially for Japanese men, is all about going out to the bars after work and socializing. It is part of our culture, you know," he nodded towards us.

"But we found a good church. And I'm very involved in BSF (Bible Study Fellowship). It is the BSF group and study that has kept me strong all these years, I believe. I meet with other businessmen, like myself. We all struggle with many of the same things. It helps."

It became clear he had a desire to maintain and grow in his faith, as well as to be a dependable husband for his wife and father for his kids.

Meanwhile, all the kids just kept eating. Plates were piling high. I was starting to worry some about the total cost. This is the issue with *kuru-kuru zushi;* you do not really have a sense of how much you're eating. It just sorta happens. And then, suddenly, you feel full. And those plates pile up.

We had a good time, all the kids seemed to be in a jovial mood, and some earlier struggle with illness seemed to have passed. Later we walked around Harajuku before saying our goodbyes.

Rain began to pour down; up went our umbrellas. We sought shelter inside shops and restaurants. As we moved around, especially through subway and train stations, I felt a lightness and ease I had not experienced for many months. I commented to Dale.

"It feels so easy here, compared to being in China. I understand what's going on. Like returning home, in a way."

He agreed. Even though my Japanese was stronger than his, our couple of years living in Japan early in our marriage had given him a good linguistic foundation, too.

It felt good to be proficient. Although I didn't get everything about Japan, my language skills were strong enough to make traveling around Tokyo – and the country – rather smooth. That day, after a little bout with a flu bug a day or two before, I also began to feel a strong sense of place and purpose, a connection to my past and present, an ability to move with ease through a culture not my own, but one steeped in familiarity. It was a thrill to share that with my family and Sonja as well. Simply, it felt good.

As we looked towards our return to China, Erika penned these thoughtful lines.

Erika's voice: 〜〜〜〜〜〜〜〜〜〜〜〜

It felt like going back in time, a piece of unknown history revealed. As my family and I traveled around Japan by bus, car, and train, I felt like I was seeing a new part of my parents' lives – and perhaps I was. I was seeing a few years of their post-college life in Japan, before my older brother was even conceived.

Although I'm used to my parents having close relationships with seemingly obscure people who I haven't seen before, I hadn't heard this part, this Japanese part, of my parents' life songs. Or maybe I had without understanding, without comprehending, without imagining it.

I could see why my parents are a part of Japan, why Japan is a part of them. Maybe it's in my blood, because I could feel that appeal of the society, the appeal of that gleaming, futuristic, and yet natural country. From the digitized, lit-up Tokyo skyline at night, to the beautiful temples and Zen gardens of Kyoto, something about this country causes an epiphany, a "yes!" I loved it.

Japan is not as big and loud as China, nor as tropical, green, and warm as the Philippines. It's unlike the smoothed-out Chinese-ness of Taiwan, and is different from the diversity and American-ness of the USA. It could be described in a few words, or in a whole book. The gracious, round-sounding language, the beautiful, almost hypnotic tea ceremonies, the silky kimonos, the gleaming skyscrapers, the city lights, the traditional baths. An intricate web of relations, traditions, advancements, and beautiful places, both modern, old, and natural. That is Japan's song.

~~~~~~

This journey back to Japan felt like both a homecoming and, in some ways, a victory trip. I was excited to share Japan with our kids and to share my kids with a number of people who represented a life lived long ago.

Keeping up those friendships was important to me. It's often said that Americans become friends fast but do not keep their friendships for long. I was determined to not be that person. And, in meeting up with so many of these people from years gone by, it not only encouraged them, but it encouraged me as well.

Springing Forward

45 | Back where we "understand what's going on!"

"What makes his world so hard to see clearly is not its strangeness but its usualness. Familiarity can blind you too."
— Robert M. Pirsig, Author
Zen and the Art of Motorcycle Maintenance: An Inquiry Into Values

When we landed in Shanghai, we headed back to Lora's place. This time she was there, and we could enjoy a pleasant evening with her over dinner out.

I asked Lora about how she managed to stay in Shanghai for so long.

"I'll be honest," she responded. "I never was aiming for this. In fact, I hoped to get married, stay Stateside, build my life there. But it's clear to me there was a different plan. I'm in my ninth year here now, and I'm wondering what's next. I think I'm getting ready for something new. But, you know, at my age it's hard to pivot."

I didn't ask her age but thought she was somewhere in her forties. Only later did I learn she had her 50th birthday coming up that year after our mutual friend Marielle alerted us to it. We got to participate in a special gift to celebrate that with her later.

This smart, talented, single, business-savvy expat in Shanghai, sat before us wondering out loud if she had missed the boat. Most people would look at her and her lifestyle as pure success. Yet it seemed to satisfy only a part of her.

Finishing dinner, most of us felt rather energetic, but Lora excused herself and went home. We instead chose to walk through a part of the city along the Yellow River (黄河 – *Huáng Hé*).

Chinese cities do nighttime well. I'm impressed with the brilliant, creative lighting along the rivers especially, at least in its first and second-tier cities. This lighting then reflects in the water, adding to the spectacle.

I sometimes wonder if the emphasis on nighttime lighting is to make up for what most of major Chinese cities lack in the day: clean air and blue skies. It's well known now how pollution blankets China's major cities, hanging over the urban landscape. The pollution often extends its tentacles into the outlying area. I believe it creates a "wall," preventing many average Chinese citizens from realizing there's a whole big, blue-skied world out there.

I also feel as if the pollution "wall" also has a spiritual dimension. For when we are spiritually "clouded," we often can't see a clearer, better way. The average Chinese person has been kept within this "wall" by a system inculcating the idea of the material world being all that exists.

Yet at night, while the stars are simply a figurative concept for most urban-dwelling Chinese, the government has done a masterful job of redirecting the focus to the "beauty" of artificial lighting, especially along its rivers, lakes and thoroughfares.

So, as we walked along the *Huáng Hé* with our family, Justin was on one arm and Erika on the other. (Locking arms is very common in China, especially between two girls and with family members. It is not seen as anything weird. I'm thankful our family still seems to feel comfortable doing this, even many years later!) Dale and Luke were bringing up the rear.

"Wow," Justin exclaimed. "It's so good to be back here in China. At least we're in a place where we know what's going on!"

A little smile came to my face as I prodded him about his comment. "What do you mean, exactly?"

"Well, in Japan I had *no idea* what was happening around me."

I let that sink in me for a moment.

"Well, of course!" I thought to myself. "Dale and I have been to Japan before. We've lived there and studied the language. It felt like familiar territory to us." It was only then I fully realized it had been anything but that for our three kids.

"I see what you mean now," I spoke up. "I guess Dad and I didn't do as good a job as we should've to make sure you understood better what was happening around you when we were in Japan. We understood pretty well, so we thought you would, too. I'm sorry!"

"It's fine, Mom. But I feel more at home here."

Both of those were amazing statements, coming from my 14-year-old son who had struggled so much in the fall. Perhaps we really were turning a corner.

The next day we met up with YZ, whom we hadn't seen for awhile. Always bubbling over with ideas, full of life, YZ remained optimistic even in the toughest of circumstances. Our kids loved him. His "angel glow" had not tarnished in the slightest.

We introduced him to Lora and then the four adults enjoyed a nice meal out while the kids ate pizza (yes, we ordered some) and watched movies at Lora's. They seemed pretty excited about this option.

The final two days before returning to Ningbo, we met up with a group of students, parent chaperones, and Joy Lin, or *Lín Lǎoshī* (林老师), the Chinese language teacher from Dale's high school back in the U.S. She was leading a trip of her middle and high school Chinese-language students over February break.

YZ joined us as we traveled. He and *Lín Lǎoshī* discovered they were alumni from the same university in Southern California, an unexpected connection. We headed first to the tradition-laden city of *Sūzhōu* 苏州 (about two hours away). Famous for silk production, we toured a factory there and also visited a traditional garden. Then it was back to Shanghai for one more day together, visiting Yuyuan Market and Shanghai Tower (上海塔 ‒ *Shànghǎi Tǎ*), plus taking in a performance of a famous Chinese acrobat troupe.

Waiting for the group in the lobby of the hotel where Joy had told us to meet, Dale went up to the front desk with YZ to ask a question. He glanced over and noticed an elegantly dressed Chinese woman, probably mid-to-late twenties, also waiting for help. As they both waited, the woman suddenly emitted a loud, extended belch. Others acted with nonchalance. It seemed as if no one noticed, except Dale.

The juxtaposition of this young woman's exterior elegance against what seemed like crass, unsophisticated behavior both startled and amused Dale.

He inquired with YZ later on.

"Yes, this happens in China. I know it is rude in the West. But many Chinese haven't learned that. So you see this kind of thing all the time," he explained.

Again we were encountering another example of how familiarity can blind us to the impression and impact of our own behavior. Of course, it's easy to see it in others; the challenge, no doubt, is recognizing it in ourselves. And that is where it's so needed.

46 | The magic of cake: A reset for our youngest

"Trust is like insurance—it's an investment you need to make up front, before the need arises."
— Erin Meyer, Author & Professor
The Culture Map

During our semester break, Dale and I had discussed Luke's school situation in great detail. We decided we would pull him out of the local elementary school and instead see if some of our students would help us by alternating care and language learning for Luke in the afternoons while we worked. We had already communicated via email with several potential students, and they seemed eager to help!

But this was *our* plan. When we brazenly announced it to Ellen upon our return from the semester break, it sent her into panic mode. The truth is, we had failed to take into account the delicate cultural and relational issues involved.

Ellen had worked hard on our behalf to secure the place at the school for Luke. Being relatively new in her position, accommodating a family with three kids was a brand new challenge. She strove to be a strong advocate for us while at the same time upholding her duties to her superiors.

Ellen told us that she wanted to make sure the relationship with this elementary school remained good, so they would accept foreign students in the future. In order to accomplish that, we needed to play by her rules.

It never would've occurred to me to purchase a cake to do this.

In reality, what we were doing was saving face. This was a concept we were well aware of after years of connections with Japan and with many other Asians. Yet in the certainty of *our* decision, we failed big time to take this into account.

Ellen insisted we purchase a cake and get printed on the top, 感谢你的帮助! (*Gǎnxiè nín de bāngzhù*) – "Thank you for your help!"

Then she suggested we get gifts for the principal, the head teacher of Luke's grade, and the English teacher. She gave us ideas of what to purchase, and we bought those items and wrapped them nicely.

Lastly, she told us to explain our reasons for removing Luke from school were because we needed more time to focus on Luke's American-based 4th grade curriculum.

Actually, this last point was complete exaggeration. Luke was progressing just fine. But Ellen needed us to agree to this so as not to give any hint the fault lay with the school.

Although telling the truth is important to us, we decided to let this one go. We calculated the cost and the long-term ramifications. We recognized our compliance would be essential for Ellen – and the school – to save face.

So we did it this way. It was an awkward moment, sitting in the principal's office, as Ellen chatted away and explained what needed to happen. And things did get better for Luke.

In the end, I believe everyone won.

The new arrangement for Luke meant a lot of reliance upon close to 20 students who "signed up" to take care of Luke each Monday through Friday in the afternoons. To start off, Dale and I got together with most of them in the coffee shop on campus.

Among them sat Eddie, Learner, Danya, Marley, Sonya, Maylin and Stuart. Bright, eager and desiring to be helpful, we thanked them for the gift they were giving us in helping Luke. We told them that, in many ways, they would become what nine-year-old Luke would remember about China. So they were "ambassadors" for their country to this little boy. Although we knew their sessions with Luke would be mostly in English, we told them whenever they could slip in some Chinese language learning, we would appreciate it.

Here's an important point. Luke was at an age where he could *decide* whether or not he wanted to learn the Chinese language. The experiences he had at the elementary school, coupled with his own stubbornness, caused him to *choose* to put a barrier up to language learning. In fact, of our three kids, he probably retained the least.

We told our Chinese students, sitting wide-eyed before us, to consider Luke and his language learning a worthwhile challenge to pursue. Approached the right way – through games, play, and discovery – Luke was still like a sponge. He still had the capacity to learn faster than anyone else in our family. His brain was still much more pliable to absorb and use language. So, we hoped, Luke would show some linguistic growth in the last half of our stay in China.

"But, truth is, the best thing you can do with Luke is have fun with him. Become his friend. He will remember you for that. And we will be very thankful," we assured them.

We worked out a schedule. For each afternoon, a few students would work together and be responsible for Luke, usually between 1–5 or 6 pm.

"Don't worry, Mrs. D. We will not let you down. We will make sure to take good care of Luke," Marley asserted.

And the classroom?

"It can be anywhere. You can meet with him at our apartment. You can take him around campus. You can come to this coffee shop. Wherever you think is good," we told them.

In the end, the "classroom" was the entire Ningbo University campus, plus the adjacent shopping areas. This seemed to work out well. The students were creative in what they did with Luke.

Some chose the safety and predictability of our apartment. But most chose to take Luke out, riding bikes somewhere, on nice days to the open field, or to explore some of the buildings, the shopping areas or the outside market. We had a ping pong room nearby, and that ended up being the destination at times. Some took him to an empty classroom and they played "classroom games."

But two things stood out from these times.

First, Luke never complained about any of his new "teachers," always looking forward to the time. Second, throughout that semester, our students *never* let us down. Sometimes one or the other could not help, but they always made sure at least one person was there for the scheduled time. Dale and I were impressed with their reliability. This was all volunteer service for them.

I should also mention about four of Dale's students – Doreen, Aurora, Trisha, and Liquid. These met with Erika a couple times each week for language learning. Dale had suggested this idea to Erika, and she was open to it. Whereas Luke was still all about play, Erika was willing to study and learn and attempt to speak Chinese. These students were eager to get to know her, too.

Years later, as I write this, I get choked up when I think about these particular students. They really helped us in a time of need, and it meant the world to us. Their faithfulness to their initial commitment left a lasting impression upon us.

47 | English as a channel for true diplomacy

"Learning is a treasure that will follow its owner everywhere."
学习是一个宝藏，随处可见。
Xuéxí shì yīgè bǎozàng, suíchù kějiàn.
– Chinese Proverb

Key to the success of the Chinese economy – and, indeed, China's interactions with the world in this first part of the 21st century – is an understanding of how to communicate well in English. That's where we stepped in. Yes, we were just a tiny part of China's quest to better understand and communicate with the outside world. But we took our jobs with these students seriously. We wanted to help them better understand us, as Americans. We also wanted desperately to understand them.

And teaching English was the vehicle for us.

While this year was, in large part, about our family's adventure and experiences, it also was about so much more. Being international diplomats, ambassadors for our country. As well, being people who follow Christ, we wanted to live out our faith in an authentic, contagious way.

No question, the students made the experience worthwhile for us. On the whole, we found them to be bright, eager, and warm-hearted. As they struggled with the challenges of growing into adulthood, many faced the reality of a nation also trying to do the same. Indeed, China sometimes seemed to resemble a gangly, enthusiastic, but sometimes angst-filled teenager.

When it comes to the Chinese people, Americans often view China as a monolith in contrast to the relatively diverse cultural, ethnic and racial backgrounds found in the U.S. When you look at those pictures online of crowds milling through Chinese train stations – a sea of black, bobbing heads – it's quite easy to miss the individuality of the people.

But that individuality *is* there! I discovered with every generalization you could make, there were dozens of people who stood in contrast. It was through my students I learned to appreciate this discovery all the more. I learned to respect the different ways many of them thought. I also recognized how so many of their ideas were just forming.

Even though I was the *lǎoshī* (老师 – teacher) and they the *xuéshēng* (学生 – students), I also felt a sense of friendship and kinship with so many of my students. Of course, I recognized the concept of hierarchy in Asian cultures. American culture tends to diminish hierarchy and elevate equality. Not always so with Asian cultures. Regardless, I found so many of my students in Ningbo also became my friends over time. Going into the classroom occasionally felt like a job, but mostly it felt like a joy – the joy of getting together with friends.

I grew closer to some students than others, of course. Eddie was one who stood out. Witty, always enthusiastic and willing to help, he found himself in an English program with female students all around him. For in a class of 30, it was common to have only four or five guys.

Eddie's natural leadership skills, his energy and authenticity, always drew me. I loved spending time with him both in class and out; as I'd walk to my next class, he would accompany me. We'd talk about what was going on in our lives. He was among the students who helped with Luke the second semester. As such, he became a permanent friend of our family.

It's worthwhile to note, Eddie later spent six months working at an amusement park in Minnesota through a U.S. Parks and Recreation program that hires temporary workers from dozens of countries abroad. At the end of his time, he came to visit our family in California, and we spent a few very precious days with him. He is now married and a father of one son, working hard in a trade-industry job near Shanghai. The connection continues.

And then there was Learner. When I asked her how she chose her

English name, she simply replied, "That's what I want to be all my life. A learner. So I thought I'd use it as a name." Well, it worked. My observation of her over time is that she has pursued just that, learning and stretching beyond her own limitations.

Learner has done a fabulous job keeping in touch with me since our years in Ningbo. She shares about her changing circumstances, jobs, family changes, information about some of the other classmates, doubts and concerns. When we exchange correspondence, it is almost as if we are sitting right next to each other in one of Ningbo University's many inexpensive eating halls, enjoying steaming hot noodles together.

I remember a talk I had with Sonya one time. Tall and winsome, wide-eyed behind Harry Potter-ish frames, Sonya possessed an innocent, almost naive way about her. She told me of her love of poetry and philosophy, how she wished she could write poetry as a career. "But it is not practical," she lamented. "Still, I imagine myself as one of those ancient scholars in Confucius' court, thinking deeply about matters of life and death, especially of living, and then writing poetry to express the heart. I wish I could do *that* for my life!"

And Aurora. She was from the western part of China, one of the Uyghur ethnic minorities. Aurora was actually one of Dale's students whom we both connected with deeply. She was one of four female students who met specifically with Erika during that second semester as well. Active with the Ningbo University radio station, she even invited Erika as her special guest one time.

But being Uyghur in a nation of ethnic-majority Han (92%) meant being different. And difference is not always prized in China, especially when it comes to job opportunities and the future. I remember Aurora sharing with me through an email about the worries she had as she thought about finding a job after college.

"I am not a thin girl, not so good looking. I think it will affect me for the rest of my life, both my career and my possibility of marriage. But I have English, and I want to use it for my career, for my life. I hope I can find something worthwhile. I do not want to go back to my hometown. It is too depressing there. There are no jobs. No future for me. And my life back home was not so good. So now I must be in this world. But it is hard."

Another student I have squarely on my heart is Stuart. Always helpful, alert, in-the-front-seat, ready-to-respond Stuart. He was proper, polite and optimistic. Tall and a natural leader, I could tell this young man would go far and pursue his dreams. He told me his dreams would lead him into law, he thought. His English was excellent, and he consistently sought to improve it whenever he had a chance. He, too, was among the "teachers" for Luke during our second semester, and I know that drew us even closer.

Finally, there was Marley. Possessing a smile that could win over a crowd in an instant, full of composure and elegant practicality, Marley won my heart over. Smart and dedicated, Marley threw herself into whatever she pursued. No wonder Marley was one of a few students who years later made it to study and later visit us in the U.S. She, too, threw herself into care for Luke – again, another reason why she stands out.

Maylin, Ellie, Danya, Amelia, Joshua, Aaron, Jack – even UFO Singer (yes, you read that right!) – these students and *so many more* remain near and dear to my heart even today. I haven't been able to keep up with all of them, but I still treasure those moments we shared. The relationships we could develop offered a lens into a culture, enabling us to understand China in a much deeper and textured way.

48 | A river runs through it... but Ningbo is cold!

"Good habits formed at youth make all the difference."
– Aristotle

It was Learner who invited me in to see her student dormitory. I had only heard about the conditions the students lived in, but had not actually set foot in a dorm. Thanks to her, I was able. I found four female students to a room, bunking 2x2. The long rooms had two built-in desks as well. If students were neat, the place was manageable, but not all were.

At any point in time, laundry hung across clotheslines strung across the space. In the colder months, it could take up to four days for the heaviest pieces (jeans, for example) to dry. There were no washers and dryers. Everything was hand washed and hung out to dry. So, of course, this meant hanging clothes were a natural part of the student dormitory landscape, underwear included.

True, this is the case in many parts of the world. The American propensity to use clothes dryers is not shared with much of the world. In fact, in most places, air drying is often preferred, both for the life of the clothing and for the environment. Not to mention affordability. Many in the developing world simply can't afford the cost of washing machines and dryers, nor the energy expense to keep them running.

Still, what was remarkable – even admirable – for these students is they did everything without any heat in the cold months (nor A/C in the hot months). No heat in their dormitories. No hot water. Clothes washing, even in sub-zero temperatures, used cold water. They had to pay a few yuan to get a hot shower in a separate facility. Not expensive, but not something you'd do every single day, like many do in America. Why was this the case? And was this true for all of China?

In fact, the Chinese have drawn a line between north and south. Traditionally, this line has fallen along the Huai River *Huáihé* (淮河), north of Nanjing (which is north of Shanghai). The *Huáihé* is a tributary of the better-known Yangtze River *Chángjiāng* (长江), which runs into Shanghai. In more recent years, the "dividing line" between north and south is considered to be along the Yangtze.

Why does this matter? First, in terms of agriculture, northern China is considered to be wheat-growing, southern China rice-growing. There are some exceptions, of course. The nation is divided more linguistically between north and south as well. In the north, Mandarin Chinese, especially *Běijīng huà* (北京话 – Beijing dialect), dominates. In the south, while Mandarin is the official language, dialects tend to rule – dozens of them. And finally, when it comes to heat – in the north, buildings are, for the most part, centrally heated. But in the south, not so. Across the board.

Ningbo is a southern city, even if its temperatures in the winter get well below freezing. Which they do. Those who are fortunate – such as foreign teachers like us – get heating systems in their living quarters. (And believe me, did we rely on it!) But the students? No heaters.

And the classrooms? Also, no heaters.

So how did they – and we – keep warm in those cold months?

Layers of clothing. Hats, scarves, heavy jackets. Hand warmers. And *rèshuǐ* (pronounced "ruh-shuay," 热水) or *kāishuǐ* (开水) – hot or boiled water. Lots of it.

I learned to love and appreciate *rèshuǐ*, like it was an exotic drink. Or, at least a lifeline. Of course, the Chinese drink tea, especially green tea. And coffee. But drinking tea and coffee nonstop can cause some trouble, both for the body and for the wallet. Hot water? It's free and can do the same thing, all day long on those very cold days.

The go-everywhere thermos is a must. And we discovered almost all of the buildings we taught in had *rèshuǐ* dispensers on the ground floor. It would not be uncommon to see lines of students waiting to fill up their thermos before the next class. I learned early that almost every building had a teacher's room as well, with the dutiful *rèshuǐ* dispensers available. During those colder months, those rooms – and specifically the dispensers – were an unquestionable go-to.

The classrooms at Ningbo University were basic and sparse, often with old-styled desks or sometimes tables for two or three. Some rooms were a bit more modern, with longer tables and, occasionally, places where students could plug in a computer. But very few were like that. Perhaps what I found most striking was the obvious lack of decoration, the stark simplicity. Maybe that was for lack of distraction? I'm not sure. As a teacher however, I aimed to create color and texture in the classroom regardless.

One of my goals was to make their experience learning English fun and memorable. And to help it stick. I would work hard to devise or discover games to help along these lines. Whenever possible, we'd move these games outdoors as the weather warmed. When I would announce we'd be doing that on any given day, you could almost feel a collective buoyancy lift up the room. We were headed out!

I also used theater and even mime. How could mime help students learn English? I would have the audience use their English to interpret the message or the story.

Another goal was to help my students better understand what America – and Americans – are all about, beyond their conventional ideas. Group discussions. Presentations. Games. Putting together a newspaper or short magazine to communicate their discoveries to others. Doing a commerce-type of activity where they would set up a "business" and "store" and run it all in English. We did stuff like that.

I took my students through the debate process several times. One debate session that stood out revolved around the question, "English or Chinese – Which should be the international language of the future?" The students really got into this debate. Even though English maintains primacy in this area, the PRO-Chinese-Language Teams in most of my classes did a pretty excellent job arguing their cases.

Although according to statistics from June 2016, English is still the most-used language on the internet (26.3% compared to 20.8%), Chinese, the second most-used language, grew at a rate of 2227.9% compared to English (at 573.9%) during the 2000–2016 period. It doesn't take a mathematician to realize Chinese *will* outpace English on the internet in the coming years. It's just a matter of time.

Traversing the Middle Kingdom

49 | Express train to heaven: Hangzhou

"Paradise above, Suzhou and Hangzhou below."
上有天堂，下有苏杭 – *Shàng yǒu tiāntáng, xià yǒu sū háng*

Both Dale and Erika had milestone birthdays that March, with Dale turning 50 and Erika officially becoming a teenager.

We felt as if a trip to nearby *Hángzhōu* (杭州) might be a good way to celebrate.

The Chinese love the cities of Suzhou and Hangzhou, equating them close to paradise. The traditional proverb *"Paradise above, Suzhou and Hangzhou below"* captures this idea well, speaking of a more provincial and less industrialized time.

The phrase above resembles the English phrase, "Heaven on Earth."

Even Marco Polo described Suzhou as "the city of the earth" while Hangzhou as "the city of heaven."

Located in eastern Zhejiang Province about an hour and a half from Ningbo, Hangzhou lies at the intersection of the busiest rail corridor in China. The Hangzhou East Railway Station ("East Station," or *Dōngzhàn* 东站) boasts 15 High Speed rail platforms available for trains criss-crossing to Ningbo, Wenzhou, Shanghai, Nanjing, Changsha, Wuhan, Hefei, and well beyond.

Hangzhou also sits at the very southern end of China's Grand Canal, which starts in Beijing. The oldest parts of the canal date back to the 5th century BC, although the Chinese finally combined various sections during the Sui Dynasty (581–618 AD) to create an uninterrupted waterway (both natural and man-made) linking Beijing with Hangzhou and dozens of cities in between.

This city's history is rich. As one of the eight ancient capitals of China (along with Beijing, Nanjing, Luoyang, Xi'an, Kaifeng, Anyang, and Zhengzhou), Hangzhou became a cosmopolitan center early on and retained its status well into the modern era. But it was also a center of conquests by Muslims from the west and Mongols from the north, as well as more commerce-minded Arab traders.

Hangzhou has always retained a mystical and ephemeral position in the minds of Chinese and foreigners alike. Poets, philosophers and scholars gravitated to Hangzhou and still do today. No wonder modern Hangzhou is a center of higher education, with close to 20 major universities and dozens of other technical and professional schools. Its U.S. sister city is Boston, which makes good sense.

Hangzhou centers around the famous West Lake – *Xīhú* (西湖), a place of lore and undeniable beauty. We stayed in a hostel nestled in the woods near the lake. Unique in design, with all sorts of attached rooms and nearby gardens and bamboo forests, the owners prided themselves on home-cooked breakfast options to suit the varied tastes of international travelers but also cater to the mostly young Chinese who fill their rooms.

We were in Hangzhou on a rainy March weekend, so umbrellas surrounded us at all times. In fact, the colorful umbrellas against the slate grey skies, with stunning new greenery and cherry blossoms all around, proved quite a photographic feast.

The kids were in an upbeat mood. We enjoyed plenty of time walking around *Xīhú* and taking the tourist ferry around part of the lake. The ferry resembles the ancient vessels that plied the lake and nearby waterways at the time – souped up for modern-day demands. We also toured the outdoor market, enjoying the occasional *mahjong* (*májiàng* – 麻将) players dueling it out, buying the occasional trinket or souvenir for someone back home.

At one point we entered a huge building, attracted by some of the animals in front. It turned out to be a pet store, but it was packed with all kinds of animals, birds and fish – from chinchillas to cockatoos to baby crocs. Luke, who always wanted a puppy, was quick to gravitate to the dogs and find the cutest ones. I'll admit, I had a hard time leaving that place, save the smell which on certain floors proved more intense than others. I had never seen a multi-story pet shop like that before. Absolutely remarkable!

50 | Our angel's roots: Wenzhou

"People of Excellence and Land of Wisdom."
人傑地靈 – *Rénjiédìlíng*

A few weekends later we found ourselves with YZ on a top-of-the-line train speeding south to his hometown of *Wēnzhōu* (温州). We wondered why this train was so luxurious, with sleeping cars, when we would only be traveling about four hours during the day.

"Well, as you know, this one comes from Shanghai, so that would be about seven or eight hours traveling," he responded. "Even though we are traveling during the day, many take the night train out of Shanghai to Wenzhou, or the other way around. And that's about seven hours."

"But there is one more important thing," you see. "Wenzhou is the place of business people. It is known for that. And it has become pretty rich through all its business. So, it makes sense to have a train like this."

Dale and I were amazed at how excellent the Chinese transportation system, at least in eastern China, had become. We recalled the China of the late 1980s, when trains were much slower and more rickety. Now, even on the basic trains, we found the travel experience to be superb.

True, sometimes you'd run into people cramming the galleys between trains, taking the train without a reserved seat. But to use most of China's trains now, you had to purchase a ticket to reserve a seat ahead of time, thus assuring a decent and much better ride.

Wēnzhōu (温州): The Chinese characters mean "mild and pleasant land." Wenzhou boasts a mild climate in summer and winter. Surrounded by mountains on three sides and the East China Sea (with over 400 islands nearby), the city is picturesque even while boasting a population of over six million (estimate, 2017).

But because of its geography, *Wēnzhōu* has been quite isolated from much of China, and the people of the region developed a distinct dialect reputed within China to be one of the most difficult. With a culture and language so different from the rest of the nation, the people have also differentiated themselves. A prosperous foreign trading port, *Wēnzhōu* has long been one of the most outward-looking areas of China.

The area is known for its emigrants, many of whom have left their home for Europe and the U.S. In fact, 90% of all Chinese residents living in Italy, France and Spain originate from *Wēnzhōu.*

The *Wēnzhōunese* have a reputation for being good entrepreneurs. Many have started up restaurants, retail and wholesale businesses, investment companies and similar ventures around the world. And interestingly, although many *Wēnzhōunese* emigrated from the city, a strong foreign settlement never really established itself there even as the city opened in 1876 for tea exports.

Wēnzhōu is the only city in China – and indeed the world – designed entirely using the principles of *Fēngshuǐ* philosophy (风水哲学 – *Fēngshuǐ zhéxué*). This is because the founder of *Fēngshuǐ*, *Guō Pú* (郭璞), left his native Shanxi Province in the north, and traveled to *Wēnzhōu* during the Jin Dynasty (265–420 AD). Viewing the valley surrounded by mountains and sea from above, he applied Fengshui principles in the orientation of buildings and the placement of streets and waterways, in an effort to create harmony between man-made and natural elements.

Because of this influence, other Chinese seem to view *Wēnzhōu* as an auspicious city, and the people of *Wēnzhōu* with reverence. So goes the well-known saying in China, reflecting the status of *Wēnzhōu* – "People of Excellence and Land of Wisdom." (人傑地靈 – *Rénjiédìlíng*).

But more recently, *Wēnzhōu* has gained distinction in another

217

way. *Wēnzhōu* has been dubbed "the Jerusalem of China." Its journey to this distinction is fascinating and, at times, disturbing. It can be traced to Overseas Missionary Fellowship's (OMF*) George Stott, who in the 19th century came to *Wēnzhōu* as a Protestant missionary. (* Previously China Inland Mission)

Stott's story itself is intriguing. He was not particularly religious until an accident left him with an amputated leg at 19 years old. Then he claims to have encountered God, and subsequently became quite devout, committing himself to the advancement of Christianity in China.

Westerners at the time looked at China with a combination of pity and hope. Some were sincere in their desire to help the Chinese people improve their livelihoods. Others were not.

A peculiar irony was not lost on the ruling elite in Peking, and even on many of the common people. From their perspective, the same people who were trying to win Chinese over to Christianity – widely seen as a "foreign religion" (外来教 – *wàilái jiào*) – were the ones oppressing China by selling it opium and forcing the nation to open its ports to foreign trade.

Stott, however, possessed a sincere heart to improve the conditions for ordinary Chinese citizens who were so often trapped in poverty. He settled on *Wēnzhōu* as a place to at least establish a beachhead. And he persevered.

His efforts proved overwhelmingly successful. The success seems to have at least some connection with *Wēnzhōu's* distance from Peking and its geographic isolation. The government simply did not crack down on the missionary effort.

And so Christianity thrived. Now, over 11% of *Wēnzhōunese* claim to be Christian, almost six times higher than the national average. As would be true in any case, some of these Christian believers are sincere, committed, and highly moral. Others, not so. A strain of "prosperity gospel" has arisen out of *Wēnzhōu* because of its commercial success, and this – like its manifestation in the U.S. – has tainted the Christian church in both countries, both within and as viewed from outside.

YZ had told us that his mother's good friend owned a hotel, but I would have never guessed we would have been able to stay in it as a free gift. But that's exactly what happened. The hotel was relatively empty at the time – "low season" the manager had told YZ when we checked in – so there were many rooms available.

We were up on the seventh floor, an expansive view before us. But what caught our attention most of all was that the interior of the hotel was easily four-to-five star, not unlike an excellent hotel in the West, but the exterior of the hotel was much less modern in its design.

This surprised me because, if anything, I would have expected it to be the other way around. But then again I was finding my expectations were often fooled in China.

YZ took us to his childhood home. No one was occupying it right now, and his aunt and uncle remained the owners, so he was able to obtain a key. We walked through rooms where he had taken his first steps as he told us story after story. He showed us the tree he used to climb, told us about boyhood antics with some friends, reminisced about his grandparents.

We also got to do some shopping in some of *Wēnzhōu's* bargain marts near its port. These bargain marts were a series of warehouses that seemed to go on and on. Merchants would bring their wares and set up shop as locals and tourists mingled among the stalls.

We had opportunities to try and buy teas, wine, leather goods, paper goods, jewelry, toys, clothing and dozens of other items. The range was limited only by our wallet and our ability to take it all away.

I learned much later that *Wēnzhōu*, in addition to being considered the birthplace of China's private economy, is also the place where Chinese Opera first took hold and is considered the cradle of Mathematics in China. In fact, on this latter point, *Wēnzhōunese* mathematician *Shu Shien-Siu* (徐賢修) is today considered as the father of the high-tech industry in Taiwan.

Wēnzhōu is a distinctive place. And I suspect, as a *Wēnzhōunese*, YZ's identity is grounded in this distinction. Visiting his hometown, even over a single weekend, helped us to understand him all the more.

51 | North to the capital: Beijing

*"The Beijing Olympics [2008] and the Shanghai Expo [2010] show
how much effort China is willing to spend to enter the global stage.
But while China desires to understand the world,
it fails to accept its universal values."*
– Ài Wèi Wèi (艾未未), Human Rights Activist

Although we also traveled to Xi'an in western China as well as
to Suzhou and Shanghai yet again during the semester, our largest trip
during the springtime took us to Beijing.

This megacity, with an estimated 21.6 million people in the city
proper (2016 figures), can be dizzying. Current estimates have it as the
third largest city in the world, after Shanghai (24.3M) and Karachi,
Pakistan (23.5M).

Beijing, formerly Peking, has evolved over three millennia. Layer
upon layer of history. Conquests. Commerce. Creativity. Chaos. And,
increasingly, cars.

The conditions of Beijing's air are well known. An oppressive
pollution hangs over the city much of the year, worsened by the annual
dust storms from the nearby desert plains. These conditions can make
living in Beijing unbearable for some.

Dale and I had first visited Beijing at a time when air quality
was much better. But political tensions and unrest simmered under
the surface. It was 1988. A year later, protests against the government
in *Tiān'ānmén* Square (天安门广场 – *Tiān'ānmén Guǎngchǎng*) by
emboldened students and activists triggered heavy-handed response.
Tanks rolled in, over 3000 were wounded and more than 10,000 taken

into custody. The world shook.

Even today, the exact number of those who died remains a mystery. Verifiable deaths come in at 155, but most China watchers believe the death toll was much higher. I personally remember being in my in-law's living room, watching the tanks roll into the square on my father-in-law's large TV.

Tiān'ānmén was a statement, both to those internally who dared to question the Communist government's ultimate authority, as well as to a watching world.

And then, silence. China's government has done much to promote revisionism when it comes to the *Tiān'ānmén* Square Massacre. The government has scrubbed all references that it even occurred – except official government-sanctioned propaganda. Indeed, the first result on search engine *Bǎidù* (Google equivalent in China) is a short article from the People's Daily concluding the incident "taught the party and the people a useful lesson."

Tiān'ānmén is not taught in Chinese schools. The government has silenced the masses, wooed them into submission by the elixir of material progress combined with restricted information. Many of our Chinese students at Ningbo University had never even heard of it.

Major anniversaries of the incident see a tightening of government control, especially online. But with each passing year, society's collective memory of the incident fades. And the government becomes increasingly skilled at preventing those who would have the truth known from getting their words out.

Why did *Tiān'ānmén* fail? Most analyses say the protesters didn't have a clear goal. They wanted more freedom and democracy, but what exactly did that mean? The Chinese government was able to crack down precisely because of the paucity of the protester's demands, their lack of clarity.

And there we were, standing in *Tiān'ānmén* Square on a day in May 2010, a little less than a year after the massacre's 20th anniversary. But for some, the memories remained. Our friend *Da Chun* was one of those who vividly remembers the day.

We walked around the grounds of the Temple of Heaven, or *Tiāntán* (天坛). It is a large, sprawling area, with ample greenery throughout, located right in the heart of Beijing. We hadn't seen *Dài Chūn* (戴春) for over five years.

As we walked along, we noted all the elderly people engaged in taichi, dance and song.

"I feel more Chinese than I ever was before," she proclaimed. "Since I'm getting older now, China is a good place for me. China is a good place for older people. It is good for the changing seasons I'm going through. American is good for youth."

Ironic. Through our conversations, we discovered that we're around the same age. Yet my husband and I didn't even consider ourselves "old" at the time. We were right in the middle of our parenting years, with kids ranging from nine through 14 years old.

When *Dài Chūn* first came back to China after two years of graduate study abroad, in our hometown, she discovered she really stood out. She spoke her mind and expected others to do the same. Gradually she learned she could no longer do that, learning to temper her ideas, at least when it came to expressing them. She found the reentry shock difficult to handle.

She told of a Chinese professor whose wife became pregnant with a second child during the time of the one-child policy. He ended up being charged with a fine and publicly decried. Refusing to pay the fine, he faced dismissal from his job.

This incident produced big headlines in Beijing when it broke. She believes he was used by the government as a scapegoat to cause others to comply. And, it worked.

Now, though, she could share openly with us as we wandered around that fabulous place of history.

Dài Chūn told of her boyfriend who lost his life in the *Tiān'ānmén* Square Massacre. The Chinese authorities at the time muted the loss of his life. She sought justice but failed to find it. This affected her for years. Finally, she got married to a colleague at work. They had a son and lived a "normal" conforming life in China as it raced towards economic primacy in the 1990's and early 21st century.

Dài Chūn moved up the ranks in her government position. In fact, she was able to secure a scholarship to do graduate work abroad. Not long after, she landed on our doorstep.

We got to know *Dài Chūn* when she was a student. But she was really a wife, mother, worker and party member. We shared openly about many aspects of life over those years.

Unfortunately, her marriage suffered during those two years away, ending in a divorce. This is a fairly "normal" arrangement – and consequence – among China's intellectuals.

She retained the custody of her son.

At the time of our visit, *Dài Chūn* was dating a Chinese Christian man – a teacher at the same school where she had done some part-time instruction. But her then 17-year-old son was not privy to that information. She didn't want to consider marriage until her son would sit through the *gāokǎo* (高考) exams in June.

Dài Chūn's research and policy roles led her to a place of prominence in the Chinese apparatus. She developed an expertise in trade policy analysis. She admitted that, while she found the Bush policy between 2000–2008 quite black-and-white, Obama's more nuanced style was proving more challenging for the Chinese government.

"Do you know what he is doing?" she queried at one point, almost as if we had an inside to White House policy makers. We smiled.

We philosophized for awhile, and then found our minds back in the present, enjoying the laughter and music in the park, the scene of a young couple getting their wedding pictures taken against the backdrop of *Tiāntán*. Children ran around squealing.

"You know, I am ready to lead a quiet, simple life. So many years of working so hard, often holding three jobs at one time. It is time to slow down, to enjoy my life."

This woman had seen so much. It seemed as if she was yet again going through another one of many changing seasons in her life. We bade her goodbye, wondering if and when we'd see her again.

52 | Tantalizing tea shop & delectable duck

*"There is something in the nature of tea that leads us
into a world of quiet contemplation of life."*
— Lin Yutang, 20th century Writer, Translator, Linguist & Inventor
The Importance of Living

We seemed to have a knack to find unusual and unique hostels and lodges as we traveled, and our place in Beijing proved no exception. It was an expansive, traditional-styled compound with ample space in our rooms and in the common areas.

The location was excellent, just off *Tiān'ānmén* Square. Dale and I found we could easily go out on our own and leave the children behind to rest, read, or play video games as we explored the surrounding areas. Of course we would encourage them to come along. But sometimes they would just prefer to lay low, and that seemed okay.

One afternoon Dale and I headed out of our hostel to explore for a bit while the kids remained. It wasn't long before we felt ourselves drawn into a tea shop we would return to again and again in the ensuing days.

When we entered the tranquil teahouse, intermingled aromas of jasmine, rose and oolong wafted through the air. We discovered this ambiance-rich space nestled in one of Beijing's remaining *hútòng* (胡同) – traditional alleyway neighborhoods created by the walls of single-story courtyard houses dating back to the Yuan Dynasty (1271–1368).

Dancing eyes and a warm smile invited us in. "*Nihao* (你好), welcome," an engaging woman sang. "Take your time and look around. Where are you from?"

We responded, "California, USA, but we live in Ningbo, China right now."

She lifted her eyebrows. Really?

"California, it must be a very nice place."

I inquired her name. "It's Alice. Well, that's my name for you!" She winked and then suggested we sit down. "I prepare you some *Lìzhī chá* (荔枝茶). You know *lìzhī?*"

I didn't, but I quickly looked it up in my dictionary. Lychee. "Oh, yes. I know that."

As Alice prepared the tea, our eyes explored the little shop, so full of character, tea and exquisite teaware. Enchanting was the only word that came to mind.

"How did you become so good at English?" I queried. "Have you travelled or lived abroad much? You speak so well."

"My customers are my teachers. They come from all over the world, to my little shop. I have run it for over 30 years. No time for travel."

I mulled over that for awhile. Nonstop work for 30+ years, no travel abroad. Yet this woman's English was impeccable. Not only was her grammar and pronunciation near native, but her fluid ease of use made us feel so welcomed. Clearly, this woman knew how to engage her customers and make each feel special.

The fragrant tea transported us to ancient times that, at the moment, seemed just a sip away. An uncommon timelessness pervaded Alice's tea shop. We almost expected to see horseback warriors charge past outside.

My husband and I are Americans who prefer tea. For us, the aromas conjure an assortment of memories of both the familiar and the mysterious.

One memory floating to the surface at that moment was the Shanghai tea house we had visited with our children shortly after our August arrival and then again three months later. I recalled our amazement at how a computer store had moved in, unknowingly stealing our "nostalgia moment" in the process.

As China has swiftly moved towards claiming a place on the world stage of industrial powers, its approach has not been without plenty

225

of controversy. The central Communist Party still wields authority allowing for rapid change that would take much longer in many parts of the world, where environmental and social impact concerns, not to mention zoning, permitting and other procedural steps, slow down the process.

Many have documented the rapid-fire bulldozing of the *hútòng* since China set out on its modernization quest. At the height of the city's headlong rush to modernity in the 1990s, about 600 *hútòng* were destroyed each year, displacing an estimated 500,000 residents. Currently, it is unknown how many *hútòng* have been demolished, but most estimates run between 2,000–5,000.

People's lives changed. Forever. By bulldozers, cranes and government edict.

That tea house in Shanghai? Its disappearance is probably more a result of "free market" activity in a still not-so-free China. Nevertheless, we couldn't help but wonder about Alice and her tea house.

We returned to visit Alice and her tea shop a few more times during our stay. Each time offered a further glimpse into this internationalized woman who had spent much of her life within the walls of her cozy shop.

Tea has a way of doing that. A relatively simple drink with unlimited variations, tea spans cultures and time. After water, it is the number two consumed beverage in the world.

Tea – liquid memories of moments, atmosphere and relationship to sip and savor long after the cup is emptied.

While in Beijing we met up with Lena, the wife of Paul, one of our Chinese student friends from long ago. After numerous go-arounds about what to do and where to meet, she insisted we join her and her sister at "a famous restaurant for *Běijīng kǎoyā* (北京烤鸭)," or Peking Duck.

We had known Paul and Lena for years. He had done an MBA at a graduate school in our town. During this time he went back to China, married Lena, and then brought her to the U.S. A few years later, they welcomed their son Nathan to this world. Dual U.S.-Chinese nationals, Paul and Lena would struggle for many years as they tried to raise their son between two countries.

Ultimately, China won out. Paul's English was strong and he felt confident moving between the two countries. He became involved in several entrepreneurial ventures connecting the two countries – exporting broccoli to China, and bringing in eyewear and IT/computer hardware to the U.S, to name just a few. But Lena always preferred her native China. Her English skill progressed slowly, always in the shadows behind her husband. She seemed more of a homebody, preferring a safer life in a land she understood.

But their life was anything but a "normal family life," from a western perspective. Paul focused most of his energies on his businesses, moving back and forth between America and China. Lena wanted to stay in Beijing. They had determined Nathan would be best with grandparents who lived a more traditional, rural life. It was at that point when we met Lena in Beijing.

In some ways the reunion with her was awkward. We expected to see them all, or at least Lena with her son. But Nathan, probably around ten by then, was nowhere to be found.

"It is best for him to be with his grandparents at this stage," Lena assured me. "They can do a better job with him than me."

I didn't question this out loud, but did struggle with the idea. Fortunately for us, the boisterous atmosphere of the restaurant and the amazing food dominated the evening. I was also dealing with a headache in the midst of all the noise (plus pollution outside), so for me the evening was a bit of a blur.

Turns out the restaurant Lena took us to was one of the two most famous establishments for *Běijīng kǎoyā* in all of China. It's name, *Quánjùdé* (全聚德), meant, according to Chinese Premier *Zhou Enlai*, "perfection, union, and benevolence." While *Quánjùdé* has eight direct branches in Beijing, Carrie took us to the original location in the *Qiánmén* (前门) section of Beijing.

This place was amazing. It serves up to 5,000 meals a day and the seven-story restaurant covers a floor area of 15,000 square meters! It even offers 40+ private dining rooms and can seat 2,000 guests at a time.

But beyond the blur for me, the savory flavor of the food lingers in my mind even now.

There's a lot of history behind *Běijīng kǎoyā*. It was first served as a food in the Southern and Northern Dynasties Period (420–589) and has remained a staple of Chinese culture ever since. Preparation of *Běijīng kǎoyā* in China holds a similar mystique as the preparation of sushi in Japan; culinary experts receive special training to do it well. The good stuff in both cases is not the food of paupers. There's a sense it holds a unique place in the collective mindset.

Wrapped in thin steamed "pancakes" with spring onions and sweet bean sauce, the flavorful meat really stands out. I personally found it so delicious – as did Dale and the kids – that I didn't know when to stop. We said our lengthy goodbyes and literally rolled out of that restaurant and onto the subway to return to our hostel that evening.

I'm glad our meeting with Lena and her sister was on Thursday, not Friday night. We needed all day Friday to "recover." More exploring of nearby *Tiān'ānmén*, along with a foray to The Forbidden City (故宫 – *Gùgōng*), rounded up the day.

This sprawling complex lies directly across the way from *Tiān'ānmén* Square, keeping our transportation for that day very simple. Yes, the famous giant picture of *Máo Zédōng*, gazing out on *Tiān'ānmén* Square, is the landmark entry of the Forbidden City. But behind the walled complex lies so much more.

Gùgōng was the home of emperors and their households, and was the political and ceremonial center of the nation for over 500 years, from the Ming Dynasty (*Míng Cháo* – 明朝) to the end of the Qing Dynasty (*Qīng Cháo* – 清朝), spanning the years 1420–1912).

Some may recall the British-Italian produced epic movie of 1987, *The Last Emperor*. This film, chronicling the life of *Pu-Yi* (Pu义皇帝 – *Puyì Huángdì*) from his ascent to the throne as a little boy to his political rehabilitation by the Communist Party of China after 1949, was the first occidental film allowed to be created almost entirely within the walls of *Gùgōng*. It gave a waiting outside world its first glimpses of a fallen empire and a rising modern China.

Gùgōng's traditional palatial architecture has played a major role in influencing design throughout Asia. UNESCO declared it a World Heritage Site in 1987.

But perhaps most notably, since 1925 *Gùgōng* has housed the Palace Museum which boasts the most extensive collection of Ming and Qing Dynasty artifacts in the world. In fact, with 16 million visitors annually (2016), the Palace Museum in The Forbidden City is the world's most visited museum.

And we could tell! But we enjoyed it anyway. Until we wanted to get away from the crowds and go back to our hostel, a 15–20 minute walk – and what seemed like another world – away.

This was important because we all needed to get to bed early that night, especially Dale and Justin. The next day we'd be waking up at 4 am to catch a bus to the main event: The Great Wall Half-Marathon.

力

53 | Running & reflecting on the Wall

"We build too many walls and not enough bridges."
– Sir Issac Newton, English mathematician, astronomer,
and physicist

Visiting the Great Wall was the primary reason we had come to Beijing at this time. Specifically, Dale had learned about the Great Wall Half Marathon through one of our colleagues, and he saw it as a perfect way to engage Justin, who had shown some real promise in middle school as a long-distance runner. It held the potential of being a perfect "bookend" for our time in China as well as a real father-son bonding opportunity.

The two had been training back in Ningbo, but it wasn't easy. The air was rarely clean; you would need to get out very early for a run, which was easy for Dale, but much less so for teenaged Justin. They would try to run along the river adjacent to our university. But all too often, the river and surrounding areas seemed cloaked in thick, yellow fog. It was hard for someone like Justin – a child who had suffered from asthma as a baby and still struggled with allergies – to run in that.

Still, they did what they could. And, ready or not, they were challenging The Great Wall Half Marathon! As a result, we found ourselves standing out in front of a Beijing Hotel at 5 a.m. in the chilly air before daybreak waiting for the bus. Fortunately, we weren't alone.

Several other *wàiguórén* and Chinese stood around, pacing and jumping to keep warm. As far as I could tell, we were the only group with children. When the bus arrived, it was a relief.

The bus wound its way out of Beijing and headed northeast, to the Great Wall at *Huángyá* Pass (*Chángchéng zài Huángyáguān*, 长城在 黄崖关). The Chinese characters for 'Great Wall' are 长城 (*Chángchéng*), literally "Long Fortress." And so it is. The Great Wall(s) of China stretches 5,500.3 miles (8,851.8 kilometers), but is not contiguous in some areas.

While the Chinese in various areas built sections of the wall, often ascribing their own names, over a long span of time, the "Long Wall," "Long Citadel," or "Great Wall," as we know it today is largely a product of Ming Dynasty builders (1368–1644). Most historians agree that this Ming Dynasty wall took approximately 200 years to build. Comprised of rammed earth, stones, wood, tiles and lime, historians estimate that a small portion of the estimated 400,000 people who built the wall actually died building it, falling inside. Disturbing, to say the least!

That day, Erika, Luke and I were spectators. But we had made our posters the day before, and we were determined to cheer Dale and Justin on well! As would be the case with spectating, we waited and waited and waited, huddled under our coats and a couple blankets at first, and then peeling off layers as the sun warmed up the day. Here, out at *Huángyá* Pass, the sky was clear and blue, with cotton-ball clouds to welcome the runners. The clear skies at *Huángyá* Pass that day proved unusual and remarkable for our year in China.

The stadium square filled with people quickly. We were surprised, since our bus didn't seem packed. And there were more foreigners in one spot than we had seen for a year! Clearly, the race was outside the mainstream Chinese experience, at least at this point.

In fact, the orchestration of races like this was a new thing in the Mainland. And aspects of this inexperience stood out every step of the way. But still, the very ambition to hold a race like this meant China was eager to capitalize on growing interest in health and fitness, both among its own citizens and, especially, among expats and destination tourists from abroad, making some money while doing it.

In some ways, being there felt a bit like being at a baseball game, but Chinese style. Vendors were plying their wares – souvenir hats, *bāozi* (包子 – dumplings), green tea, keychains and other memorabilia – as they walked through the aisles of people and around the perimeter of the stadium.

Organizers faced their largest crowd ever, with a record number of

1,748 participants from around the world running the four distances: 5K, 10K, Half-Marathon and full Marathon. We needed to watch the 5K and 10K races first, so Dale and Justin huddled with us in those early hours, doing their best to stay warm.

Like many 5K races in the U.S., a bevy of children participated with their parents. These, mostly local Chinese, were cute and fun to watch. The course only involved one steeper ascent up a portion of the wall, then circled around the stadium on mostly flat ground. The 10K runners just continued for a second circuit. It would not be long before the half-marathoners and marathoners would be up. Like the 5K and 10K, the marathoners would simply run the half-marathon twice.

The course Dale and Justin would follow had them running about a mile leading up to the wall, 4-5 miles on the wall, then switching back and running through a part of the stadium again, before heading out for a 7-mile loop that eventually led back to the finish line. That latter part had them winding in and out of the local village streets. I could only imagine what a scene that would be!

Both Justin and Dale seemed to start out strong. The race was not as sophisticated as many were in the West at that time, so our two runners did not stagger start. But, within a few seconds, it became clear Justin, especially, was off fast.

We caught sight of Justin first, as he doubled back and passed through the stadium. He seemed to be in good form, running strong! And he was easily among the first 25 runners coming through the chute.

Dale followed. Although not among the leaders like Justin, he was easily in the first quarter of the pack.

When Justin sped through the finish line of the race, we had no idea of the drama – both inside and out – he had been through to make it there. Apparently Justin had gone out too fast and "hit the wall" (his own personal wall, not the Great Wall) about mile 10 with three miles yet to go. His dad, the tortoise chasing the hare, found him sitting on the side of the trail as runners flowed past him. After much cajoling, he got Justin to his feet and walked with him. When the stadium came in sight with about a half mile to go, Justin rediscovered his legs and sped to the finish. Dale followed about a minute afterwards. Both of them looked flushed but fulfilled. We were proud of our boys!

The Great Wall Half Marathon proved a metaphor for Justin's

year, I believe. Full of struggle, discouragement at times, and yet hopeful and victorious. We knew this young man, soon to celebrate his 15th birthday, was on his way to overcoming the emotional, physical, and spiritual obstacles he had encountered during our year abroad.

Dale was wise, yet again, in realizing how much a race like this could help our oldest son grow up.

Home stretch

54 | Blue sky, fresh air & baseball!

*"Remember me and smile, for it's better to forget
than to remember me and cry."*
— Dr. Seuss

During the spring we also visited a couple remote areas in *Zhèjiāng* (浙江), the province we were living in. We got to these places because others had invited us.

The first trip was with our Ningbo International Christian Fellowship group to a "retreat house" a few hours east of the city. We all piled in vans and headed to the location. Most noteworthy from that time were the blue skies and the warm times of sharing, singing and praying. Dale and Justin had been invited to lead the worship music, and I think both enjoyed contributing that way.

But blue skies! And fresh air! This was something we had very little of during our year in Ningbo. They were quite a gift!

The second opportunity came when a group of my students invited Luke and me on a camping trip over the Labour Day / Youth Day weekend. The camping trip was over two nights.

Eddie, Learner, Stuart, Maylin and Ellie were among the students who were already meeting up with Luke each week, so the connections were easy. The lively group of about 40 meant a group outing much different from our camping experiences back in the U.S.

We headed to a lake about three hours away by bus. We played games on the bus, and, even though a lot around us took place in Chinese, the students made deliberate effort to keep many of their conversations in English. I was impressed!

As I exited the bus, I looked up. Blue skies! Again! What a treat. It's amazing how much you learn to appreciate this natural phenomenon when you don't get it often.

It seemed this lake was a common place for young people to gather. And to camp. There were many buses there with lots of other college-aged students taking advantage of the four-day weekend.

We walked a distance before the group settled on a wide open space to set up our 20 or so tents. The students had made sure to secure one for me and Luke, so we got right to work. Luke was good at it and was having fun. I was recalling how, almost two years ago, as we traversed the U.S., Luke was involved in the setting up of the campsite with his dad. This "training" seemed to be paying off!

The students had prepared the food well, skewering all sorts of meat, seafood and vegetables for shish kabobs to grill over the long barbeque at the campsite. They also had prepared noodle dishes and a bunch of other savory delights, as well as plenty of rice.

I was amazed by the amount of meat they had brought with them. Tons! And my little Luke was one happy camper! He could not get enough.

We hung out. We sang around a campfire that evening. A couple of the students played guitars and led us in some songs. Mostly Chinese songs, but even a few English ones. We played games. It was so much fun interacting with them! We even told stories – funny ones, scary ones, and ones I simply couldn't understand because of the language. But everyone seemed engaged, so I'm sure they were funny or gripping as well.

We even enjoyed the stars together, picking out different constellations and imagining the stories behind them. I'm not sure we would have ever been able to do that in Ningbo because the stars were hidden most of the time.

Luke seemed to love the whole camping experience – reading in his sleeping bag with flashlight, receiving a boatload of attention, collecting and skipping rocks, playing games. And eating plenty of meat.

As we neared the end of May, it seemed as if the days tumbled into one another. We began to glimpse the "finish line" of our family year abroad. On one hand, with the warming weather, it felt good. But on the other hand, as the humidity set in, we began to fantasize about the temperate climate back home.

We were determined to finish strong, both as a family, and with our schooling / jobs. We kept focused with our eyes on the goal, but also did our best to be mindful of each day. It was a season of deep relational moments with our students – as well as with our other friends in Ningbo.

We would soon be giving our final exams to students, but before we did, we held a bargain sale of many of our items and a going-away party, side-by-side, at our apartment building, making use of the common room on the ground floor.

We encouraged the kids to come up with a number of items they were willing to part with. Erika, in particular, priced a few dozen items and made some extra money. We, too, had a number of items we wanted to pass on and thought doing so through a bargain sale made sense.

Students poured into our tiny apartment for those few hours, purchased items here and there, and then joined us downstairs for a variety of dishes prepared by Jack. Of course, some of the students had gifts for us, though when we publicized the event, we specifically asked them not to bring any gifts – cards would be just fine, thank you! Usually one of them would say, "This is really just a very small item (perhaps jewelry)...I really hope you can take it home with you to remember me, Mrs. D!" Of course I would oblige.

So I'm not sure if our net result, in terms of number of items, ended in our favor or not. But the time was fun, we all hung out and enjoyed one another. Ellen and a few administrators, some of the other foreign English teachers, as well as Soo-jin and her sons, came to say goodbye.

Our final exams administered, papers graded, and final grades submitted, we were in the closing days of our time in Ningbo. Before we left, however, we wanted to find a way to thank the group of students that had volunteered faithfully to care for Luke throughout the second semester.

After some brainstorming, we decided to put together small handmade memory gifts and hold a "baseball and pizza" party for them. We figured, what could be more American than baseball? And we again hired Jack to prepare food, this time a number of pizzas for us, American style.

The memory gifts were little photo albums featuring Luke together with them, as well as our family. I found a number of quotations to include, printed them, and assembled each one.

The party took place on a mostly-sunny June day right after finals were over, days before we'd be leaving Ningbo for the U.S. It was full of fun and laughter. Others passing would stop and watch for awhile. Maybe they wanted to join in, but this time it was a private party. We taught our students the rules of baseball and split into two teams. Our kids – especially the boys – really got into it. And Luke? He enjoyed being the center of the show, of course.

Several of our students later told us through email how much they enjoyed that laughter-filled time, how it would be a memory they'd hold on to for years to come. That's exactly what we wanted. I, too, can close my eyes and see that simple baseball-game-pizza-party-thank-you almost as if it were just yesterday.

55 | Epilogue: Higher, deeper still

"We shape our dwellings and afterwards our dwellings shape us."
— Sir Winston Churchill

I sit writing this last section at a massive wooden table in the center of a local juice bar and café in Monterey, California. It's the wee hours of the morning, before the crowd arrives. The sky and world are waking up – a pastel-painted, glowing, ephemeral moment quickly passing – in this coastal California city we have called home for almost 25 years. This place has been good to us.

It is here we moved to so I could pursue my graduate studies. It is here where my husband found a job he loves, teaching high school students to appreciate literature and writing, while engaging them in discussion and pouring into their lives. And it is here where we grew our family from two to five people.

It is here we became involved with international students – first studying among them (me) and then seeking to serve and love on them (both of us). Now, after almost 25 years, we have cultivated thousands of relationships with people from countries around the world. We recognize the immense gift this has been to *our* lives.

How did our family's year abroad change us? And what lasting lessons and influences remain? Here are my top five:

1 **Our family grew closer.**
During the year abroad, sibling rivalry was an issue, especially when we were traveling. I remember many times when Dale and I

would exchange glances and wonder, "Will this bickering *ever* end?" At times it proved deeply discouraging.

But since we returned to the U.S., I can honestly say our kids have rarely fought. This is *not* an exaggeration. Of course, some of that could be attributed to simply growing up. But I believe a large part of this is due to our shared experiences abroad, and a deep sense of doing and completing it together.

2 Each of our children grew in character and confidence.

All three of our children are now confident travelers and not intimidated as they move around, figure out bus and travel routes, and forge out on their own. Traveling inside or outside of the country is not intimidating to them. Nor are the people they encounter, even if very different from themselves. They have become globally savvy young people.

But, on a deeper level, all three have become much more circumspect, mature people with an understanding of the privileges we in America enjoy.

3 We created lasting memories.

No one can take that year away from us. We have many memories of that year together we often will reference. (And a ton of photos and videos as well!) Not only was it a turning point in our lives, but memories from that year often connect with experiences we have now. Collectively and individually we grew. There are moments even now that remind us of that year, or of a person from that season of our lives.

4 All of us grew in our global mindset.

All three kids continued with their study of Chinese language in middle school (Luke) and high school (Justin, Erika and Luke). In fact, although he didn't need it for his Mechanical Engineering major, Justin took some Chinese language classes during college, and it is in one of these where he met his wife, Jacqueline. Whether or not China is in their future is anyone's guess. But he took his nascent language skills and developed them to a higher level.

Due to our family's year abroad, I believe our children are more open to future work – in whatever field they choose – that prizes a global approach and mindset.

Indeed, spending the year abroad opened all of our eyes to new perspectives, views of the world, ways of doing things, and even an understanding of what may become food (although I still don't do insects well!).

5 **We learned how to *receive* help.**
This may seem like a strange one. But especially for Dale and me, being on the receiving end was a good thing because, for so many years, *we* were the ones helping others. As good as that may sound, without an understanding of how it feels to be dependent upon help *from* others, you miss an important component of understanding the helping / serving and receiving relationship.

It's humbling to accept help. To admit dependency on another. Most of us don't do this very well.

But when you're forced to? Like when we needed Andy in Shanghai, or relied on Ellen in Ningbo, or trusted YZ all the year through? This grew us a lot. And I think it's made us more sensitive and understanding to those who need our help now while we're in the U.S. and they are the *wàiguorén*.

A two-thousand-year-old Chinese proverb aptly sums up the sentiment surrounding our family's year abroad:

"One can never know the height of the sky
nor the depth of the earth
without climbing up a high mountain
and looking into the depths of the waters."

不登高山，不知天之高也; 不临深溪，不知地之厚也.
Bù dēng gāoshān, bùzhī tiān zhī gāo yě;
bù lín shēn xī, bùzhī dì zhī hòu yě.

When Master Xun (荀子 – *Xúnzǐ*), the student of Mencius (孟子 – *Mèngzǐ*), who was the protegé of Confucius (孔子 – *Kǒngzǐ*), penned these words, I'm pretty sure he didn't have us in mind.

But what he did know was the stir in the human spirit to live life in all its fulness, to stretch beyond one's comfort zone and discover the height of a sky and the depths of an earth beyond the familiar. He seemed to understand the lure of adventure and both the internal and external obstacles necessary to overcome.

On these points we resonate.

For indeed, our year abroad stretched each of us in really hard ways. And, upon our return each one of us faced unique challenges readjusting to the life in the U.S. Dale, Justin and I seemed to grapple with reverse culture shock the most.

But as we worked through the re-entry process, we also gained greater appreciation for what we had experienced, a year of jumping out of our mainstream American life, climbing and descending all at once. What we gained along the journey still impacts us in both overt and subtle ways today.

We plan to continue climbing and descending beyond what we know, for new mountains and ever deeper waters beckon.

What about you?

If you've been inspired by our story, please check out our website
as well as our how-to course, *YourFamilyAbroad.*
Give your family the experience of a lifetime.

CultureWeave.com
cultureweave.com/yourfamilyabroad

yourGlobalFamily.com

Acknowledgements

I owe a great debt of gratitude to so many who have inspired, cheered me on, and supported me in this process.

Thanks, Phil (& Sophia), for help in those early stages. We share common hearts and minds. Our friendship stands the test of time.

Dale and I are grateful to Jon, who led us to Helen, who welcomed us to our positions at Ningbo University with such enthusiasm and warmth. We're grateful for all you poured into us.

The young Chinese adults who filled our classrooms during our year in China remain in our hearts, long after our family's year abroad. With some we keep in good contact; sadly, with many others we do not. But thank you for helping us see the humanity of your nation at a very real level.

Our "angel" YK remains among our closest friends today. We love you and your excellent wife (whom you found!), deeply.

We remain grateful for Lisa, Leon, William, Michael, Marissa, Christina, Sharon, Simon, our NICF family, Hillary & Win, as well as the scores of brothers and sisters in the Philippines, Taiwan, Japan, and China with whom we broke bread and celebrated life. Each one of you holds a treasured space in our hearts.

Thank you to the leadership at Carmel High School for granting Dale a sabbatical year. Thanks too for the leadership, as well as our friends & donors, with International Students, Inc. You enabled a change of assignment for me so we could take this special year living abroad with our children. Many of you followed our journey with interest, and prayed for us when we were in need. Which was a lot.

More recently, I have benefitted so much from the experiential wisdom and practical advice of author and entrepreneur Jeff Goins. Your *TribeWriters* course & community, the *Tribe Conference*, and your inspiring books play a large role in what got me to this place. Keep doing what you do; it matters!

Without Laura, my writing buddy in the early morning hours for most of my first draft, I'm not sure I would've made it to this point. The accountability made such a difference. I'm glad we built a solid friendship in the process.

I could never have gotten the Chinese characters right without the expertise, time, and passion of my two Chinese friends, Serene and Holly. Three language nerds around the table, I'm so grateful we could make sure those Chinese characters accurately convey the heart of each section and chapter.

Two friends over the last few years, Ewelina and Finot, encouraged me to write time and again, cheering me on. I am ever grateful. Your friendship means the world to me, literally.

My friend Kelly, perhaps unwittingly, became one of my earliest readers. I cannot tell you how much your enthusiasm for this book touched me. I am so grateful for our longtime friendship.

Our home church, Calvary Monterey, plus another local church, Mayflower Presbyterian, prayed for and supported us wholeheartedly during our year in China. We so appreciate these wonderful brothers and sisters!

Thank you, Sue, my mentor and dear friend, for not only teaching me the beauty of flowers, but also the wonder of Jesus. We appreciate yours and Jack's rock-solid support of our family and unwavering prayers over the years.

Of course, thank you to my parents, Tony & Joan. You have been there for me through thick & thin, even when you haven't always understood me! Thanks, too, for your dedication to my husband and children. I love you both.

Justin, Erika and Luke, you trusted us to travel across an ocean (though you didn't have much choice!); we trusted God we wouldn't mess you up (too much). You have all grown into impressive young adults. I'd like to think our year in China helped shape you along the way. Thank you for the many ways you contributed to the final product here. I love each of you wholeheartedly.

There is no one who has been more supportive and crucial to this project's success than Dale. You encouraged me to go the distance. Thank you. I love you to the moon and back (a million times, which means almost 38,953,204 times back-and-forth to China!). Thanks for being my partner in life, adventure, and fine dark chocolate. I think we make a good team!

Finally, thanks be to God, in whom (as the Apostle Paul quoted), "*[I] live and move and have my being.*" (Acts 17:28) Making You smile is my greatest joy & highest motivation.

About the author

Caroline DePalatis has worked in the field of international education and service for over 20 years. A graduate of Stanford University and the Middlebury Institute of International Studies at Monterey, she's still doing much of what she was trained in: bringing people of the world together. A committed Christ-follower, Caroline longs to shine light on the Master Designer's awesome creativity expressed through the cultures, languages, peoples and places of our world. She has a passion for families and believes every parent should raise their child(ren) to be engaged global citizens.

Caroline and her husband, Dale, are the founders of *CultureWeave* (www.cultureweave.com), a venture aiming to:
*   make cultural immersion more accessible to all;
*   educate families to proactively overcome barriers, misunderstandings and conflicts in their cross-cultural encounters;
*   improve children's perspective of the world ; and
*   help family units to build meaningful & lasting cross-cultural relationships to influence change for good.

You can find Caroline with her husband Dale, youngest son Luke, and a supply of 60%+ dark chocolate at their home in Monterey, California whenever she is not out exploring new corners of our world (or revisiting favorites).

Jumping Out of the Mainstream is her first book.

Visuals

Our family in the Shanghai Tea House, days after arrival.
– August 2009 –

Our family now, with Justin's new wife, Jacqueline.
– August 2017 –

Pictures do speak thousands of words in an instant!
For a quick visual tour of our year, take a look at:

cultureweave.com/jumping-out-book/photos

Chinese character glossary

梦   *mèng* | dream
1 | 茶   *chá* | tea

备   *bèi* | prepare
2 | 开   *kāi* | open
3 | 和   *hé* | peace
4 | 动   *dòng* | act
5 | 道   *dào* | path
6 | 心   *xīn* | heart
7 | 光   *guāng* | light

至   *zhì* | arrival
8 | 慌   *huāng* | disorientation
9 | 寻   *xún* | find
10 | 惧   *jù* | fear
11 | 不   *bù* | not

适   *shì* | fit
12 | 续   *xù* | next
13 | 内   *nèi* | inside
14 | 进   *jìn* | progress
15 | 奇   *qí* | unexpected
16 | 教   *jiào* | teach
17 | 外   *wài* | outside
18 | 食   *shí* | food

Chinese character glossary

	学	*xué*	learning
19	醒	*xǐng*	wake up
20	校	*xiào*	school
21	小	*xiǎo*	small, elementary
22	中	*zhōng*	middle
23	言	*yán*	language
	索	*suǒ*	quest
24	敬	*jìng*	respect
25	老	*lǎo*	elderly
26	异	*yì*	difference
27	庆	*qìng*	celebrate
28	月	*yuè*	moon
29	上	*shàng*	up, Shanghai
30	变	*biàn*	changed
31	共	*gòng*	together, Communism
32	难	*nán*	difficult
	越	*yuè*	overcome
33	苦	*kǔ*	hardship
34	信	*xìn*	belief
35	得	*dé*	gain
36	念	*niàn*	thankful
37	旦	*dàn*	New Year's Day

Chinese character glossary

息　　　*xī* | rest, vacation
38 | 逃　*táo* | flee
39 | 悦　*yuè* | joy
40 | 佑　*yòu* | blessing
41 | 臺　*Tái* | Taiwan (traditional)
42 | 归　*guī* | return
43 | 旧　*jiù* | old
44 | 织　*zhī* | woven

跃　　　*yuè* | leap
45 | 熟　*shú* | familiar
46 | 正　*zhèng* | correct
47 | 英　*yīng* | English
48 | 寒　*hán* | cold

游　　　*yóu* | tour
49 | 杭　*háng* | Hangzhou
50 | 繁　*fán* | prosperous
51 | 京　*jīng* | Beijing
52 | 味　*wèi* | taste
53 | 力　*lì* | power

终　　　*zhōng* | end
54 | 净　*jìng* | clear, pure
55 | 敢　*gǎn* | dare

Helpful resources

We mentioned our Decision-Analyst friend, Phil, early in the book. If you are interested in his services, he can be reached at phil@beccue.com.

For 25 years we've been involved with International Students, Inc., a Christian friendship outreach to college and university international students. Currently I run a local outreach to international wives, couples and families. If you live anywhere in the vicinity of a university, college or community college, it's likely there are international students who would appreciate and benefit from local hospitality, organized or organic (or a mixture of both). Involvement can be as simple as hosting an international student or two for dinner, providing needed household goods (both volunteer), or as involved as fulltime staff. Check it out at isionline.org.

This book would not have been possible without the mentoring & guidance of Jeff Goins (goinswriter.com), his Tribe Writer's course (tribewriters.com) and community, and the annual Tribe Conference (tribeconference.com). When I attended TRIBE 2016, I made a promise to myself I'd return with a book in 2017 – and I did (not without a ton of hardwork, sweat, and too much chocolate!). I recommend all these without reservation if you want to stop procrastinating and really become serious about your writing – and connect with a simply astounding community in the process.

The resources and camaraderie available through NaNoWriMo (National Novel Writing Month, nanowrimo.org) proved instrumental in getting me laser-focused to actually write this book. Check it out if you have your own writing project you want to pursue.

Notes

Chapter 11 | Learning the art of *Bù yào!*

1. Wikipedia, s.v. "Century Egg," accessed November 7, 2016, https://en.wikipedia.org/wiki/Century_egg.
2. China Expats, "How To – Other Produce," accessed November 11, 2016, http://www.china-expats.com/HowTo_CnOther_Eggs.htm.

Chapter 12 | Onwards to Ningbo!

1. Wikipedia, s.v. "Ningbo," accessed November 9, 2016, https://en.wikipedia.org/wiki/Ningbo.
2. Wikipedia, s.v. "List of Cities in China by Population and Built-Up Area," accessed November 9, 2016, https://en.wikipedia.org/wiki/List_of_cities_in_China_by_population_and_built-up_area.
3. World Population Review, "Population of Cities in China (2016-17)," accessed November 9, 2016, http://worldpopulationreview.com/countries/china-population/cities/.
4. World Economic Forum, "You knew China's cities were growing. But the real numbers are stunning," accessed November 9, 2016, https://www.weforum.org/agenda/2016/06/china-cities-growing-numbers-are-stunning/.
5. Wikipedia, s.v. "Xihoumen Bridge," accessed November 15, 2016, https://en.wikipedia.org/wiki/Xihoumen_Bridge.
6. China Highlights, "China's 10 Most Popular Street Foods," accessed November 9, 2016, https://www.chinahighlights.com/travelguide/chinese-food/street-food.htm.
7. Wilson, Allan, Live Less Ordinary, "Top 10 Chinese Street Food," accessed November 9, 2016, https://www.live-less-ordinary.com/top-10-chinese-street-food-in-china/.

Chapter 19 | Ningbo University wakes up

1. Wikipedia, s.v. "National Higher Education Entrance Examination," accessed November 16, 2016, https://en.wikipedia.org/wiki/National_Higher_Education_Entrance_Examination.
2. Lu, Shen and Griffiths, James, CNN, "Gaokao: Can you pass China's grueling Entrance Exam?," June 7, 2016, accessed November 16, 2016, http://www.cnn.com/2016/06/07/asia/gaokao-quiz/index.html.

Chapter 23 | Encountering the language dragon

1. Wikipedia, s.v. "Chinese Language," accessed November 19, 2016, https://en.wikipedia.org/wiki/Chinese_language.
2. Lin, Kathy, EthnoMed, "Chinese Language," accessed November 19, 2016, https://ethnomed.org/culture/chinese/chinese-language-profile.

Notes

Chapter 27 | The PRC celebrates 60 & we join in

1. Wikipedia, s.v. "60th Anniversary of the People's Republic of China," accessed November 22, 2016, https://en.wikipedia.org/wiki/60th_anniversary_of_the_People%27s_Republic_of_China.

Chapter 28 | Mooncakes, lanterns, Máo & memories

1. Wikipedia, s.v. "Mid-Autumn Festival," accessed November 22, 2016, https://en.wikipedia.org/wiki/Mid-Autumn_Festival.
2. Rodgers, Greg, Trip Savvy, "Chinese Moon Festival," accessed November 22, 2016, https://www.tripsavvy.com/chinese-moon-festival-1458337.

Chapter 35 | Hard lessons, unexpected gifts

1. Butch, Taylor, The Diplomat, "How Does Starbucks Succeed in China?", July 4, 2016, accessed November 28, 2016, http://thediplomat.com/2016/07/how-does-starbucks-succeed-in-china/.
2. Zhang, Shuai, CBS MoneyWatch, "1 U.S. brand booming in China, in spite of economic woes," January 14, 2016, accessed November 28, 2016, https://www.cbsnews.com/news/starbucks-china-open-2500-new-stores-chinese-customers-coffee-culture/.

Chapter 38 | Fleeing the world's largest annual migration

1. Wikipedia, s.v. "Chinese New Year," accessed November 30, 2016, https://en.wikipedia.org/wiki/Chinese_New_Year.
2. Wikipedia, s.v. "Chunyun," accessed November 30, 2016, https://en.wikipedia.org/wiki/Chunyun.
3. CNN Travel, "What does the biggest human migration on earth look like on a map?", February 18, 2015, accessed Novemer 20, 2016, http://www.cnn.com/travel/article/china-spring-migration-chunyun/index.html.
4. Shadbolt, Peter, CNN Travel, "What happens when all of China goes on vacation at once," January 12, 2016, accessed November 30, 2016, http://www.cnn.com/travel/article/travel-china-chunyun/index.html.
5. McDonald, Mark, New York Times, "Direct flights between China and Taiwan begin," December 15, 2008, accessed November 30, 2016, http://www.nytimes.com/2008/12/15/news/15iht-15TAIWAN.18675854.html.

Chapter 41 | A visit to the 'Other China'

1. The Skyscraper Center, "Taipei 101," accessed December 1, 2016, https://www.skyscrapercenter.com/building/taipei-101/117.
2. Wikipedia, s.v. "Taipei 101," accessed December 1, 2016, https://en.wikipedia.org/wiki/Taipei_101.

Notes

Chapter 42 | Layer upon layer: Return to Japan

1. Wikipedia, s.v. "Tōkaidō Shinkansen," accessed December 3, 2016, https://en.wikipedia.org/wiki/T%C5%8Dkaid%C5%8D_Shinkansen.
2. Nippon.com, "Shinkansen Route Map," accessed December 3, 2016, http://www.nippon.com/en/features/h00077/.
3. Oi, Mariko, BBC News, "The man who saved Kyoto from the atomic bomb," August 9, 2015, accessed December 4, 2016, http://www.bbc.com/news/world-asia-33755182.
4. Wikipedia, s.v. "Kyoto," accessed December 4, 2016, https://en.wikipedia.org/wiki/Kyoto.
5. Sato, Hiroaki, The Japan Times, "Stimson's love of Kyoto saved it from A-bomb," December 4, 2015, accessed December 4, 2016, https://www.japantimes.co.jp/opinion/2015/12/04/commentary/japan-commentary/stimsons-love-kyoto-saved-bomb/#.WaifNNOGOYU.
6. Wikipedia, s.v. "Geisha," accessed December 4, 2016, https://en.wikipedia.org/wiki/Geisha.

Chapter 48 | A river runs through it...but Ningbo is cold!

1. Wikipedia, s.v. "Northern and southern China," accessed December 8, 2016, https://en.wikipedia.org/wiki/Northern_and_southern_China.
2. Internet World Stats, "Internet World Users by Language," accessed December 9, 2016, http://www.internetworldstats.com/stats7.htm (This site is periodically updated.).
3. Young, Holly, The Guardian, The British Academy for the Humanities and Social Sciences, "The digital language divide: How does the language you speak shape your experience of the internet?", accessed December 9, 2016, http://labs.theguardian.com/digital-language-divide/.

Chapter 49 | Express train to heaven: Hangzhou

1. Wikipedia, s.v. "Hangzhou," accessed December 12, 2016, https://en.wikipedia.org/wiki/Hangzhou.
2. Lonely Planet, "Hángzhōu," accessed December 12, 2016, https://www.lonelyplanet.com/china/zhejiang/hangzhou.
3. Wikipedia, s.v. "West Lake," accessed December 12, 2016, https://en.wikipedia.org/wiki/West_Lake.

Chapter 50 | Our angel's roots: Wenzhou

1. Wikipedia, s.v. "Wenzhou," accessed December 13, 2016, https://en.wikipedia.org/wiki/West_Lake.

Notes

Chapter 51 | North to the capital: Beijing

2. Wikipedia, s.v. "Beijing," accessed December 12, 2016, https://en.wikipedia.org/wiki/Beijing.
3. History.com, "1989: Tiananmen Square Massacre Takes Place, accessed December 12, 2016, http://www.history.com/this-day-in-history/tiananmen-square-massacre-takes-place.
4. Encycleapedia Brittanica, "Tiananmen Square Incident," accessed December 12, 2016, http://time.com/2822290/tiananmen-square-massacre-facts-time/.
5. Rayman, Noah, Time, "6 things you should know about the Tiananmen Square Massacre," June 4, 2014 (updated May 19, 2016), accessed December 12, 2016, http://time.com/2822290/tiananmen-square-massacre-facts-time/.
6. Wikipedia, s.v. "Tiananmen Square Protests of 1989," accessed December 12, 2016, https://en.wikipedia.org/wiki/Tiananmen_Square_protests_of_1989.

Chapter 52 | Tantalizing tea shop & delectable duck

1. Wikipedia, s.v. "Hutong," accessed December 14, 2016, https://en.wikipedia.org/wiki/Beijing.
2. Nix, Elizabeth, History.com, "In China, It's Out With the Old, In With the New," January 23, 2013, accessed December 14, 2016, http://www.history.com/news/in-china-its-out-with-the-old-in-with-the-old.
3. China Highlights, "Beijing Hutongs," accessed December 14, 2016, https://www.chinahighlights.com/beijing/hutong/.
4. Wikipedia, s.v. "Peking Duck," accessed December 15, 2016, https://en.wikipedia.org/wiki/Peking_duck.
5. Wikipedia, s.v. "Peking Duck," accessed December 15, 2016, https://en.wikipedia.org/wiki/Quanjude.
6. Wikipedia, s.v. "Forbidden City," accessed December 15, 2016, https://en.wikipedia.org/wiki/Forbidden_City.

Chapter 53 | Running & reflecting on the Wall

1. Wikipedia, s.v. "Great Wall of China," accessed January 5, 2017, https://en.wikipedia.org/wiki/Great_Wall_of_China.
2. Great Wall Marathon website, http://great-wall-marathon.com/.
3. Wikipedia, s.v. "Great Wall Marathon," accessed January 6, 2017, https://en.wikipedia.org/wiki/Great_Wall_Marathon.

Chapter 55 | Epilogue: Higher, deeper still

1. Wikipedia, s.v. "Xun Kuang," accessed August 19, 2017, https://en.wikipedia.org/wiki/Xun_Kuang.
2. Proverb of Xun Kuang, [不登高山，不知天之高] on Baidu, accessed August 19, 2017, https://baike.baidu.com/item/不登高山，不知天之高].

Made in the USA
San Bernardino, CA
25 September 2017